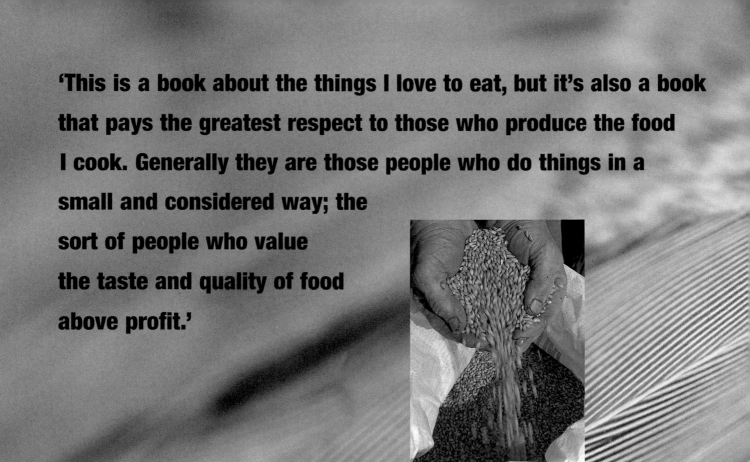

'This is a book about the things I love to eat, but it's also a book that pays the greatest respect to those who produce the food I cook. Generally they are those people who do things in a small and considered way; the sort of people who value the taste and quality of food above profit.'

rick stein's food heroes

rick

stein's food heroes

BBC

To Jill, Edward, Jack and Charles

food photography
james murphy

location photography
craig easton

This book is published to accompany the television
series entitled *Rick Stein's Food Heroes*.
The series was produced for BBC Television by
Denham Productions.
Producer and Director: David Pritchard
Executive Producer for the BBC: Andy Batten-Foster

First published by BBC Books, BBC Worldwide
Limited in 2002
80 Wood Lane
London W12 0TT

Reprinted 2002

ISBN: 0 563 53474 5

Set in Helvetica neue
Printed and bound in Great Britain by Butler and
Tanner Limited, Frome and London
Colour separations by Radstock Reproductions
Limited, Midsomer Norton
Jacket printed by Lawrence Allen Limited,
Weston-super-Mare

introduction 6

eggs and cheese 10

salads, soups and first courses 22

fish and shellfish 40

poultry 64

meat and offal 86

contents

Commissioning Editor: Vivien Bowler
Project Editor: Rachel Copus
Copy Editor: Rachel Connolly
Art Director: Sarah Ponder
Designer: Paul Welti
Home Economist: Debbie Major
Stylist: Helene Lesur
Production Controller: Susan Currie

To quote the legendary Irish cook Myrtle Allen, this book is about people producing 'common things uncommonly well'. More than that, it's a book of my favourite recipes; it's the cookery book I've wanted to write for some time.

I'm best known for cooking fish and that is still my first love. A builder who worked for us for many years in the early days of the restaurant once said, 'Can you cook real food?' Those were the days when fish was not considered to be nourishing enough for men. Well, I do cook 'real' food. I grill chops and make deeply aromatic Chinese pork hotpots smelling of tangerine and star anise. I love a good navarin of lamb filled with sweet early carrots, turnips, peas and little new potatoes. I eat free-range chicken roasted with garlic and tarragon. I love a rib of aged beef grilled over coals with chips, a simple salad and béarnaise sauce. I cook vegetables such as spring greens with butter and shallots, or courgettes sliced

introduction

and gently fried with chervil and chives. I fry eggs and serve them up with Mexican ranchero sauce and tortillas on special Sunday mornings. I make puddings like Sussex pond, fragrant and sweet-and-sour, with whole lemons and demerara sugar. I consider rhubarb crumble to be the finest British pudding going.

But just as I insist on the best and freshest fish, I do the same with meat, game and vegetables. I've always felt that the most important point about cooking good food is getting the best produce in the first place. This is a book about the things I love to eat, but it's also a book that pays the greatest respect to those who produce the food I cook. Generally they are those people who do things in a small and considered way; the sort of people who value the taste and quality of food above profit.

Not only have I incorporated their produce into my recipes, but I've taken the slightly adventurous step of listing all of them – some 300 – in the back of the book. I've also included producers of good food in those other countries that enjoy my cookery books: Ireland, Australia and New Zealand. The problem with doing this is that as soon as the book is published, the list becomes out of date. It's time to use the internet for such things. This list will be updated regularly on our own website (www.rickstein.com) and the BBCi Food website (www.bbc.co.uk/food) will carry details of regional producers and suppliers in the UK. I hope these listings will become an important source of reliable information for you.

You could make all the recipes in this book with food from any large supermarket. I'm not opposed to supermarkets. All of us would be the poorer without the incredible wealth of raw materials they offer. One has

recently opened just outside Padstow. There was a lot of opposition to it but now it's here everyone uses it. Who would have thought five years ago that I could buy fresh coriander and basil, chillies, Illy espresso coffee, Australian Barossa Shiraz, crème fraîche, duck breasts, olive oil and fish sauce in a small Cornish town?

Yet in spite of the variety there is better-tasting food to be bought from small producers. Take a delicatessen like Valvona and Crolla in Edinburgh, for example. They thrive because they buy from producers too small to supply supermarkets; growers who do nearly everything by hand and who take their time. You'll see bent and twisted peppers, 13 types of tomato – some deep red, others misshapen and even green – all designed for different uses: in sauces, salads, to go with buffalo mozzarella and basil, or with pasta. There are varying sizes of hand-made goats' and ewes' milk cheeses with wonderful aromas, and bread with scorched, cracking crusts and white interiors with giant air bubbles.

You only need to go to a good farmers' market to appreciate this; knobbly, ungraded vegetables, local bread, cheese, geese and milk, too regional to be taken up by the multiples. There's a whole band of people out there producing small quantities of food with passionate commitment, who look after their land properly, treat their flocks or herds with affection and respect and take their time to grow or rear crops or animals. Supermarkets are driven by shareholders who want returns, so profit is king. Great food is about love not money.

The TV series that accompanies this book is a culinary journey around Britain. I remember saying at the beginning that it was a journey to find where we're at with food in Britain today. Are we still a nation that eats to live, or are we becoming more and more enchanted with the life-enhancing joy of good food? The journey and lots of subsequent trips and research have led me to believe that we are seriously moving on. There is a growing groundswell of people who really want to eat food that is produced properly.

I am fascinated by the current debate about fox hunting and the wish by many to have it banned. There probably is a polarization between urban and rural dwellers, which I also witnessed in letters I read about the recent foot and mouth tragedy. The most important argument of the anti lobby is the cruelty of hunting down and killing a wild animal with a pack of dogs. As a farmer's son, the way hunts used to gallop over our land without asking permission was more important, but the cruelty argument is interesting. Nothing's perfect, but isn't the cruelty inflicted on millions and millions of animals – chickens, ducks, pigs, and probably fish – in the interests of producing cheap food a wrong out of all proportion to fox hunting? Yet we all quietly condone it because we don't think about it. I feel that we have a moral duty to care about the way the food we eat and love is produced.

The people whose recipes have inspired me don't ram their pigs into little concrete cages; they let them roam free. You can go to a farm like that of Stuart Pierce, of the Isle of Wight Bacon Company, and watch the piglets having piglet races down a grassy track in the setting sun, or drive into the farmyard of James Graham, of Peele's, at Thuxton, near Norwich, and watch a flock of Norfolk Black turkeys in a stubble field having a communal change of wattle colour (the males, anyway) from pink to deep red and back again. Or you can stand with Edward Hamer high above the Severn Valley at Llanidloes in Powys, surveying his herd of Welsh Black cattle in the pasture below, having just been to his cold room and seen the quality of the sides of beef there. You can feel perfectly happy with being a meat eater: these beasts have not had a mean life.

I found you don't need to try hard to make an engaging television programme if you are talking to people who care about their livelihood – they talk naturally and eloquently about why their produce is so special. It's a real excitement to visit people like Aeneas and Minty Mackay of Ardalanish Farm on the Isle of Mull and taste their highland beef, with its crisp fat and deep, rare red meat, and to feel the tingle of realization that there really is a world of difference between this beef, those turkeys, and the stuff you get more or less everywhere else. That's why these people are my food heroes.

But I've taken it further than that. I haven't just listed primary producers; I've also written about those who acquire the best ingredients from elsewhere – they're my heroes, too. Firms like Brindisa, a cornucopia of the best Spanish produce – chorizos, Ortiz tuna and anchovies, sublime butter beans, smoked paprika, little beautifully coloured boxes of saffron – or the Italian supplier Esperya, with an addictive finocchio salami, jars of sun-dried tomatoes and capers from the island of Panteleria near Sicily, or jars of whole anchovies in sea salt from Cetara near Positano that are so good because they are salted down at sea seconds after they are caught, and have a sweet, warm flavour to be seriously sought out. I've also included people who have written passionately about food and inspired me to cook: people like Claudia Roden, who unfurled the charm and sophistication of Middle Eastern cookery; Elizabeth David, who above all had an instinctive economy and elegance both in her writing and her food, and Alan Davidson, whose seafood books have taught me so much about fish and shellfish biologically, historically and gastronomically.

I think it's important to identify those people, the champions of good food, who keep the whole idea of excellence afloat. At a time when mothers no longer teach their children how to cook and the whole art of cookery is regarded as being on a par with metal turning in our schools, we need some heroes to turn to.

1 eggs and

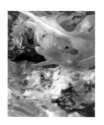  

WE'VE FEATURED MRS KIRKHAM'S LANCASHIRE
CHEESE ON OUR MENU AT THE SEAFOOD RESTAURANT
FOR YEARS. TO ME SHE ALWAYS SEEMED A
LEGENDARY FIGURE, POSSIBLY SOMEONE WHOSE
PARTICULAR STYLE OF THAT TART, WHITE, CRUMBLY
CHEESE MADE IT A SPECIAL, ALMOST *GRAND CRU*
VERSION OF LANCASHIRE. THEN I MET HER — WE
FILMED AT HER TINY FARM AT GOOSNAGH — AND SHE
TOLD ME THAT SHE OFTEN FELT THAT PEOPLE
BELIEVED SHE WAS NO MORE REAL THAN MR KIPLING.
I USE THE WORDS *GRAND CRU* INTENTIONALLY,
BECAUSE WHEN YOU TALK TO GREAT CHEESE-
MAKERS LIKE RUTH AND HER EQUALLY ENTHUSIASTIC
SON, GRAHAM, YOU REALIZE THAT THE SAME
DEDICATION AND INTELLECTUAL CURIOSITY DRIVES
THEM AS DRIVES GREAT WINE-MAKERS.

cheese

The interesting thing about cheese is that, as it is treated with a living culture during the separation of the curds and whey, there is the same fascinating uncertainty about the finished quality as with making wine. Some batches are definitely more successful than others, and it is this pleasing inconsistency that leads to the individuality of the best cheese. This isn't to say, though, that consistency in manufacture and attention to hygiene aren't treated seriously.

The same dedication seems to exist in all the small cheese-makers I visited. Talking to Richard Rowlett, the Stilton maker at Colston Bassett, I was struck by the same commitment. It's more of a factory there, surrounded by lush Leicestershire pasture and organized by a co-operative of local dairy farmers, but there's still almost a serenity about producers like this; a passionate involvement in doing something right. One of the things that struck me about Richard when talking about cheese was his comment that Colston Bassett Stilton tastes different from, say, Cropwell Bishop, because the pastures in each village are different.

Mike Davies, of the Dorset Blue Cheese Company at Sturminster Newton in Dorset, is also a man with a mission. He reinstated Blue Vinny cheese, a completely different type of blue cheese, made as it is from skimmed milk, which gives it a leaner, chalkier taste. Incidentally, the blue in Vinny comes from the same mould that grows on leather shoes left in a damp, dark scullery or dairy for months, presumably

how a once ordinary cheese first became permeated by the mould. I can't help but remember the day I visited Mike, because we were sitting under a cider apple tree eating the apples with Blue Vinny and watching Chalky, my dog, being seen off by some irascible dairy cows on a sunny afternoon last autumn, when someone came out of the farmhouse to say that a plane had crashed into the World Trade Center – an image of pastoral bliss forever shattered.

In another life I would love to be a cheese-maker, or indeed to grow things rather than cook them. We had a period of some five years of keeping chickens, and I must say I sometimes wonder why we don't still do it – I suppose it's because we all got depressed when they stopped laying and started to die, but the pleasure of looking after those chickens and gathering the eggs, and the unbelievable quality of those eggs with their deep yellow yolks exemplify the point of this book. I've listed as many local free-range suppliers as I can find, but really I would hope that the *Salad of poached eggs* (see page 16), the *Huevos rancheros* (see page 19) and the *Fried Eggs with Shallots* (see page 21) would all be made with free-range eggs; the difference is everything.

Of all blue cheeses, Blue Vinny is perhaps the leanest, as it is made with skimmed milk; it is the produce of thrifty Dorset farmers looking to make extra money from the remains of the milk after the prized cream has been skimmed off. It's good for cooking with, though, because sometimes a relatively low-fat cheese is just what's required. I think of this tart as being a light first course or lunch. It also works very well when made with other blue cheeses, and with robustly flavoured sheep's milk cheeses such as feta or pecorino. I like the veining in Vinny, though; it gives the dish a sort of faint taint which I find pleasing.

oven-dried tomato and thyme tart with blue vinny, olive oil and rocket

SERVES 8

750 g (1½lb) vine-ripened
or plum tomatoes
450 g (1 lb) puff pastry
100 g (4 oz) Blue Vinny,
thinly sliced
1 teaspoon fresh thyme leaves
1 tablespoon olive oil
A handful of wild rocket leaves
1 tablespoon extra virgin olive oil
Maldon sea salt flakes and
freshly ground black pepper

1 Preheat the oven to its highest setting. Cut the tomatoes in half lengthways and place them cut–side up in a lightly oiled, shallow roasting tin. Sprinkle over 1½ teaspoons of Maldon salt and some black pepper and roast for 15 minutes. Lower the oven temperature to 150°C/300°F/Gas Mark 2 and roast them for a further 1¼–1½ hours until they have shrivelled in size but are still slightly juicy in the centre. Remove and set aside.

2 Increase the oven temperature to 200°C/400°F/Gas Mark 6. Roll out the pastry on a lightly floured surface into a 30 x 37.5 cm (12 x 15 in) rectangle. Lift it onto a lightly greased baking sheet, prick here and there with a fork and bake blind for 18–20 minutes until crisp and golden. Remove from the oven, carefully turn it over and bake for a further 5 minutes.

3 Arrange the tomatoes haphazardly over the tart base, leaving a narrow border free around the edge. Crumble over the slices of Blue Vinny, sprinkle over the thyme leaves and drizzle over the olive oil. Return the tart to the oven for 5–6 minutes until the cheese has melted.

4 Remove the tart from the oven and scatter the rocket over the top. Cut it into 8 pieces, sprinkle with a little extra virgin olive oil and serve.

This is my version of the classic salade tiède, in which I've included a poached egg; the yolk, when broken, mixes with the dressing and coats the salad leaves in a pleasing way. I've included a few rocket leaves just to lift the colour a little. Don't try using a bag of mixed salad leaves – I find them a bit boring, really. The crowning glory of this dish is the bacon. It celebrates the dry-cured middle cut bacon of Sillfield farm in Cumbria (see page 191) where Peter Gott rears nice, old-fashioned fatty pigs like Gloucester Old Spots, Berkshires and Middle Whites. He ages the bacon after curing which produces a taste almost like pancetta, and inevitably generates the response: 'This is how bacon used to taste'.

salad of poached eggs with bacon and croûtons

SERVES 4

2 slices white bread, crusts removed
Sunflower oil, for shallow frying
4 rashers rindless, thick-cut middle bacon, cut across into short, fat strips (lardons)
1 tablespoon white wine vinegar
1 tablespoon salt
4 medium eggs
The pale green centre of 1 frisée (curly endive), leaves separated, washed and dried
25 g (1 oz) wild rocket leaves

FOR THE MUSTARD DRESSING:
1 teaspoon Dijon mustard
2 teaspoons white wine vinegar
¼ teaspoon salt
2–3 tablespoons sunflower oil

FOR THE PERSILLADE:
2 small garlic cloves
A small handful of flatleaf parsley leaves

1 Cut the bread into 1 cm (½ in) cubes. Shallow fry in 1 cm (½ in) oil until crisp and golden. Drain briefly on kitchen paper.

2 For the mustard dressing, whisk together the mustard, vinegar and salt. Gradually whisk in the oil to make a creamy dressing. For the persillade, chop together the garlic and parsley, leaving it a little bit coarse.

3 Heat a little sunflower oil in a frying pan, add the bacon strips and fry for 2–3 minutes until crisp and golden. Keep warm.

4 Bring a couple of inches of water, the white wine vinegar and salt to a simmer in a large, shallow pan. Break in the eggs and poach for 3 minutes. Lift out with a slotted spoon and drain.

5 Toss the frisée and rocket leaves with a little of the mustard dressing and spread over 4 plates. Put a poached egg into the centre of the leaves and scatter over the bacon. Sprinkle with some of the persillade, drizzle over a little more dressing and then scatter over the croûtons. Serve immediately.

The aubergines are the only warm ingredient here, but when oiled, salted and griddled they make this salad special. However, the most important ingredient is the mozzarella. I decided to include this recipe in the book after visiting Ribblesdale Cheesemakers in Yorkshire (see page 181). I often find British copies of excellent food products from elsewhere in the world to be, not unnaturally, not as good, the felicitous symbiosis of climate and terrain being the reason for the excellence of the genuine article. I've yet, for example, to come across a famous foreign beer, brewed under licence in the UK, to be anything like the original. Here, however, is an exception: this mozzarella is excellent.

warm aubergine and mozzarella salad

SERVES 4

2 large aubergines
150 ml (5 fl oz) extra virgin olive oil
4 large vine-ripened tomatoes, skinned
2 x 150 g (5 oz) mozzarella cheeses
6 good-quality anchovy fillets preserved
in olive oil, drained
1 tablespoon lemon juice
1 tablespoon balsamic vinegar
2 sun-dried tomatoes in olive oil, drained
and thinly sliced
25 g (1 oz) wild rocket leaves
Salt

1 Cut the aubergines diagonally into 5 mm (¼ in) thick slices. Brush them well on both sides with some of the olive oil and sprinkle with a little salt. Heat a ridged cast-iron griddle until smoking hot, add the slices of aubergine a few at a time and cook for about 1½ minutes on each side until nicely golden. Remove and keep warm.

2 Thinly slice the tomatoes and the mozzarella and cut the anchovies diagonally into 5 mm (¼ in) pieces. Whisk together the lemon juice, balsamic vinegar and ½ teaspoon of salt to make the dressing.

3 These types of salad are made up just before they are served. Lay out 4 large, cold plates and build up 4 natural-looking piles on each one: start with a base of tomato, mozzarella and aubergine slices with a few rocket leaves. Add the pieces of anchovy, sun-dried tomato and a light sprinkling of salt, then add another layer of tomato, mozzarella, aubergine, rocket and a little more salt. Finally, pour about 1–1½ tablespoons of the remaining extra virgin olive oil over each plate and then sprinkle a teaspoon of the balsamic dressing over each salad and around the outside edge of the plates.

Thank heavens for restaurants like Chez Bruce in Wandsworth, South London. In a cooking world gone mad with relentless experimentation it's reassuring that there are people like Bruce Poole, who has an innate sense of style and an appreciation of good, everyday French cooking with a serious nod towards the Mediterranean. This recipe was originally made with Gorgonzola, but it works equally well with an excellent full-fat Stilton like Colston Bassett.

stilton with walnuts and honey

SERVES 4

4 x 50 g (2 oz) thin wedges of
Stilton cheese
24 walnut halves, lightly toasted
4 tablespoons clear honey

1 Arrange a piece of the cheese, a little pile of 6 walnut halves and a puddle of honey on each plate and serve.

This is the best-known breakfast egg dish in Mexico. As rather a cautious twenty-one-year-old, I found some of the food and drink there distinctly alarming, things like fried grasshoppers, ants' eggs, chicken with chocolate sauce and tequila with a worm in it. I loved the street food though: tacos, burritos and tamales, and became a real enthusiast for tequila, salt and the bite of a lime – so much so that I seem to have spent too many a morning in Mexico seeking out this revitalizing combination of corn tortilla, tomato, chilli and egg, normally served with refried beans and strong black coffee. I still like to cook this on a long Sunday morning after a particularly lively Saturday night. You will need a tortilla press to make the corn tortillas. These can be bought quite inexpensively from The Cool Chile Company (see page 193).

huevos rancheros (ranch-style eggs)

8 large eggs
Sunflower oil for shallow frying
Salt and freshly ground black pepper

FOR THE TOMATO SAUCE:
2 garlic cloves, finely chopped
1 medium onion, finely chopped
2 tablespoons vegetable oil
4 serrano, jalapeño or medium-hot red Dutch
chillies, roughly chopped
1 x 400 g (14 oz) can chopped tomatoes

FOR THE CORN TORTILLAS
(MAKES APPROXIMATELY 12):
250 g (9 oz) masa harina (maize flour)
(see The Cool Chile Company, page 193)
325 ml (11 fl oz) warm water

FOR THE REFRIED BEANS (OPTIONAL):
350 g (12 oz) dried black, pinto or red kidney
beans, soaked overnight
A large pinch of dried chilli flakes
1 medium onion, finely chopped
2 garlic cloves, chopped
1 bay leaf
40 g (1½oz) lard
3 tablespoons finely grated Cheddar cheese

1 For the refried beans, drain the beans and put them into a large pan with the chilli flakes, onion, garlic and bay leaf. Cover with lots of cold water, bring to the boil and simmer for anything up to 2 hours until tender. Drain, discarding the bay leaf and reserving the cooking liquor. Heat the lard in a large frying pan, add the beans and mash them into a rough paste with a potato masher – leave some of the beans whole to give them a better texture. Stir in the Cheddar cheese and cook over a medium heat for 5 minutes, stirring frequently and adding a little of the reserved cooking liquor now and then, until you have a thick, creamy paste – you might not need to add it all. Season to taste with salt, cover and set aside.

2 For the tomato sauce, soften the garlic and onion in the oil without browning them. Add the chillies and cook for a couple of minutes, then add the chopped tomatoes and simmer until slightly reduced and thickened – you want a pourable sauce. Season to taste with salt and pepper and set aside.

3 For the tortillas, put the masa harina, a good pinch of salt and the water into a bowl and mix together into a slightly moist dough. Mould the dough into 25 g (1 oz) balls. You need to line the tortilla press with a couple of 15 cm (6 in) squares of polythene or baking parchment. You'll soon get the hang of pressing them out and peeling the liner away. Cook in a dry heavy-based frying pan for about a minute on each side until lightly coloured with little brown spots. Wrap the tortillas in a tea towel and keep warm.

4 When you are ready to serve, gently reheat the tomato sauce and the refried beans. Heat some sunflower oil in a large frying pan over a medium heat. Break in the eggs and fry to your liking, spooning a little of the hot oil over the yolks as they cook. Slightly overlap 2 tortillas in the centre of each warmed plate and put 2 of the eggs on top. Spoon a generous quantity of the sauce over and around the eggs and serve with the rest of the tortillas, some good coffee and a bowl of refried beans.

While we were on holiday in South Africa recently, Jill and her best friend Terri rounded on me for not serving up salads like those they were eating – cheese, bacon, salad leaves, beetroot – in any of our restaurants. We were on a terrace overlooking Gansbaai, watching a couple of whale tails flopping in the sunny sea, and surrounded by fynbos, the wispy grey-green bushes which flow all over the hills along the Atlantic coast east of Cape Town. I said, 'You mean a "ladies who lunch" salad?' 'Precisely,' they said, without acknowledging my pathetic joke. So this is it – a big plate of salad designed to fill the need for something exciting but not too heavy at lunchtime. Mrs Kirkham's Lancashire (see page 180) is the perfect cheese for this, being quite surprisingly piquant, but if you can't get this, Parmesan is great, too.

a salad of lancashire cheese, with pancetta in balsamic vinegar and chilli beetroot

SERVES 4

2 x 50 g (2 oz) cooked beetroot
3 tablespoons sherry vinegar
1 small garlic clove, finely chopped
1 teaspoon caster sugar
¼ teaspoon dried chilli flakes
225 g (8 oz) Lancashire cheese
4 tablespoons extra virgin olive oil
75 g (3 oz) thinly sliced
smoked pancetta
1 tablespoon balsamic vinegar
100 g (4 oz) mixed baby salad leaves,
such as lambs' lettuce, baby beet
leaves and rocket
Salt and freshly ground black pepper
A few small flatleaf parsley leaves

1 Halve the beetroot and cut it into thin slices. Put them into a small bowl with the sherry vinegar, garlic, sugar, chilli flakes and ½ teaspoon of salt and leave for 1 hour.

2 Thinly slice the cheese and crumble it into smallish pieces. Put a little olive oil in a heavy-based frying pan and fry the pancetta (in batches if necessary) on each side until crisp and golden. Add the balsamic vinegar and allow it to bubble away to nothing. Remove the pancetta from the pan, leave it to cool, and then break it into small, chunky pieces.

3 To serve, toss the salad leaves with the remaining olive oil and a little seasoning to taste. Pile onto 4 large plates and tuck the bacon, beetroot and cheese in amongst the leaves. Sprinkle over the parsley leaves and serve immediately.

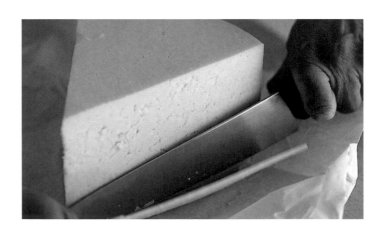

This is the perfect breakfast dish to accompany exceptional bread; something like a blistering, brown, crusty sourdough with a slightly chewy interior and a faintly tart aroma. The combination of the reduced vinegar, olive oil, shallots and egg, early morning sunshine and some characterful bread with which to wipe the plate clean, conjures up memories of villas by Mediterranean rocky beaches. This is one of Elizabeth David's recipes and exemplifies the unforced naturalness of her recipes. Not the work of an over-active imagination, but of someone who saw eggs cooked like this somewhere in the Mediterranean.

fried eggs with shallots and vinegar

SERVES 2

2 tablespoons olive oil
4 medium free-range eggs
1 medium-sized shallot, finely chopped
1 teaspoon white wine vinegar
Salt and freshly ground black pepper

1 Heat the olive oil in a frying pan over a moderate heat. Break in 2 of the eggs and fry briskly to slightly crisp up the edges of the whites. Remove to a warm plate and repeat with the other 2 eggs, adding a little more oil.

2 Return the pan to a moderate heat, add the shallots and turn them over for 10 seconds only. Pull the pan off the heat, add the vinegar and let it bubble for 3–4 seconds, season with some salt and pepper and pour over the eggs. Serve with bread and coffee.

2 salads, soups

EVERY DISH IN THIS CHAPTER CAN BE MADE
PERFECTLY SATISFACTORILY WITH THE PRODUCE
FROM ANY LARGE SUPERMARKET. VEGETABLES ARE
THE ONE AREA WHERE ALL EXCEL, SO WHY NOT NAME
MARKS AND SPENCER, SAINSBURY, TESCO, WAITROSE,
AND ALL THE OTHERS AS FOOD HEROES? IN MANY
WAYS THEY ARE. SUPERMARKETS HAVE ENABLED US
ALL TO GET HOLD OF THE RAW MATERIALS TO COOK
FRESH, HEALTHY FOOD. HOW COULD WE SATISFY OUR
THIRST FOR ALL THINGS MEDITERRANEAN – THE
TOMATO, MOZZARELLA AND BASIL SALADS, THE THICK
GREEK YOGHURT AND WILD-THYME HONEY, THE OLIVE
OILS FROM TUSCANY TO ANDALUCIA – WITHOUT
THEM? HOW, TOO, COULD WE TRY OUT THE CUISINES
OF ALMOST EVERY COUNTRY ON EARTH WITH
AUTHENTIC INGREDIENTS?

and first courses

RIGHT AND BELOW
Bill Allam of Test Valley Watercress in Hampshire, gathers bunches of cress and herbs. The chalky ground of Hampshire generates particularly pure water, creating the perfect conditions for growing lush, green watercress.

Think of the varieties of tomatoes: vine, plum, cherry, beef. These are available everywhere; perhaps not quite as stunning as the best varieties from Tomatoes Direct on the Isle of Wight, one of the producers listed in the directory (see page 183), but very good. The purple sprouting broccoli I bought from my local Tesco this spring was nearly as good as that which I grew myself. I had to go out and

buy some – the pigeons ate most of mine. I boiled it briefly and we had it as a first course with hollandaise sauce, a fitting way to focus on the delight of the first tender shoots of the season.

Consider too the salads now available. At the restaurant we like to be ahead of the game, but we find it very hard to have salad leaves that the multiples don't with the accessibility of wild rocket, radicchio, lamb's lettuce, baby chard and spinach leaves, all washed, fresh and ready to be dressed. Those trays of growing herbs they sell – parsley, coriander, chives and basil – are a godsend. You could use them to make my *Parsley soup with chive cream* (see page 29). It wouldn't be quite as minerally as that made with a big bunch from The

Organic Farm Shop near Cirencester, or Rod and Ben's, Bickham Farm at Kenn near Exeter, but it would do. Small growers like these are where the best vegetables come from, many of them organic and certified by The Soil Association.

I suppose I'm never satisfied. I want the supermarkets to go that little bit further: forge links with lots of local growers and eliminate the need to send everything back to the central distribution depots; buy the vegetables locally and stock them direct; put more money into the local economy, just as we should do, whenever possible, by buying locally. I'm afraid supermarkets do lead to the demise of most local food shops. I know – I had to close our general deli and reopen as one specializing in seafood soon after a large supermarket opened on the outskirts of Padstow. Our turnover had dropped by 30 per cent. The big companies argue that quality local shops will always survive, but lots of good ones go too. And supermarkets don't yet offer back enough of what they've taken away: good local produce. We filmed a game auction in Louth in Lincolnshire last summer. Louth is that rare phenomenon: a fair-sized town without a large supermarket. The result is a town alive with butchers, greengrocers and delis and a thriving market. It gives you a pang to see what so many other towns have lost, the buzz at the centre of the town, the human scale of lots of small competitive shops. That part of Lincolnshire is flat and fertile and produces excellent vegetables; Abbey Parks Asparagus at East Heckington near Boston will deliver freshly-picked asparagus to you with which to make my simple but exciting *Asparagus with Parmesan and olive oil* (see page 33). Incidentally, the Italians often finish this dish with a free-range egg fried in olive oil. Try it too.

I first came across the Brindisa company (see page 193) on a visit to Borough Market, where they sell Spanish ingredients of superb quality and are one of the few sources of that best-of-all air-dried ham, Ibérico. Another of their delicacies is air-cured tuna loin called mojama. It comes in a block and has the same sort of pungent odour as a barrel of long-salted herrings, but when shaved paper-thin and served in a salad alongside the bitterness of radicchio and the saltiness of good Parmesan, it adds an intriguing and exciting dimension to this crisp salad.

a seasonal salad of fennel and radicchio with shaved tuna and parmesan

SERVES 4

2 x 225 g (8 oz) fennel bulbs, trimmed
175 g (6 oz) radicchio leaves, broken into small pieces
8 teaspoons extra virgin olive oil, plus extra to serve
2 teaspoons lemon juice
25 g (1 oz) piece of mojama (dried tuna loin)
25 g (1 oz) piece of Parmesan cheese
Salt and freshly ground black pepper

1 Remove the outer layer of each fennel bulb, if damaged. Slice the bulbs across into thin slices, preferably on a Japanese mandolin, and put them into a bowl with the radicchio leaves, olive oil, lemon juice and some salt and pepper to taste. Toss together briefly.

2 Shave very thin slices off the dried tuna and Parmesan cheese, again with a mandolin if possible – the pieces must be very thin.

3 Arrange the fennel and radicchio salad on 4 plates and drizzle a little more oil around the outside edge of the plates. Scatter over the shaved tuna and Parmesan cheese. I like to finish the salad with a drizzle of olive oil around the edge, scattered with a little cracked black pepper and Maldon sea-salt, which has a pleasing flaky texture to it.

Most home-made soups end up tasting too much like the tinned ones, so why bother? Well, here I've taken care to make sure that the tomatoes are hardly cooked at all, and also added some black-olive tapenade, chilli, garlic, extra virgin olive oil and fresh basil. I created this recipe after a trip to Tomatoes Direct on the Isle of Wight (see page 183). Before then I had always assumed that growing good tomatoes was all a matter of having more sunshine than we do in the UK, but it seems that's not so; it's more a question of the varieties grown. Tomatoes from Italy and Spain may have a luscious juiciness, but our best varieties have a fragrant acidity, particularly when sold still on the vine.

fresh tomato soup with tapenade

SERVES 4

900 g (2 lb) vine-grown tomatoes with their stalks (but not the stems)
50 ml (2 fl oz) extra virgin olive oil, plus extra to serve

1 For the tapenade, blend the olives, anchovies, capers and garlic in a food processor, then add the oil in a thin, steady stream through the hole in the lid. I prefer to leave the finished tapenade a little on the coarse side. Stir in some black pepper to taste.

6 garlic cloves, roughly chopped
¼ teaspoon dried chilli flakes
Salt
A few basil leaves, very finely shredded, to garnish

FOR THE TAPENADE:
75 g (3 oz) pitted good-quality black olives
4 anchovy fillets in olive oil, drained
25 g (1 oz) capers, drained and rinsed
3 garlic cloves, roughly chopped
85 ml (3 fl oz) olive oil
Freshly ground black pepper

2 For the soup, coarsely chop the tomatoes and their stalks. Put the olive oil, garlic and chilli flakes into a large saucepan and set over a low heat for a few seconds until the garlic just begins to sizzle. Add the tomatoes and turn over a low heat for just 2 minutes until their juices begin to run.

3 Tip the mixture into a food processor or liquidizer, blend until finely chopped and then pass through a conical sieve into a clean pan, pressing out as much liquid as you can with the back of a small ladle. Stir in 2 tablespoons of the tapenade.

4 Reheat the soup gently until warm but not hot – you want to retain the fresh flavour of the tomatoes. Season the soup to taste with some salt, ladle into warmed bowls, and serve drizzled with a little more oil and garnished with the finely shredded basil.

Last summer we filmed in the idyllic walled kitchen garden of the Stone House Hotel at Rushlake Green near Heathfield on the Sussex/Kent border. We had eaten there the previous evening and were much taken by the Englishness of it all. The house, built in 1495, has been the home of the Dunn family ever since. It is filled with antiques, family heirlooms and portraits of the Dunns through the centuries. The stairs are old, oak and creaky, there are log fires, probably alight even in summer, and the house is surrounded by a vast estate where sheep and cattle graze. You feel delightfully lost in some of the most considered rural scenes in the world – Glyndebourne and Sissinghurst are almost next door – and it felt as though we were in *A Midsummer Night's Dream*. Jane Dunn cooked our dinner, and there happened to be parsley soup on the menu. It was as straightforward as one would have hoped: just parsley from the garden, a few leeks, cream and some excellent stock.

parsley soup with chive cream

SERVES 4

2 large leeks
2 x 100 g (4 oz) bunches of curly leaf
parsley, well washed
75 g (3 oz) butter
275 g (10 oz) floury potatoes such as
Maris Piper, peeled and chopped
1.2 litres (2 pints) *Chicken stock*
(see page 176)
50 ml (2 fl oz) double cream
Salt and freshly ground black pepper

FOR THE CHIVE CREAM:
50 ml (2 fl oz) double cream
1 teaspoon very finely chopped chives

1 Remove and discard the darker green tops of the leeks. Slice the rest and wash well.

2 Pull the leaves off one of the bunches of parsley and set them aside to add to the soup just before liquidizing to give it a vivid greenness. Roughly chop the second bunch and the stalks of the first.

3 Melt the butter in a large pan, add the chopped parsley and leeks and cook gently for 5 minutes until soft. Add the potatoes and chicken stock, cover and simmer gently for 20 minutes.

4 Add the reserved parsley leaves and simmer for 2 minutes, then liquidize in batches until smooth and return to a clean pan. Stir in the cream and season with salt and freshly ground black pepper.

5 For the chive cream, lightly whip the cream with a small pinch of salt and pepper so that it thickens slightly but is still runny. Stir in most of the chopped chives.

6 Ladle the soup into warmed bowls and swirl in some of the chive cream. Scatter over the remaining chives.

I've been to Hampshire recently in search of wild brown trout in the Rivers Itchen and Test. I was disappointed that it wasn't possible to eat simply-fried brown trout from the local chalk streams in any of the local restaurants. I was more than cheered up, however, by the availability of watercress soup in all the local pubs. The substrata of chalk in this part of Hampshire, just north of Winchester, acts as a filter, producing particularly pure water for beds of clean watercress. I think that the soup is better using water rather than stock: stock gives the soup a greater depth, but water leads to concentration of the clean pepperiness of this pungent plant.

potato and watercress soup

SERVES 4

50 g (2 oz) butter
2 medium onions, chopped
2 large bunches watercress
(about 200 g/7 oz in weight)
750 g (1½ lb) floury potatoes, such as Maris
Piper, peeled and cut into small pieces
1.2 litres (2 pints) water
150 ml (5 fl oz) double cream
Salt and freshly ground white pepper

1 Melt the butter in a large pan, add the onions and cook gently for 5–7 minutes until very soft but not brown.

2 Roughly chop the watercress and add half of it to the pan with the potatoes and water. Bring to the boil, cover and simmer for 20 minutes, or until the potatoes are very soft.

3 Add the rest of the watercress and liquidize the soup until smooth. Return the soup to the pan, bring back to a simmer, then stir in the cream and plenty of salt and pepper to taste.

This is the sort of breakfast dish I reserve for Sundays. Other days, I'm normally to be found with a slice of toast and a cup of coffee, running for the door. I think a simple sauté like this is the best way to enjoy mushrooms picked straight from the fields or woods. Try to avoid washing them: most just need a brush or a wipe with a damp cloth. This is particularly important with absorbent mushrooms like penny buns (ceps) or parasols, which take on water like a sponge. Morels are often sandy and trap dirt but take to washing in cold water well, being quite waxy. I have rather a novel way of toasting the bread for this recipe: I like to singe the bread lightly over a gas flame before toasting it normally.

wild mushrooms and devilled kidneys on hot buttered toast

SERVES 2

4 slices of sourdough bread, or a similar rustic white bread
175 g (6 oz) wild mushrooms, such as pieds de mouton, pied bleu, girolles and chanterelles, cleaned
3 lambs' kidneys
1 tablespoon plain flour
¼ teaspoon cayenne pepper
¼ teaspoon mustard powder
40 g (1½ oz) salted butter
1 tablespoon chopped curly leaf parsley
25 g (1 oz) unsalted butter
Salt and freshly ground black pepper

1 Toast the slices of bread over a naked gas flame until nicely singed on either side and set aside.

2 Cut the mushrooms in half, or into quarters, or leave whole, depending on their size. Cut the kidneys in half lengthways and snip out the cores with scissors. Mix together the flour, cayenne pepper, mustard powder, ¼ teaspoon of salt and some black pepper in a bowl, add the kidneys and toss well.

3 Heat half the salted butter in a large frying pan over a moderate heat. Add the kidneys, leaving behind any excess flour, and cook for 1½ minutes on each side until lightly browned on the outside but still pink and juicy in the centre. Lift onto a plate and keep warm.

4 Add the rest of the salted butter to the pan and as soon as it is foaming add the mushrooms and increase the heat to high. Season them with salt and pepper and fry briskly for a couple of minutes. Return the kidneys to the pan, add half the chopped parsley and toss together briefly. Remove the pan from the heat.

5 Toast the bread and spread each slice with the unsalted butter. Put one piece of toast onto each plate and spoon the mushrooms and kidneys on top. Sprinkle with the remaining chopped parsley and serve the remaining toast separately.

'Chile rellenos' – poblano or Anaheim chillies (stuffed with cheese, coated in a crisp cornmeal crust and served with a dried red chilli and tomato sauce) – is one of my favourite Mexican dishes and the sort of thing that must set the tastebuds of every vegetarian alight. It's really hard to get the right chillies, though, so I have rearranged the recipe using Romano peppers, those long chilli-shaped red peppers that most supermarkets now sell. You might like to add a pinch of chilli powder to the cheese stuffing to re-create the heat. I've changed the cheese, too, as it's difficult to get the special Mexican cheese for stuffing, but felicitously our own Cornish Yarg is ideal for the job as it melts easily. David Gray, the cheese-maker and another food hero of mine, makes a mild, Cheddar-like cheese, distinguished by a rind of nettles which gives it a faint herby flavour (see page 180).

stuffed romano peppers with guajillo chilli sauce fried in polenta

SERVES 4

4 good-sized Romano peppers
225 g (8 oz) Cornish Yarg cheese
2 eggs, beaten
2 tablespoons milk
50 g (2 oz) polenta or cornmeal
Sunflower or groundnut oil, for frying
Salt and freshly ground black pepper
Corn tortillas (see page 19), to serve

FOR THE GUAJILLO CHILLI SAUCE:
3 dried Guajillo (little gourd) chillies
(see The Cool Chile Company,
page 193)
1½ tablespoons sunflower oil
75 g (3 oz) onion, roughly chopped
2 tinned plum tomatoes
1 fat garlic clove, crushed
½ teaspoon ground cumin
1½ teaspoons caster sugar
2–3 teaspoons lemon juice

1 Slit open the dried chillies and remove the stalks and seeds. Put them into a small bowl, cover with hot water and leave to soak for 20 minutes. Meanwhile, preheat the oven to 220°C/425°F/Gas Mark 7. Roast the Romano peppers for 10–12 minutes, then remove, put them into a plastic bag and leave to cool.

2 For the chilli sauce, heat 1 tablespoon of the oil in a small pan, add the onion and fry over a medium–high heat, stirring now and then, until richly browned.

3 Drain the chillies, reserving the soaking liquor. Put the soaked chillies, tomatoes, fried onion, garlic, cumin, sugar and ½ teaspoon salt into a liquidizer with 120 ml (4 fl oz) of the chilli soaking liquor and blend to a smooth paste.

4 Heat the remaining ½ tablespoon of oil in a medium-sized saucepan. Add the paste and simmer for 10 minutes, stirring now and then, until it has reduced to a good sauce consistency. Stir in the lemon juice and some seasoning to taste. Keep hot.

5 Carefully peel the skin off the peppers, then make a slit down one side, leaving the stalks in place, and scoop out the seeds, taking care not to tear the flesh. Season them well inside and out. Remove the rind from the cheese and cut it into long pieces, about 2.5 cm (1 in) wide and 1 cm (½ in) thick. Fill the whole length of each pepper's cavity with pieces of cheese, putting a tapering piece in towards the tip. Push them back into shape and tie in 2 places with string to keep everything in place.

6 Beat the eggs and milk together in one large, shallow dish and put some seasoned polenta into a second dish. Dip the stuffed peppers in the polenta, then the egg and milk, then the polenta once more. Heat 1 cm (½ in) of oil in a large, deep frying pan to 180°C/350°F. Add the peppers and fry them gently for 5 minutes on each side until crisp and richly golden. Carefully lift out with a fish slice and drain on kitchen paper. Serve with the chilli sauce and warm corn tortillas.

The classic accompaniment to simply boiled asparagus is hollandaise sauce, or sometimes sauce mousseline (hollandaise sauce with a little lightly whipped double cream folded through), but the alternative addition of a very good olive oil, shaved Parmesan and sea salt is equally satisfying.

asparagus with parmesan and olive oil

SERVES 4

450 g (1 lb) (about 24 stalks) of
fine asparagus
100 ml (3½ fl oz) extra virgin olive oil
A small chunk of Parmesan cheese,
to serve
Maldon sea salt flakes and coarsely
ground black pepper

1 Trim the woody ends from the asparagus by bending each stalk near the bottom and discarding the bit where it naturally breaks. Bring some well-salted water (1 teaspoon of salt per 600 ml/1 pint of water) to the boil in a shallow wide pan, add the asparagus and cook for 3–4 minutes until just tender.

2 Lift the asparagus out of the water, drain well and divide between 4 plates. Drizzle about 2 tablespoons of oil over each one and then shave over 4–6 thin pieces of Parmesan. Sprinkle with a few Maldon sea-salt flakes and some black pepper and serve immediately.

I came up with this recipe as a celebration of the organic vegetables I had tasted at Coleshill Organics near Swindon (see page 182). Cultivating vegetables without recourse to chemicals is very hard work, but there does seem to be more flavour in a leek grown organically. I thought that to make a vegetable (which is mostly just added to flavour other ingredients) the star of the dish would do justice to Peter Richardson and Sonya Oliver's hard work. If you can't get provolone piccante, other good cheeses for this would be Beaufort or Gruyère.

leek cannelloni with lemon thyme and provolone piccante

SERVES 4

50 g (2 oz) butter
900 g (2 lb) leeks, cleaned and thinly sliced
2 garlic cloves, crushed
2 teaspoons lemon thyme leaves
2 tablespoons water
250 g (9 oz) ricotta cheese
250 g (9 oz) (12 sheets) fresh lasagne pasta
Salt and freshly ground black pepper

FOR THE TOMATO SAUCE:
2 tablespoons olive oil
1 medium onion, finely chopped
1 garlic clove, crushed
400 g (14 oz) can chopped tomatoes
50 ml (2 fl oz) red wine vinegar
2 teaspoons caster sugar

FOR THE CHEESE SAUCE:
1 small onion, peeled and halved
3 cloves
450 ml (15 fl oz) full cream milk
1 bay leaf
½ teaspoon black peppercorns
30 g (1¼oz) butter
30 g (1¼oz) plain flour
2 tablespoons double cream
150 g (5 oz) provolone piccante, coarsely grated
1 egg yolk

1 For the cheese sauce, stud the onion with the cloves and put it into a pan with the milk, bay leaf and black peppercorns. Bring the milk to the boil and set it aside for 20 minutes to infuse.

2 For the tomato sauce, heat the oil in a medium-sized pan. Add the onion and garlic and cook gently until softened. Add the tomatoes and simmer gently for 15–20 minutes, stirring now and then, until reduced and thickened. Put the vinegar and sugar into a small pan and boil rapidly until reduced to 1 teaspoon. Stir into the tomato sauce with some salt and pepper to taste, then spoon the sauce over the base of a large, shallow ovenproof dish.

3 For the cannelloni filling, melt the butter in a large pan. Add the sliced leeks, garlic, lemon thyme leaves and water and cook gently, uncovered, for 15 minutes, until they are tender and all the excess liquid has evaporated. Transfer to a bowl and leave to cool. Then beat in the ricotta cheese and season to taste with salt and pepper.

4 Bring a large pan of salted water to the boil. Drop in the sheets of lasagne pasta one at a time, take the pan off the heat and leave them to soak for 5 minutes. Drain well and leave to cool. Spoon some of the leek filling along one short edge of each sheet and roll up. Arrange the cannelloni seam-side down on top of the tomato sauce.

5 Preheat the oven to 200°C/400°F/Gas Mark 6. Strain the milk for the cheese sauce. Melt the butter in a non-stick pan, add the flour and cook over a medium heat for 1 minute to cook out the flour. Gradually beat in the milk, bring to the boil, stirring, and leave to simmer very gently over a low heat for 10 minutes, giving it a stir every now and then. Remove the pan from the heat and stir in the cream, 75 g (3 oz) of the grated provolone, the egg yolk and some seasoning to taste.

6 Pour the sauce over the cannelloni, sprinkle over the rest of the cheese and bake in the oven for 30 minutes until golden and bubbling.

SALADS, SOUPS AND FIRST COURSES LEEK CANNELLONI

The hero of this piece is the pasta. I have no real insider knowledge of the best factory-made pasta, but I do know what I like and that is, above all, 'De Cecco', particularly the linguine no 7. The most important element in a good pasta is the flour – hard semolina – but almost as important is the length of time it is dried. The longer it takes, the harder the finished pasta and the better it keeps its al dente quality during cooking. De Cecco is amazingly robust in this way and it makes all the difference, even in the way that it falls on the plate, retaining bounce and shape, served with this simple olive oil, parsley and dried porcini sauce clinging to it.

linguine with porcini, garlic and truffle oil

SERVES 4

25 g (1 oz) dried porcini mushrooms
450 g (1 lb) dried linguine
5 tablespoons extra virgin olive oil
4 small garlic cloves, thinly sliced
1 teaspoon minced truffle
8 tablespoons roughly chopped flatleaf parsley
Salt
Truffle oil, to serve

1 Cover the dried porcini with warm water and leave to soak for 30 minutes.

2 Drop the linguine into a large pan of well-salted boiling water (1 teaspoon of salt per 600 ml/1 pint of water), bring back to the boil and cook for 7–8 minutes or until al dente.

3 Meanwhile, drain the mushrooms and slice them thinly.

4 Put the oil into a large pan with the garlic and leave to sizzle gently for 1 minute. Add the mushrooms and cook them for another minute.

5 Drain the pasta, add to the garlic, mushroom and oil pan with the minced truffle and chopped parsley. Toss together.

6 Spoon the pasta into 4 warmed bowls, sprinkle each one with a little truffle oil and serve immediately.

Panzanella is a bread, tomato and olive-oil salad from Tuscany, and is a way of using up stale bread – no less practical than our own bread pudding. To make stale bread palatable, it is usually well soaked in water. Having eaten a salad made like this I had previously marvelled that anyone would actually want to eat such slop. Then Debbie Major, with whom I work on all my cookery books, showed me this panzanella made with really rugged bread, which was lightly toasted and mixed with the rest of the salad ingredients, only five minutes before serving.

Of course the heart of it is the bread. It's got to be interesting, and I favour a slightly chewy, waxy bread like a ciabatta or the pain au levain from a good baker such as Baker and Spice in Walton Street, London (see page 191). Or, indeed, at our own deli on the quayside in Padstow.

panzanella

(see page 191)

SERVES 4

1 good-sized loaf of ciabatta bread
½ cucumber
1 small red pepper
750 g (1½lb) medium vine-ripened
tomatoes, skinned
2 fat cloves of garlic
2 tablespoons red wine vinegar
4 tablespoons extra virgin olive oil,
plus extra to serve
1 small red onion, very thinly sliced
2 tablespoons capers in brine,
drained and rinsed
100 g (4 oz) small, well-flavoured
black olives
25 g (1 oz) basil leaves, torn into pieces
Maldon sea salt flakes and freshly
ground black pepper

1 Preheat the grill to high. Cut the bread into 1 cm (½ in) thick slices and toast them very lightly on both sides until just starting to colour. Leave to cool and then break into rough 2.5 cm (1 in) pieces.

2 Peel the cucumber, cut it in half lengthways and scoop out the seeds with a teaspoon. Cut across into slices. Grill the red pepper for 7–8 minutes, turning it now and then, until the skin has blistered and blackened. Put in a plastic bag and leave to cool. Then peel off the skin, remove the stalk and seeds, and cut the flesh into chunky strips.

3 Cut the tomatoes into quarters, scoop out the seeds and juice and press the seeds through a sieve into a large bowl. Cut the flesh of the tomatoes into rough 2.5 cm (1 in) pieces.

4 Crush the garlic and add to the tomato juice in the bowl. Stir in the vinegar, olive oil and some seasoning.

5 Five minutes before serving, add the pieces of bread to the salad bowl and toss together well with the tomato dressing. Add the cucumber, red pepper, tomatoes, red onion, capers, olives and basil and check the seasoning. Set aside for 5 minutes to allow time for the bread to soften slightly.

6 To serve, pile the mixture into the centre of 4 large plates, drizzle over a little more extra virgin olive oil and sprinkle with a little Maldon salt and freshly ground black pepper.

3 fish and

IN THIS CHAPTER THERE'S A RECIPE FOR *SEARED ESCALOPES OF WILD SALMON WITH A WARM OLIVE OIL, BASIL AND CARAMELIZED VINEGAR DRESSING* (SEE PAGE 60). WHEN I THOUGHT THIS UP I HAD IN MIND A DAY SPENT ON THE RIVER TYNE WITH A LOCAL FLY FISHERMAN CALLED MIKE ZELLAS, WATCHING THE SALMON LEAP UP THE WEIR AT HEXHAM. I HAD MET MIKE A FEW WEEKS PREVIOUSLY AT RATHER A GOOD RESTAURANT AT HAYDON BRIDGE CALLED THE GENERAL HAVELOCK INN; HE HAD DROPPED OFF A CARDBOARD BOX OF PARTRIDGES WHICH HE HAD JUST SHOT AND WE GOT TALKING ABOUT THE SALMON IN THE TYNE — A WELCOME RETURN OF THE FISH TO A PREVIOUSLY MUCH POLLUTED RIVER.

shellfish

I was fairly depressed at the time, having just been to the centre of what was the last big outbreak of the foot and mouth epidemic. I'd interviewed a farmer's wife who had lost all her stock and who was almost as bereaved as she would have been at losing close friends. Seeing the cattle dropped like pieces of rag from the jaws of a crane-shovel into a burial pit was a sight I shall not forget; nor the silence and emptiness in the fields all around.

I needed a tonic and Mike was it. He was exactly the sort of character this book is a celebration of: filled with an enthusiastic respect for the quality of those partridges and the wild salmon of the Tyne. It's a respect we all need to have in large quantities for the seafood around our shores; already there are signs of rapid decline in stocks through overfishing. Despite suggestions that my attempts to make seafood more popular only exacerbate the situation, I feel that the more we love our seafood the harder we'll strive to protect it. There are clear signs of this now: the efforts of the Marine Stewardship Council to certify sustainable fisheries and the attempts of the Worldwide Fund for Nature to have areas of sea

declared 'no take zones' to allow for stock generation, are becoming increasingly understood and supported.

Our seafood school in Padstow is popular, largely, I suspect, because the quality of the seafood we work with there is a revelation to most of our students. So often when demonstrating fish cookery someone asks the question, 'how do we buy seafood like you use?' It is difficult; I still find it hard to be ecstatic about supermarket fish, which is where most people will buy it. I think the time between catching and sale is too long, though quality is improving all the time: Asda has taken the vital step of selling day-boat fish at two of its stores in Cornwall.

The suppliers in this book tend to buy from day boats for freshness, whenever possible, and they know which boats they like to buy from – they have built relationships with the best fisherman. It's these relationships that lead you to the sort of fish I use for dishes like *Hake with sauce verte and butter beans* (see page 57) and *Langoustine and clotted cream quiche with tarragon and parsley* (see page 50).

Combinations of thick fillets of fish and shellfish are always popular at my restaurant. I've chosen cod here because the local fish from Matthew Stevens in St Ives (see page 184) is the best I've tasted. I would also suggest using the little-known but excellent wolf fish (sometimes called catfish or rock turbot); I've included a couple of suppliers in the directory at the back of the book. Any thick fillet of white fish would work well here. In Australia, large murray cod, perhaps, if you can get it, or king dory, coral trout or jewfish. The brown shrimps are very important. You can use a combination or just one type of the other shellfish. I like to leave one or two in the shell when I serve the dish.

grilled cod with shellfish in garlic butter

SERVES 4

350 g (12 oz) each of small mussels, cockles and carpet shell clams, washed
50 ml (2 fl oz) dry white wine
4 x 175 g (6 oz) pieces of thick, unskinned cod fillet
2 tablespoons melted butter
175 g (6 oz) cooked brown shrimps, peeled
Salt and freshly ground black pepper
Plain boiled new potatoes (see page 172), to serve

FOR THE GARLIC BUTTER:
2 large garlic cloves
100 g (4 oz) unsalted butter, softened
1 teaspoon lemon juice
1 teaspoon brandy
25 g (1 oz) chopped parsley

1 Put the mussels, cockles and clams into a large pan with the white wine. Cover and cook over a high heat for 3–4 minutes until just opened. Tip into a colander set over a bowl so that you can collect all the juice. Remove the meats from most of the shells. Leave a few intact.

2 Return 300 ml (10 fl oz) of the cooking liquor to the pan and boil rapidly until reduced to 2 tablespoons.

3 For the garlic butter, crush the garlic cloves with a little salt, put into a bowl with the butter, lemon juice, brandy, parsley and some freshly ground black pepper and beat together well.

4 Preheat the grill to high. Brush the pieces of cod on both sides with melted butter and season well with salt and pepper. Put skin-side up onto a lightly buttered grilling tray or the rack of the grill pan and grill for 8–10 minutes.

5 Melt the garlic butter in a pan, add the reduced cooking liquor, cooked shellfish and the peeled brown shrimps and stir briefly over a low heat until heated through. Lift the cod onto warmed plates. Spoon some of the shellfish butter over the top of the cod and the rest onto the plate. Serve with boiled new potatoes.

I wrote this recipe for the excellent sweet smoked haddock from the Swallow Fish smokery in Seahouses, Northumberland (see page 185), but it's possible to get really good-quality undyed smoked haddock from lots of sources: Alfred Enderby Ltd in Grimsby (page 183) and Quayside Fish in Porthleven, Cornwall (page 184), to name but a couple. This dish appears on the menu at our Bistro in St Petroc's frequently – the combination of the flakes of smoked haddock, the new potatoes and Little Gem lettuce with a creamy dressing is irresistible and all the work of our chef there, Alistair Clive. You can make this with other smoked fish – if you can get unsliced smoked salmon and poach a thick steak, you would be in for a treat. In New South Wales, Australia, there's a really good product, smoked silver perch, which comes hot-smoked, so you wouldn't need to poach it first.

salad of smoked haddock, warm potatoes and little gem lettuce

SERVES 4

12 medium-sized new potatoes, scrubbed clean
600 ml (1 pint) milk
600 ml (1 pint) water
550 g (1¼ lb) undyed smoked haddock fillet, or other smoked fish
4 baby Little Gem lettuces, broken into leaves (discard the outer leaves if necessary)
4 tablespoons roughly chopped flatleaf parsley

FOR THE DRESSING:
2 shallots, thinly sliced and separated into rings
1 tablespoon good-quality red wine vinegar
2–3 tablespoons double cream
Salt and freshly ground black pepper

1 For the dressing, toss the shallots and vinegar together in a bowl. Set aside for at least 15 minutes and up to 4 hours to soften the shallots.

2 Cook the potatoes in well-salted water (1 teaspoon of salt per 600 ml/1 pint of water) for 15–20 minutes, until just tender. Drain and slice thickly.

3 Meanwhile, bring the milk and water to the boil in a shallow pan. Add the smoked haddock and poach for about 4 minutes until just cooked through. Lift out onto a plate, and when cool enough to handle, break the fish into large flakes, discarding the skin and any bones.

4 To serve, scatter the lettuce leaves over the base of 1 large or 4 smaller plates. Arrange the warm sliced potatoes and pieces of warm, flaked poached haddock in amongst the leaves.

5 Stir the cream into the dressing and season to taste with some salt and pepper. Spoon the dressing over the salad and scatter over the parsley.

I came up with this recipe after a few days spent near Winchester in Hampshire looking for trout. There seemed to be plenty of them in the Itchen and Meon every time I stopped in villages like Titchborne and Itchen Abbas to look over a bridge. However, I couldn't find a restaurant or pub that sold a pan-fried trout, even ones by the river. I was denied a simple pleasure; the countryside there is so conducive to such innocent enjoyment. Finally I met a local fly fisherman, John Holt, who caught me a couple. You can occasionally buy farmed brown trout in supermarkets; otherwise use rainbow trout. Like farmed salmon, farmed trout can be extremely good if well looked after, and taste of pond water if not.

pan-fried brown trout with bacon, hazelnuts and frisée

SERVES 2

75 g (3 oz) dry-cured streaky bacon
rashers, rinds removed
Sunflower oil
2 x 350–450 g (12 oz–1 lb) brown trout,
fins trimmed
25 g (1 oz) plain flour
25 g (1 oz) skinned hazelnuts,
roughly crushed
15 g ($\frac{1}{2}$ oz) butter
50 g (2 oz) prepared frisée (curly endive)
Salt and freshly ground black pepper

FOR THE DRESSING:
1 small garlic clove, finely chopped
2 tablespoons cider vinegar
1 teaspoon Dijon mustard
3 tablespoons sunflower oil
1 tablespoon chopped parsley

1 Cut the bacon across into short, thin strips. Put the strips into a frying pan with a little oil and leave over a medium heat until the fat from the bacon begins to run. Meanwhile, season the trout inside and out with salt and pepper, coat them in flour and pat off the excess. Add the hazelnuts to the pan and fry with the bacon until both are golden brown. Remove with a slotted spoon to a plate and keep warm.

2 Add the butter and the trout to the pan and fry them over a medium heat for 4–5 minutes. Turn them over and fry for another 4–5 minutes. Lift the trout onto 2 warmed serving plates.

3 For the dressing, add the chopped garlic to the pan, leave it to cook for a few seconds, then add the cider vinegar and boil until it has reduced to about 1 tablespoon. Whisk in the mustard, sunflower oil, parsley, $\frac{1}{2}$ teaspoon of salt and 10 turns of the black pepper mill.

4 Pile the frisée alongside the trout and spoon over some of the dressing. Scatter the bacon and hazelnuts over the trout and the frisée.

Few fish go together so well with such flavours as saffron, chilli, coriander, garlic and olive oil as skate. Like all members of the shark family, it needs strong flavours to accompany it, being almost overassertive after the first half-a-dozen mouthfuls. I came up with this hot-climate dish after a cold day at Start Bay in Devon, spent with some divers whose hobby is to go spear fishing for skate in the bay and bring it back to the Start Bay Inn, where they serve an excellent plate of battered skate and chips which you can eat contendedly with a pint or two, and reflect on those 50-year-old men who prefer to do something uncomfortable, like skate diving, rather than play golf. This dish works well with any member of the shark family, often referred to as flake in Australia.

warm poached skate with the sunny and aromatic flavours of morocco

SERVES 4

2 x 450 g (1 lb) prepared skate wings,
or shark steaks

FOR THE COURT BOUILLON:
1 onion, sliced
2 celery sticks, sliced
1 fresh bay leaf
3 tablespoons white wine vinegar
2 teaspoons salt
6 black peppercorns
1.2 litres (2 pints) water

FOR THE SAUCE:
A pinch of saffron strands
2 plum tomatoes, skinned, seeded
and diced
¼ teaspoon crushed coriander seeds
A pinch of ground cumin
1 small *Roasted red pepper*
(see page 177), skinned, seeded and
cut into thin strips
1 medium-hot Dutch red chilli, seeded
and finely chopped
2 garlic cloves, finely chopped
150 ml (5 fl oz) extra virgin olive oil
1 tablespoon lemon juice
2 teaspoons each of shredded coriander
and mint
Salt and freshly ground black pepper

1 For the court bouillon, put all the ingredients into a large, shallow pan. Bring to the boil and simmer for 20 minutes.

2 Cut each skate wing in half. Add them to the court bouillon and simmer gently for 10 minutes.

3 Meanwhile, for the sauce, steep the saffron in a couple of teaspoons of warm water for 5 minutes. Then put the saffron and its water, tomatoes, coriander, cumin, red pepper, chilli, garlic, oil, lemon juice, 1 teaspoon of salt and 10 turns of the black pepper mill into a small pan and, just before the skate is ready, warm the sauce through over a very gentle heat.

4 Lift the pieces of skate out of the court bouillon, drain off the excess liquid and put onto 4 warmed plates. Stir the coriander and mint into the sauce, spoon some over each piece of skate and serve.

Bill Baker, our main wine supplier and a good friend, knocked this up for me one Sunday lunch at Trebetherick. I think it's one of the best recipes in the book – there's something about the clotted cream mixed with milk which gives it an almost curd-like finish, and of course seafood and tarragon are a match made in heaven. This is equally good made with lobster. It makes a little lobster go a deliciously long way.

langoustine and clotted cream quiche with tarragon and parsley

SERVES 6–8

1 quantity of *Rich shortcrust pastry* (see page 177)
1 egg white
750 g (1½lb) cooked langoustines in the shell
175 ml (6 fl oz) milk
100 g (4 oz) clotted cream
3 large eggs
2 teaspoons finely chopped tarragon
2 teaspoons finely chopped parsley
Salt and freshly ground black pepper
Soft green lettuce salad with olive oil and garlic dressing (see page 174), to serve

1 Preheat the oven to 200°C/400°F/Gas Mark 6. Roll out the pastry on a lightly floured work surface and use it to line a 4 cm (1½ in) deep, 22½ cm (9 in) loose-bottomed flan tin. Prick the base here and there with a fork and chill for 20 minutes.

2 Line the pastry case with a sheet of crumpled greaseproof paper and baking beans. Bake blind for 15 minutes. Remove the paper and beans and return it to the oven for 5 minutes. Remove once more and brush the base of the case with the unbeaten egg white. Return to the oven for 1 minute. Remove and lower the oven temperature to 190°C/375°F/Gas Mark 5.

3 While the pastry case is baking, remove the langoustine meats from their shells. In a bowl, gradually mix the milk into the clotted cream until smooth. Beat in the eggs and stir in the tarragon, parsley, ¾ teaspoon of salt and some freshly ground black pepper.

4 Scatter the langoustine meats over the base of the pastry case and pour over the egg mixture. Bake the quiche for 25–30 minutes until just set and lightly browned. Remove and leave it to cool slightly before serving with the salad.

While the scallops have got to be impeccable, the hero of this dish is the cider vinegar. I spent an enjoyable week nosing around cider-making farms in the Somerset Levels last autumn. I wouldn't say they all made the most impeccable cider, and actually, I think the long-aged vinegar some of them make is almost more interesting. The idea for this, scallops with puff pastry, stems from adventurous fish cooking in the 80s when dishes such as Rendezvous de Fruits de Mer, a mixture of seafood in a white wine sauce served in a deep puff pastry case, were all the rage. This is much lighter but still celebrates the combination of buttery puff pastry, intense creamy sauce and sweet seafood. I would recommend the cider vinegar from Aspall's in Suffolk (see page 193) for use in this dish.

scallops in puff pastry with aged cider vinegar and dill

SERVES 4

225 g (8 oz) fresh puff pastry
50 g (2 oz) block of chilled unsalted butter
12–16 prepared scallops, each cut horizontally into 2 discs
2 tablespoons aged cider vinegar
6 tablespoons *Fish stock* (see page 176) or *Chicken stock* (see page 176)
1 teaspoon chopped fresh dill
2 teaspoons double cream
Salt and freshly ground white pepper
Small sprigs of dill, to garnish

1 Roll out the pastry on a lightly floured surface and cut out four 10 cm (4 in) discs. Prick them here and there with a fork, place them onto a lightly greased baking sheet and chill for 1 hour.

2 Preheat the oven to 200°C/400°F/Gas Mark 6. Remove the tray of pastry discs from the fridge. Lightly grease the underside of a second baking tray and rest it on top of the discs. Bake them for 20 minutes, or until crisp and golden. Remove and keep warm.

3 Rub the base of a large, non-stick frying pan with a little of the butter and cut the remainder into small pieces. Put the pan over a high heat and as soon as the butter begins to smoke, add the scallop slices and sear them for 30 seconds on each side, seasoning them with a little salt and pepper as they cook. Lift them onto a plate and keep warm.

4 Quickly remove the pan from the heat, add the cider vinegar and stir with a wooden spoon to lift all the caramelized juices from the base of the pan. Return the pan to the heat, add the stock and bring back to the boil. Whisk in the butter pieces a few at a time, then stir in the dill, double cream and some seasoning to taste.

5 Put the discs of warm puff pastry into the centre of each plate and pile the scallop slices on top. Drizzle a little of the sauce over the scallops and the rest around the outside of the plate. Garnish with the dill sprigs.

This dish is part of my continuing obsession with oily fish and the curry pastes of southern India. They go together so well that I just don't think it's true that all that spice ruins the taste of a perfectly fresh fish. I wrote this as a tribute to the Cornwall Hand Liner's Association, whose mackerel fishery has recently received Marine Stewardship Council accreditation, indicating that they are practising fishing methods that allow long-term stability of fish stocks. The masala paste makes more than you need for this recipe but it keeps very well in the fridge.

red chilli mackerel with fresh onion chutney

SERVES 4

8 x 225–275 g (8–10 oz) mackerel, cleaned and fins trimmed
6–8 tablespoons sunflower oil
Salt
Lime wedges, to garnish
1 quantity of *Pilau rice* (see page 175), to serve

FOR THE MASALA PASTE:
20 g (³⁄₄ oz) dried Guajillo (little gourd) chillies (see The Cool Chile Company, page 193)
1 teaspoon black peppercorns
1 teaspoon cloves
1 tablespoon light muscovado sugar
6 garlic cloves, roughly chopped
4 cm (1¹⁄₂ in) piece fresh root ginger, peeled and roughly chopped
4 tablespoons red wine vinegar

FOR THE FRESH ONION CHUTNEY:
1 medium-hot red chilli, seeded and thinly sliced
4 tablespoons red wine vinegar
1 medium red onion, quartered and sliced
Juice of ¹⁄₂ a lime
A handful of fresh coriander, roughly chopped

1 For the masala paste, slit open the dried chillies and remove the stalks and seeds. Cover with hot water and leave to soak for 20 minutes. For the fresh onion chutney, cover the red chilli with the vinegar and set aside.

2 Drain the soaked dried chillies, reserving the soaking liquor. Grind the peppercorns and cloves and put them into a food processor with the soaked chillies, sugar, garlic, ginger, vinegar and ¹⁄₂ teaspoon of salt. Blend, adding a little of the chilli soaking liquor if necessary, to make a smooth paste.

3 Make 3 deep diagonal slashes on each side of the mackerel. Season inside the cuts and the gut cavities with salt and then spread plenty of the masala paste inside the cavities and into the cuts with a palette knife.

4 When cooking 8 mackerel for 4 people I would tend to use 2 frying pans rather than cook them in batches, so do this if you can. Heat 3–4 tablespoons of sunflower oil in each large frying pan over a medium heat. Add the fish and fry them for 6–7 minutes on each side until cooked through. Meanwhile, drain the vinegar off the red chilli and mix with the rest of the ingredients for the fresh onion chutney, with some salt to taste. Serve the fish with the chutney and pilau rice, garnished with a wedge or two of lime.

You might like to try this as an alternative to grilling kippers, particularly if they are nice thick ones with a pronounced smoky flavour like those from Swallow Fish (see page 185). These are not to everybody's taste, being particularly tarry – they use beech-wood logs rather than sawdust – but they're certainly to mine. I love kippers served with Lapsang Souchong tea, which has a similarly outdoor sort of flavour. I also like kippers for lunch with a glass of good beer.

jugged kippers

SERVES 2

2 x 300–350 g (10–11 oz) kippers
25 g (1 oz) unsalted butter
Juice of ½ a small lemon
1 teaspoon finely chopped herbs of your
choice (I like chopped chives)
Brown bread and real ale, to serve

1 Put the kippers into a large, shallow pan and pour over enough boiling water to cover. Cover with a lid and leave for 6–7 minutes. Then lift the fish out of the water and drain well.

2 Take a ladleful (about 3 tablespoons) of the poaching water, bring to a rapid boil in a small pan and whisk in the unsalted butter, lemon juice and chopped herbs to make a beurre fondue. Put the kippers onto warmed plates, pour over the beurre fondue and serve with some brown bread and butter and a glass of beer.

It's extraordinary, but when I first experienced this excellent way of eating smoked salmon and scrambled eggs a couple of years ago at the Berkley Hotel, I'd never heard of it before. It was served in chef Paul Knight's office with considerable aplomb: white tablecloth, napkins, little vase of flowers, senior waiter, that sort of thing. Now I come across it everywhere I go in the world, and everyone seemed to know about it but me, but I'm still filled with the enthusiasm of finding something new.

smoked salmon with scrambled eggs, capers and onion

SERVES 2

175 g (6 oz) smoked salmon, thinly sliced
(see pages 183–5, for suppliers)
3 large eggs
25 g (1 oz) butter
2 teaspoons double cream
½ small red onion, thinly sliced
2 teaspoons nonpareilles capers,
drained and rinsed
Salt and freshly ground black pepper

1 Divide the smoked salmon between 2 plates.

2 Break the eggs into a bowl, add some salt and pepper and lightly break up with a fork – don't whisk them, I like the finished egg to be a bit lumpy. Melt the butter in a pan, add the eggs and stir with a wooden spoon until you have reached the degree of firmness that you like – I like them to just hold their shape. Remove from the heat and stir in the cream.

3 Spoon the eggs alongside the smoked salmon, with a little pile of thinly sliced onion and some capers.

I'm very partial to pilau rice. I like to gently sauté the rice in flavoured oil or butter and then cook with liquid for only about 15 minutes so that the grains remain firm and separate. I've contrasted this with a fair bit of chilli, toasted cumin and black mustard seeds and lovely moist, fresh mussels. I serve this with a fresh, astringent relish of tomato, coconut and lime.

mussels in pilau rice with roasted cumin and mustard seeds and a coconut, cucumber and tomato relish

SERVES 4

1.5 kg (3 lb) mussels, cleaned
300 ml (10 fl oz) water
1 teaspoon cumin seeds
1 teaspoon black mustard seeds
1 large leek, cleaned
50 g (2 oz) butter
½ teaspoon turmeric
½ teaspoon chilli flakes
350 g (12 oz) basmati rice
Salt

FOR THE COCONUT, CUCUMBER AND
TOMATO RELISH:
½ cucumber, peeled, seeded and diced
2 vine-ripened tomatoes,
seeded and diced
50 g (2 oz) fresh coconut
(about ½ a small coconut),
peeled and finely grated
1 mild green or red chilli,
seeded and chopped
A small bunch of fresh coriander,
roughly chopped
4 teaspoons lime juice

1 Put the mussels and water into a large pan, cover and cook over a high heat for 3–4 minutes, shaking the pan every now and then until the mussels have all just opened. Tip them into a colander set over a bowl to collect the cooking liquor. Pour all but the last tablespoon or two of the liquor into a measuring jug and make up to 600 ml (1 pint) with water, if necessary.

2 Heat a dry, heavy-based frying pan. Add the cumin seeds and mustard seeds and shake them around for a few seconds until they darken slightly and start to smell aromatic. Remove from the heat.

3 Cut the leek lengthways into long, thin strips, then bunch the strips together and slice them across quite finely. Melt the butter in a 20 cm (8 in) heavy-based saucepan, add the leeks and spices and cook over a medium heat for 2–3 minutes until the leeks have softened. Add the rice and fry briefly until all the grains are well coated in the butter.

4 Add the mussel cooking liquor and ½ teaspoon of salt and bring quickly to the boil. Stir once, cover with a tight-fitting lid, reduce the heat to low and cook for 15 minutes.

5 Meanwhile, remove all but 12 of the mussel meats from their shells and season them with a little salt. Mix the relish ingredients together with a large pinch of salt.

6 Uncover the rice and gently fork in the mussel meats. Garnish with the mussels in their shells and serve with the coconut, cucumber and tomato relish.

Here's a little pat on the back for supermarkets. It would be unfair to ignore the progress they have made in bringing good products within the reach of everybody, yet still moan about their track record of closing down small butchers, grocers and fishmongers, and not really trying to stock the best local produce. A fish like farmed sea bass doesn't have the same flavour as the larger wild fish, but they are nevertheless good, being always fresh and of consistent quality. This is a recipe which is made for those small, firm fillets from a 400–500 g (14–18 oz) fish. Because this dish is cooked in less than five minutes, make sure that all the ingredients for the stir-fry are ready before you start. In Australia and New Zealand I would suggest using farmed barramundi, red snapper, bream or silver perch fillets for this.

grilled sea bass fillets with stir-fried asparagus, red pepper and sugar snap peas

SERVES 4

4 x 175 g (6 oz) unskinned sea bass fillets
Maldon sea salt flakes and freshly
ground black pepper

FOR THE STIR-FRIED ASPARAGUS,
RED PEPPER AND SUGAR SNAP PEAS:
3 tablespoons sunflower oil
2 garlic cloves, sliced into fine
matchsticks (julienne)
2.5 cm (1 in) fresh ginger, peeled and cut
into julienne
100 g (4 oz) sugar snap peas
1 small red pepper, seeded and cut
lengthways into long, thin strips
1 bunch of fine asparagus, trimmed and
halved, or 175–200 g (6–7 oz)
asparagus tips
2 heads of pak choi, cut lengthways into
4 or 6 wedges
1 teaspoon roasted sesame oil
2 tablespoons dark soy sauce
1 tablespoon Thai fish sauce
1 bunch spring onions, halved lengthways
and cut into 5 cm (2 in) pieces
A small bunch of fresh coriander,
roughly chopped
1 teaspoon lightly toasted sesame seeds
A small handful of picked
coriander leaves, to garnish

1 Preheat the grill to high. Season the fillets of sea bass on both sides with salt and pepper and place skin-side up on a lightly oiled grilling tray or the rack of the grill pan. Grill the sea bass fillets for 3–4 minutes until the skin is crisp and golden brown.

2 While the fish is cooking, make the stir-fry: heat the oil in a wok or large, deep frying pan, add the garlic and ginger and stir-fry for a few seconds. Add the sugar snap peas, red pepper and asparagus and stir-fry over a high heat for 2 minutes. Remove the sea bass from the grill and keep warm. The underside of the fish will be slightly underdone at this stage but will continue to cook after you remove it from the heat. Add the pak choi to the wok and stir-fry for another 1 minute, until it has started to wilt slightly. Add the sesame oil, soy sauce, fish sauce and toss everything together well. Add the spring onions and coriander and toss over a high heat for another 30 seconds.

3 Spoon the stir-fry into the centre of 4 warmed plates and put the grilled sea bass on top. Sprinkle both the fish and the stir-fry with a few sesame seeds and then scatter over a few coriander leaves. Serve immediately.

Hake is an excellent fish, soft and fibrous in texture and meltingly tender. One of my favourite contrasts in fish cookery is to partner hot fish with a cold sauce, particularly a mayonnaise-based sauce like sauce verte. That combination, together with some butter beans mixed with tomato and chilli, made this a dish which had to go straight onto the Seafood Restaurant menu. The recipe came from a trip to Borough Market in London. I wish there were more markets like it in the country. Too often city-centre produce markets seem to be in decline; not so this one. The hake from the stall of Morecambe Bay Seafood had to be matched by some butter beans from the stall of Spanish produce called Brindisa (see page 193). The beans come from the Sierra de Gredos mountains between Madrid and Salamanca. In Australia and New Zealand I would suggest using coral trout, blue cod or orange ruffy fillets for this.

hake with sauce verte and butter beans

SERVES 4

4 x 175–200 g (6–7 oz) pieces of thick, unskinned hake fillet
Salt and freshly ground white pepper

FOR THE COURT BOUILLON:
1.2 litres (2 pints) water
1 slice of lemon and the juice from the rest of the fruit
2 fresh bay leaves
6 black peppercorns
1 small onion, sliced

FOR THE BUTTER BEANS:
225 g (8 oz) dried butter beans
15 g (½ oz) butter
2 vine-ripened tomatoes, seeded and diced
½ medium-hot red Dutch chilli, seeded and finely chopped
1 tablespoon chopped curly leaf parsley

FOR THE SAUCE VERTE:
15 g (½ oz) each flatleaf parsley leaves, chervil leaves, tarragon leaves and chives
25 g (1 oz) watercress sprigs
25 g (1 oz) baby spinach leaves
2 egg yolks
2 teaspoons lemon juice
1 teaspoon Dijon mustard
½ small garlic clove, crushed
300 ml (10 fl oz) light olive oil

1 Put the dried butter beans into a pan and cover with plenty of cold water. Bring them to the boil, lower the heat and leave them to simmer until just tender – about 40 minutes – adding ½ teaspoon of salt 5 minutes before the end of cooking. Drain well and set aside.

2 For the sauce verte, bring a large pan of water to the boil. Add the herbs, watercress and spinach, cook for a few seconds then drain and refresh well under cold running water. Dry well in a clean tea towel. Put the blanched leaves, egg yolks, lemon juice, mustard, garlic and ½ teaspoon of salt into a food processor and blend together for a few seconds until smooth. Then, with the motor still running, add the oil in a slow, steady stream until you have a thick mayonnaise. Transfer it to a bowl, cover and chill until needed.

3 For the court bouillon, put all the ingredients and 2 teaspoons of salt into a large, shallow pan which will take all the pieces of fish in one single layer. Bring to the boil, cover and leave to simmer for 20 minutes.

4 Add the pieces of hake, skin-side up, to the court bouillon, bring back to a very gentle simmer and cook for 4–6 minutes. Melt the butter for the butter beans in a pan, add the beans, tomatoes, chilli, parsley and some seasoning to taste and stir over a low heat until warmed through.

5 Spoon the butter beans onto 4 warmed plates. Remove the hake from the court-bouillon with a fish slice and drain well. Lay slightly on, slightly off the butter beans. Spoon some of the sauce verte alongside and serve.

This is for those who like picking crab meat out of the shell with their fingers. I've merely removed all the unwanted bits of shell and cut the crab up in a way that makes it easy to pick. Of course you can use precooked crabs for this dish, though they will never be quite as good as those you cook yourself.

hot crab in the shell with mace and tarragon butter

SERVES 2

2 x 1.25–1.5 kg (2½–3 lb)
live brown crabs

FOR THE MACE AND TARRAGON
BUTTER:
175 g (6 oz) butter
¼ teaspoon ground mace
¼ teaspoon cayenne pepper
1 tablespoon chopped fresh tarragon
2 teaspoons lemon juice

1 To kill the crabs, turn them on their backs with their eyes facing you. Drive a thick skewer or long, thin-bladed knife between the eyes into the centre of the crab. Then lift up the tail flap and drive the skewer through the underside of the crab. When the crab is dead it will go limp.

2 Bring a large pan of salted water to the boil (150 g/5 oz of salt per 4.5 litres/8 pints of water). This is roughly the same salinity as sea water. Lower the crabs into the water, bring the water back to the boil and cook them for 22–25 minutes. Lift them out of the water and leave them to cool slightly. Meanwhile, melt the butter in a small pan over a low heat.

3 Place each crab, back-shell down, on a board. Lift up and break off the tail flap and discard. Then break off the claws (but not the legs) and crack the shells of each section with a hammer. Now insert the blade of a large knife between the body and the back shell and twist to release it. Push upwards on the body with both thumbs and it will come away from the back shell in one piece, with the rest of the legs still attached. Discard the back shell unless there is plenty of hard roe inside. If so, remove the roe and serve it with the rest of the crab. Pull the feathery looking gills or 'dead man's fingers' from the body and discard and then, using a large knife, cut the body section in half down the centre so that you are left with 2 pieces, each with 4 legs attached. Crack the shells of each little section of each leg.

4 Arrange 2 pieces of the body and the claws in the centre of 2 warm bowl-like plates. Stir the mace, cayenne pepper, tarragon and lemon juice into the warm melted butter and spoon it over the crab. Serve immediately with finger bowls and lots of paper napkins.

This soup really celebrates the subtle flavours of oysters. The flavours are clean but restrained, allowing for the oyster meats, just slipped in at the last minute, to sing out loud. It's almost good enough to warrant using the native oysters from West Mersea near Colchester, but in the end I think that natives should be served au naturel, and this dish is better made with the much cheaper Pacific oysters, which, incidentally, are also grown in that pretty part of Essex. For perfect results with this soup the stock that you use needs to be chilled until the fat sets on the top and can be strained off, otherwise there will always be disappointing droplets on the top of your otherwise beautifully clear soup.

oyster soup

SERVES 4

12 Pacific oysters
1.5 litre (2½ pints) cold *Chicken stock*
(see page 176)
2 teaspoons Thai fish sauce
1 teaspoon light soy sauce
1 green chilli, seeded and
roughly chopped
1 cm (½ in) fresh ginger,
peeled and sliced
100 g (4 oz) cheap white fish fillet,
finely chopped
50 g (2 oz) leeks, thinly sliced
1 egg white
1 teaspoon salt
A few tarragon, chervil and young
flatleaf parsley leaves, to garnish

1 Open the oysters and pour off the juices into a bowl. Release the oyster meats from their shells and keep them chilled until needed.

2 Put the cold chicken stock, oyster juice, Thai fish sauce, soy sauce, green chilli, ginger, chopped fish, leeks, egg white and salt into a large pan. Place over a medium heat and slowly bring to the boil, giving the mixture a stir every now and then. Allow the stock to boil vigorously for 5–10 seconds, then lower the heat and leave it to simmer undisturbed for 30 minutes.

3 Pass the soup into a clean pan through a fine sieve lined with a double thickness of muslin .

4 Slice the oyster meats lengthways into 2 or 3 slices, depending on their size. Bring the soup back to the boil, add the oyster slices and leave them to cook gently for just 5 seconds. Then ladle the soup into warmed bowls and scatter each one generously with the herb leaves. Serve immediately.

As I said in the introduction to this chapter, this dish is designed for cooking with wild salmon. It is very much a last-minute dish so make sure everything is ready before you start. If using farmed salmon, pay a little extra and go for the best. In Australia and New Zealand the quality of farmed salmon is consistently good – firm flesh with not too much fat and as there is no wild Atlantic salmon, Tasmanian salmon would be ideal for this.

seared escalopes of wild salmon with a warm olive oil, basil and caramelized vinegar dressing

SERVES 4

1 tablespoon caster sugar
4 tablespoons Cabernet
Sauvignon vinegar
5 tablespoons extra virgin olive oil
4 teaspoons lemon juice
1 x 550 g (1¼ lb) piece of unskinned wild
(or best-quality farmed) salmon fillet,
taken from a large fish
A small bunch of fresh basil
Salt and freshly ground black pepper

1 Put the sugar into a small saucepan and leave over a low heat until it has turned into a light brown caramel – about the colour of golden syrup. Immediately remove from the heat, add the vinegar, then return to a low heat and stir with a wooden spoon until all the caramel has dissolved. Bring to the boil and reduce to 1½ tablespoons, leave to cool a little and then stir in 4 tablespoons of the oil, the lemon juice, ½ teaspoon of salt and 5 turns of the black pepper mill. Keep warm.

2 Put the salmon skin-side down on a board and, using a long, thin-bladed knife, cut at a 45-degree angle down towards the skin into twelve 5 mm (¼ in) thick slices. Brush them on both sides with the remaining oil and season lightly with salt and quite generously with black pepper.

3 Heat the ridged cast-iron griddle until smoking hot. Cook the escalopes, no more than 2 at a time, for 15 seconds on each side, turning them with a palette knife, then quickly lifting them onto a warmed baking tray.

4 Slightly overlap 3 of the salmon slices on each warmed plate. Very finely shred the basil leaves and sprinkle them around the outside edge of the plate. Spoon the warm dressing over the shredded basil. You can, if you like, garnish the salmon with some deep-fried basil leaves – just drop them into hot oil for a few seconds and then drain.

The best choice of lobster for this dish is one that has only recently been cooked so that it is still lukewarm and fresh, but it's worth making with a previously cooked lobster. The dressing ingredients are kept to a minimum so that they remain a subtle excitement in the background. This is a tribute to the excellent lobsters of Argyllshire in western Scotland.

lobster salad with chive dressing

SERVES 2

1 x 750 g (1½lb) cooked lobster
Maldon sea salt flakes and freshly
ground black pepper

FOR THE CHIVE DRESSING:
3 tablespoons extra virgin olive oil
2 teaspoons lemon juice
1 tablespoon shallots,
very finely chopped
2 teaspoons chives, chopped

FOR THE SALAD:
A small handful of watercress sprigs
A small handful of prepared frisée
(curly endive)
A small bunch each of chervil
sprigs and young flatleaf
parsley sprigs

1 Remove the meat from the lobster: pull the tail away from the head, turn the tail over and cut along either side of the flat belly shell with strong scissors. Lift back the flap of shell and lift out the tail meat. Cut the meat lengthways into thin slices and remove the dark intestinal tract. Remove the claws from the head and break them into pieces at the joints. Crack the shells with a knife. Remove the meat from the pincers, in one piece if you can, and the pieces of meat from each of the joints. Cut the head in half, remove the stomach sac, which is situated just behind the mouth. Using a teaspoon, scrape out the soft greenish liver, called tomalley, and any red coral.

2 Whisk together the ingredients for the dressing, with the tomalley, the coral and some salt and pepper to taste. Mix together the salad leaves.

3 Arrange the lobster meat slightly to one side of 2 large plates and pile the salad leaves alongside. Spoon a little of the dressing over the leaves and the rest around the outside edge of the plates.

I wanted to create a sort of dry Thai curry; I'd been to a chilli festival at West Dean near Chichester in Sussex and had been amazed by the enthusiasm so many people have for the searing heat of capsaicin. I came to the conclusion that, just as we used garlic with everything as a way of cutting a bit of a dash as foodies in the 60s, people are doing the same with chilli now. There's a farm in Dorset whose owners grow just about any chilli you may have heard of and send them to you by post; they call themselves 'Peppers by Post' (see page 183). They were at the show, as was Dodie Miller who will send you any dried or smoked chillies from her ironically named Cool Chile Company (see page 193). I came away with this idea of taking most of the ingredients of a Thai red curry but omitting all but a little liquid so that the ingredients, when stir-fried with the prawns, would end up coating them. This could then be served directly onto a salad as a first course. It is really good.

spring onion, lettuce and coriander salad, with hot stir-fried red chilli prawns, lime leaves, garlic and basil

SERVES 4

1 kg (2¼lb) raw, unpeeled prawns
2 tablespoons sunflower oil
3 garlic cloves, finely chopped
25 g (1 oz) ginger, peeled and very finely chopped
2 tablespoons Thai fish sauce
2 teaspoons light soft brown sugar
1 fresh kaffir lime leaf, finely sliced
4 medium-hot red Dutch chillies, seeded and finely chopped
1 lemon grass stalk, outer leaves removed and the core finely chopped
1 tablespoon roasted salted peanuts, coarsely chopped
1 tablespoon coconut cream
½ teaspoon salt
A large handful of basil leaves (Thai basil if you can get it)
1 lime, cut into 4

FOR THE SALAD:
1 romaine lettuce, outer leaves removed and the rest broken into small pieces
6 spring onions, halved and thinly shredded
A handful of coriander sprigs

1　For the salad, mix together the romaine lettuce, spring onions and coriander sprigs and divide between 4 plates.

2　Peel the prawns. Heat the oil in a wok or large, deep frying pan. Add the garlic and ginger and stir for a few seconds. Throw in the prawns and stir-fry for 1 minute. Add the Thai fish sauce, sugar, kaffir lime leaf, chillies and lemon grass and stir-fry for another minute until the prawns are cooked through. Add the peanuts, coconut cream and salt and stir for a few seconds until the prawns are lightly coated, then add the basil leaves and toss together briefly. Scatter the prawns and red chilli mixture over the salad leaves, squeeze one quarter of the lime over each plate and serve.

CHAPTER 4 poultry

IN THE 1950S MY MOTHER USED TO TAKE ME TO LUNCH AT
THE S & F GRILL, JUST OFF PICCADILLY, AFTER WE'D BEEN TO
MADAME TUSSAUD'S OR THE NATURAL HISTORY MUSEUM. I'D
ALWAYS HAVE GRILLED CHICKEN, WHICH CAME WITH CHIPS
AND TOMATO KETCHUP – TWO DAZZLINGLY MODERN DELIGHTS
UNKNOWN IN OUR FARMHOUSE KITCHEN IN OXFORDSHIRE.
CHICKENS WE HAD IN PLENTY, REARED IN ONE OF OUR
FIELDS; MAYBE THE TOP WOODSIDE, THE HOMEGROUND, OR
THE BOTTOM-END OF THE NINETEEN ACRE. THEY WERE KEPT
IN LONG, MOVEABLE COOPS. EACH DAY THEY WOULD BE
HOOKED UP ON A TWO-WHEELED TROLLEY AND MOVED A FEW
YARDS DOWN THE FIELD, LEAVING A BROWN PATCH DENUDED
OF GRASS, WHICH WOULD SOON SPRING UP WITH DARK
GREEN VIGOUR FROM ALL THE RICH DROPPINGS. THEY HAD
FRESH GRASS TO EAT EVERY DAY, GRUBS TO PECK UP AND
A SUPPLEMENTARY DIET OF GRAIN.

BELOW AND RIGHT
My food heroes pay high regard to the condition in which their animals live. The ducks of Long Grove Wood Farm (available from Manor Farm Game) lead a happy existence.

Those chickens, simply roasted, were what chickens ought to taste like. You hardly ever see plain roast or grilled chicken on the menus of good restaurants these days unless it's Poulet de Bresse or Poulet Noir. Few of us have any knowledge of varieties of chicken in Britain: fowls bred for flavour like Black Orpington or Devon Red. Chicken seems to be just blandish white meat designed to carry other flavours – in breast form for making Thai green curry, fajitas, Creole chicken or Kievs.

Turkey also lacks flavour. A commercial white turkey is almost ball-shaped as it is bred to put on breast meat fast, whereas an old breed like a Norfolk Black looks more like a game bird. Ducks now

appear in all supermarkets, fast-reared and lacking the delicious flavour of crisp skin: smooth, endlessly tempting fat, and meat soft and comfortingly flavoured.

The suppliers of poultry in this book do nothing more elaborate than rear their birds outdoors, allowing them to forage and exercise their muscles. They are kept alive much longer and therefore develop flavour, and when they are killed they are hung for 1–3 weeks to allow the flavour to develop further. The breeds too are chosen for taste rather than fast, hormone-aided growth. It all costs money. Why keep a fowl two months longer, eating costly feed, when you can fatten it quickly and get a return on your money? The Sasso chickens and the guinea fowl from The Ellel Free Range Poultry Co., near Lancaster, and Barry Clark's Trelough ducks from English Natural Foods, cost about 30 per cent more than supermarket birds. Neither Barry nor the Charles's at Ellel are getting rich, any more than James Graham of Peele's is from selling almost wild-tasting Norfolk Black turkeys; they just believe in a better, more honest product. As Richard Charles said at Ellel, the French have their Bresse chickens, why don't we value our own breeds, like Norfolk Grey or Derbyshire Redcap?

It would be too doctrinaire to suggest that none of the recipes in this chapter should be prepared with run of the mill chickens; I use them just like everyone else. I just think that suppliers such as those listed on pages 185–7 should be supported more. Just order from one of them and you'll see why. It's easy to forget what it's like in those intensive long, wooden sheds, with the characteristic silos at the end for automatic feeding and watering of chickens in small cages. Yet we all eat, and we all benefit from, the cheapness and convenience of intensively reared poultry.

I remember driving into Claire Symington's farm at Billesdon in Leicestershire. The green pasture running down to the farm was white with a swirling flock of chattering geese; they really seemed to be enjoying each other's company. We had a spirited chat about gravy with roast goose; never put wine in a gravy to go with a British roast, we both agreed. When the dressed goose arrived at my house it was carefully packed with aromatic herbs, branches of thyme, sage and bay, and when roasted the fat was crisp and the meat moist and as full of flavour as good brisket of beef.

As with everything else in this book, the success of this dish lies in getting the best-quality raw materials, and the livers from Holly Tree Farm Shop (see page 186) and English Natural Foods (see page 186) are very special. The flavour of free-range ducks does, of course, extend to their livers. If you are using livers from a supermarket, make sure they haven't been frozen long; they should be a nice bright red rather than tinged with brown. This combination is classic; the onion confit recipe is pleasingly sweet and acidic and the walnut bread is worth making just to accompany this recipe.

duck liver parfait with onion confit and walnut bread toast

SERVES 10–12

450 g (1 lb) duck livers, trimmed of any white sinews
1 garlic clove, crushed
2 tablespoons port
1 tablespoon brandy
225 g (8 oz) unsalted butter, melted and cooled slightly
Salt and freshly ground white pepper
Thin slices of lightly toasted *Walnut bread* (see page 167), to serve

FOR THE ONION CONFIT:
100 g (4 oz) butter
750 g (1½ lb) onions, peeled and thinly sliced
75 g (3 oz) granulated sugar
7 tablespoons sherry vinegar
250 ml (8 fl oz) red wine
Freshly ground black pepper

1 Preheat the oven to 110°C/225°F/Gas Mark ¼. Put the duck livers, 1 teaspoon of salt, 20 turns of white pepper, garlic, port and brandy into a food processor and blend for 1 minute until smooth. Add the cooled melted butter and then press the mixture through a fine sieve into a bowl.

2 Pour the mixture into a 450 g (1 lb) loaf tin lined with cooking grade cling film, cover with a sheet of lightly buttered foil and put into a roasting tin half-filled with hot water. Transfer to the oven and cook for 1¼ hours. Remove from the roasting tin, leave to cool, then remove the foil, re-cover with cling film and leave to chill overnight.

3 For the onion confit, heat the butter in a large pan until a light nut-brown. Add the onions and sugar and cook slowly for about 45 minutes, stirring now and then, until the onions are very soft and richly caramelized. Add the sherry vinegar and red wine and cook for a further 10 minutes, stirring now and then, until the mixture has reduced and thickened and turned a dark mahogany colour. Stir in 1 teaspoon of salt and 1 teaspoon of black pepper and leave to cool, but don't chill.

4 To serve, uncover the parfait and invert it onto a board. Peel off the cling film and cut it across into approximately 5 mm (¼ in) thick slices – you don't want them to be too thick as it's very rich. Put a slice of the parfait slightly to one side of each plate and spoon a heaped tablespoon of the onion confit alongside. Serve with the walnut bread toast.

Spatchcock refers to the method of flattening out a chicken to make it easy to grill. The Oxford English Dictionary says it is probably an abbreviation of 'dispatch cock'. I like the French expression for the same dish, grillé en crapaudine, which means grilled like a toad. This refers to my preferred method of cutting a chicken horizontally below the point of the breast bone, over the top of the legs and down to the wing joints. The breast is then folded out and it does indeed come to look like a toad. The chicken in this recipe is grilled, but I often cook them this way on the barbecue, slipping in a few mesquite wood chippings to give them a slightly smoky flavour. In Australia the name spatchcock has come to refer simply to a young poussin rather than the method of preparation. Poussins are ideal for flattening and grilling. It's hard to find them free range, though. If using poussins allow one per person and allow a total cooking time of about 30 minutes.

grilled spatchcock with cherry tomatoes, spring onions and rocket

SERVES 4

1 chicken, weighing about 1.5 kg (3½ lb)
2 tablespoons olive oil
3 tablespoons balsamic vinegar
2 garlic cloves, crushed
Salt and freshly ground black pepper
3–4 tablespoons *Chicken stock* (see page 176) or water
1 quantity of *Thin chips* (see page 172–3), to serve

FOR THE CHERRY TOMATOES, SPRING ONIONS AND ROCKET:
350 g (12 oz) vine-ripened cherry tomatoes
25 g (1 oz) rocket leaves
6 spring onions, trimmed

FOR THE DRESSING:
2 tablespoons extra virgin olive oil
1 teaspoon white wine vinegar
¼ garlic clove, crushed

1 To spatchcock the chicken, put on a chopping board, back-side down, and make a horizontal cut from the cavity end, just under the point of the breastbone, through the ribs on either side, over the top of the legs and stopping at the neck, just before you cut the whole breast away from the body. Lift the breast up, over and down onto the chopping board, still hinged at the neck. Spread-eagle the legs apart onto the board. Turn the chicken over so that it is skin-side down and flatten the chicken as much as possible. Now you can see the toad shape.

2 Take a large roasting tin and add the olive oil, 2 tablespoons of balsamic vinegar, the garlic, 1 teaspoon of salt and lots of black pepper. Add the chicken and rub the marinade into both sides of the bird. Leave for 30 minutes.

3 For the salad, chop each tomato once or twice into rough-shaped pieces. Bunch up the rocket leaves and slice them across into 2.5 cm (1 in) slices and thinly slice the spring onions on the diagonal. Put them into a salad bowl and mix together briefly. Whisk together the dressing ingredients with a pinch each of salt and pepper and set aside.

4 Grill the chicken, carcase-side up for about 15–20 minutes, then turn it over and cook it for a further 15 minutes until it's a good colour (but not too dark) and the skin is crispy.

5 Remove the chicken from the roasting tin and keep warm. Pour most of the excess oil from the tin (leave just a little), place it on the hob over a medium heat and add the chicken stock or water and the rest of the balsamic vinegar and stir around with a wooden spoon to make a gravy. Pour into a jug. Cut the chicken into pieces and stir the dressing into the salad. Serve with the gravy, salad and chips.

I first ate this in the 1980s at the legendary restaurant Berowra Waters, on the Hawkesbury River, north of Sydney. You could only get to the restaurant by boat or seaplane from Rose Bay or Palm Beach, so even the arrival was memorable, as was the food. Gay Bilson, who ran the restaurant with her husband Tony, and latterly with another fantastic cook, Yanny Kyritsis, had a restaurant which, with one or two others, created modern Australian cookery, and this combination of salt duck, sweet melon, pickled ginger and soy, is a perfect example.

cured duck breasts with melon, soy and pickled ginger

SERVES 4

2 large duck breasts
½ a melon, preferably Charentais or Canteloupe
Salt

FOR THE SALT CURE:
½ teaspoon black peppercorns
½ teaspoon coriander seeds
1 tablespoon fresh thyme leaves
2 bay leaves
50 g (2 oz) salt
40 g (1½ oz) sugar

FOR THE PICKLED GINGER:
75 g (3 oz) fresh ginger
1 medium-hot red Dutch chilli, seeded and thinly sliced
25 g (1 oz) sugar
200 ml (7 fl oz) white wine vinegar
6 allspice berries
2.5 cm (1 in) cinnamon stick

FOR THE SOY SAUCE DRESSING:
2 teaspoons red wine vinegar
2 teaspoons dark soy sauce
3 tablespoons groundnut oil
A pinch of Sichuan peppercorns, crushed

1 For the salt cure, put the peppercorns, coriander seeds, thyme leaves, bay leaves and salt into a spice grinder and grind to a powder. Mix with the sugar. Put half the cure into a shallow dish and lay the duck breasts, flesh-side down, on top. Cover with the rest of the cure and refrigerate for at least 12 hours.

2 For the pickled ginger, peel the ginger and slice it thinly. Pile up a few slices at a time and cut them into fine matchsticks. Mix the ginger and chillies with 1 teaspoon of salt and then transfer them to a glass jar or small bowl. Put the rest of the ingredients into a small pan, bring to the boil and simmer for 5 minutes. Pour over the ginger and chillies, leave to cool, then cover and leave for at least 24 hours.

3 Preheat the oven to 160°C/325°F/Gas Mark 3. Rinse the salt cure off the duck breasts, put them into a small ovenproof casserole and add 300 ml (10 fl oz) of water. Cover and cook for 25 minutes (or until the internal temperature of the duck reaches 60–65°C, if you have a meat probe). Remove them from the casserole to a plate and leave them to cool.

4 Just before serving, whisk together the ingredients for the soy sauce dressing. Remove the seeds from the melon with a spoon and cut it into 4 wedges. Slice the flesh neatly away from the skin and then cut it diagonally into thin slices. Slice the duck breasts lengthways, slightly on the diagonal, into long, very thin slices. Arrange the duck and melon slices on 4 plates and put about 1 tablespoon of ginger alongside. Sprinkle the dressing around the edge of the plate and serve.

There's no real reason why we shouldn't eat turkey on occasions other than Christmas – certainly if you choose Norfolk Black turkeys, such as those from James Graham of Peele's (see page 186), which are more lean and gamey than the common white turkeys that everyone seems to order. This Italian-influenced roast imbues the bird with the aromatic flavours of garlic, sage, olive oil and fennel. I had in mind a large celebratory dinner where you might accompany the turkey with one of those exceptionally individual Italian chardonnays like Angelo Gaja's Rossj Bass, Silvio Jermann's Where the Dreams Have No End, or Avignonessi's Il Marzocco.

dry-roasted turkey with fennel seeds and rosemary and olive oil potatoes

SERVES 10

1 x 3.5 kg (8 lb) oven-ready turkey
6 tablespoons extra virgin olive oil
2 whole large heads of garlic, broken into cloves but left unpeeled
16 sage leaves
2 teaspoons fennel seeds
150 ml (5 fl oz) dry white wine
Finely grated zest and juice of ½ a lemon
Maldon sea salt and cracked black pepper
2 quantities of the *Italian radicchio, rocket and carrot salad* (see page 174), to serve

FOR THE GIBLET STOCK:
The turkey giblets
1 bulb of fennel, sliced
2 celery stalks, sliced
2 fresh bay leaves
1 large carrot, peeled and sliced
1 onion, peeled and sliced
1.2 litres (2 pints) water

1 Preheat the oven to 230°C/450°F/Gas Mark 8. Take a roasting tin large enough to hold the turkey, add the oil and place over a medium heat to get hot. Throw in the garlic cloves, sage leaves and fennel seeds, some Maldon salt and cracked black pepper and turn them over in the hot oil for a minute or so. Remove the tin from the heat, cool slightly, then add the turkey and turn it over in the flavoured oil. Turn the turkey breast-side up and spoon most of the garlic and sage leaves into the cavity of the bird. Spoon over more of the oil so that the skin becomes sprinkled with fennel seeds and season it with more salt and pepper.

2 Roast the turkey for 30 minutes. Remove and lower the oven temperature to 170°C/325°F/Gas Mark 3. Add the wine to the tin, which should bubble up immediately and reduce slightly, followed by the lemon zest and juice. Baste the turkey with this, then cover with a large sheet of foil, sealing it well all around the edges of the tin, and return it to the oven for at least another 1¾ hours, until the juices run clear when the thickest part of the thigh meat is pierced with a skewer. Uncover the turkey 20 minutes before the end of cooking to crisp up the skin.

3 For the giblet stock, put all the ingredients into a pan, bring to the boil and simmer for 1 hour until reduced and well-flavoured. Strain and set aside.

4 For the rosemary and olive oil potatoes, cut the potatoes into 2 cm (¾ in) dice. Put them into a second roasting tin with the rosemary sprigs, olive oil, salt and pepper and toss together well. Spread them out into an even layer. Roast with the turkey for the last hour.

5 Remove the turkey from the oven, lift it onto a board, re-cover with the foil and leave it to rest.

6 For the gravy, pour off the excess oil from the roasting tin and put it over a medium heat. Add the giblet stock and deglaze the tin, rubbing all the caramelized juices from the base with a wooden spoon. Pass

**2.75 kg (6 lb) large, even-sized floury
potatoes such as Maris Piper, peeled
The leaves from 2 x 15 cm (6 in) sprigs
of rosemary
250 ml (8 fl oz) olive oil**

through a sieve into a small pan and boil rapidly until reduced to 300 ml
(10 fl oz) of well-flavoured gravy. Season to taste with salt and pepper.

7 Carve the turkey and arrange the meat on a warmed serving platter
with the garlic cloves from inside the cavity. Serve with the gravy,
rosemary and olive oil potatoes and a large bowl of the radicchio salad.

The Aylesbury ducks from Long Grove Wood Farm in Chesham, Buckinghamshire (available from Manor Farm Game, see page 186),
reinforce the fact that free-range poultry tastes so much better than intensively reared fowl. I've done nothing in this recipe but
assemble the ingredients that I love best with roast duck: peas cooked à la Française, gravy made with a little redcurrant jelly,
and a simple milk-and-butter mashed potato. The choice of wine is a matter of some importance with this dish. I'm very fond of
Pinot Noir with my duck, so I would choose a red Burgundy like Gevrey Chambertin or a good Pinot Noir from the Mornington
Peninsular in Victoria in Australia, Martinborough in New Zealand or Carneros in California.

roast duck with petit pois à la française

SERVES 4

**1 x 2.75 kg (6 lb) oven-ready duck
2 teaspoons redcurrant jelly
1 teaspoon *Beurre manié* (see page 177)
Salt and freshly ground black pepper
1 quantity of *Mashed potatoes*
(see page 172), to serve (reserving
the potato water for the gravy)**

FOR THE PETIT POIS À LA FRANÇAISE:

**25 g (1 oz) butter
1 bunch spring onions,
trimmed and halved
2 Little Gem lettuces, each cut into
6 wedges through the root
450 g (1 lb) frozen petit pois
150 ml (5 fl oz) water
1 teaspoon *Beurre manié* (see page 177)**

1 Preheat the oven to 230°C/450°F/Gas Mark 8. Sprinkle salt and
pepper inside the cavity and over the skin of the duck. Put it into a
roasting tin and roast it for 20 minutes. Then lower the oven temperature
to 180°C/350°F/Gas Mark 4 and roast the duck for a further 1 hour
10 minutes, pouring off the fat from the tin every 20 minutes or so.

2 For the petit pois à la Française, melt the butter in a large, shallow
pan, add the onions and cook gently for 2 minutes until beginning to
soften. Add the quartered lettuce hearts and turn them over in the
melted butter. Add the peas, water and ½ teaspoon of salt, cover and
simmer for 10 minutes until the vegetables are tender.

3 Take the duck out of the oven, lift it onto a board, cover it loosely
with some foil and leave it to rest for 10 minutes. Pour off all the fat
from the roasting tin, put the tin on the hob over a medium heat and
add 300 ml (10 fl oz) of reserved potato-cooking water. Scrape up all
the browned juices from the base of the pan with a wooden spoon,
then whisk in the redcurrant jelly and some seasoning to taste. Whisk in
the beurre manié and leave it to simmer while you carve the duck.

4 Lift the duck onto a board and cut off the legs. Cut the legs in half
at the joint. Cut each breast away from the carcase in one piece and
then carve each one lengthways into long, thin slices. Arrange the meat
on a warmed serving platter.

5 Stir the beurre manié into the peas and simmer for 1 minute. Adjust
the seasoning if necessary. Spoon them into a warmed serving dish,
the mashed potatoes into another dish and the gravy into a boat or
small jug. Serve with the roast duck.

This is the way my mother always used to cook chicken. Putting lots of tarragon inside the chicken imbues the flesh with a slightly mouth-numbing, aniseedy flavour. Though I love tarragon with fish, nothing matches its affinity with chicken, particularly the fantastic chickens from Higher Hacknell Farm at Umberleigh in Devon (see page 186). If you use a chicken with giblets for this recipe, make the stock for the gravy as on page 76 for the *Roast goose with sage and onion stuffing and apple sauce*. Serve with *Sautéed potatoes* (see page 172) and *Soft green lettuce salad with an olive oil and garlic dressing* (see page 174). Don't forget to let the chicken rest for at least 15 minutes before carving.

roast chicken with tarragon

SERVES 4

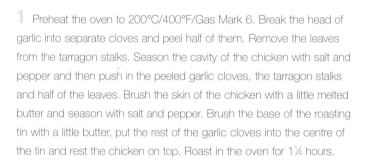

1 large head of garlic

25 g (1 oz) bunch of fresh tarragon

1 x 1.75 kg (4 lb) chicken

25 g (1 oz) butter, melted

150 ml (5 fl oz) *Chicken stock* (see page 176) or giblet stock (see above)

1 teaspoon double cream

Salt and freshly ground black pepper

Sautéed potatoes (see page 172) and *Soft green lettuce salad with an olive oil and garlic dressing* (see page 174), to serve

1 Preheat the oven to 200°C/400°F/Gas Mark 6. Break the head of garlic into separate cloves and peel half of them. Remove the leaves from the tarragon stalks. Season the cavity of the chicken with salt and pepper and then push in the peeled garlic cloves, the tarragon stalks and half of the leaves. Brush the skin of the chicken with a little melted butter and season with salt and pepper. Brush the base of the roasting tin with a little butter, put the rest of the garlic cloves into the centre of the tin and rest the chicken on top. Roast in the oven for 1¼ hours.

2 Remove the chicken from the oven and tip all the juices, garlic and tarragon from the cavity back into the roasting tin. Pick off a few of the tarragon leaves and set them aside. Put the chicken onto a carving board, cover it with foil and leave it to rest while you make the gravy.

3 Put the roasting tin over a medium–high heat, add the stock and mash the garlic cloves lightly with a potato masher to release the cooked purée from the skins. Boil until reduced by half, rubbing all the caramelized juices off the base of the tin with a wooden spoon. Add the rest of the butter and the cream and strain into a warmed sauce boat. Chop the remaining fresh tarragon leaves and stir in.

4 Carve the chicken and add the juices from the tray to the gravy. Divide the chicken between warmed plates and scatter over some of the reserved cooked tarragon leaves from the cavity. Serve with the sautéed potatoes and soft green lettuce salad.

I can understand why the turkey overtook the goose as the preferred bird for Christmas in the nineteenth century – turkeys are much meatier – but having roasted one of Claire Symington's geese, from the charmingly named Seldom Seen Farm, near Billesdon, Leicestershire (see page 186), I wonder if we're not missing a treat. The flavour, particularly of the fat, is so much more interesting. I tried lots of different types of stuffing but in the end I think a simple sage and onion and breadcrumb is best. Anything with more punch, like apricots, prunes, chestnuts or sausagemeat, merely competes for attention with the sublime flavour of goose.

roast goose with sage and onion stuffing and apple sauce

SERVES 8

1 x 4.5–5 kg (10–11 lb) oven-ready goose
Sunflower oil
2 kg (4½lb) floury potatoes,
such as Maris Piper
Salt and freshly ground black pepper
Steamed sprouts (see page 170) and
A purée of swede, carrot and potato
with rocket (see page 171),
to serve

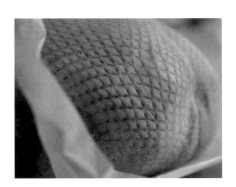

FOR THE GRAVY:

4 rashers streaky bacon, chopped
The goose giblets
1 small onion, chopped
1 carrot, chopped
2 celery stalks, chopped
1.2 litres (2 pints) water
2 bay leaves
6 black peppercorns

1 Preheat the oven to 220°C/425°F/Gas Mark 7. Remove all the clumps of excess fat from the inside of the goose cavity. Put them into a pan with a little sunflower oil and leave on a very low heat until melted, then pass through a fine sieve into a bowl. (This makes a beautiful frying medium, particularly for chips.)

2 For the stuffing, fry the onions in about 75 g (3 oz) of goose fat until soft and very lightly browned. Stir into the breadcrumbs with the lemon zest, sage, parsley and plenty of salt and pepper to taste. Stir in enough beaten egg to bind the mixture together.

3 Season the cavity of the goose with salt and pepper and then spoon in the stuffing. Seal the opening with a metal skewer.

4 Season the skin of the goose with salt and place it on a rack set over a large roasting tin. Roast the goose for 30 minutes. Remove it from the oven and lower the temperature to 180°C/350°F/Gas Mark 4. You need to pour off the excess fat from the roasting tin. The easiest way to do this is to lift the goose onto a board with 2 clean tea towels (you don't want to pierce the skin by using forks), pour off the fat and then replace the goose on the rack. Return it to the oven and roast for a further 1½–2 hours, pouring off more fat after another 30 minutes.

5 In the meantime, for the gravy, fry the bacon, giblets and vegetables in a little goose fat until golden brown. Pour off the excess fat, add the water, bay leaves and peppercorns and simmer for 1 hour. Strain through a sieve and set aside.

6 Peel the potatoes, cut them into large chunks and boil them for 7 minutes in water salted at the rate of 1 teaspoon per pint. They should be soft on the outside but still slightly hard in the centre. Drain well, then shake them around in the pan with a lid on to give the edges a sandy texture. After the goose has been cooking at the lower temperature for 1 hour, remove from the oven and lift it and the rack off the roasting tin. Add the potatoes to the tin and turn them over so that they become well coated in the fat. Pour off any excess fat, replace the goose and continue to roast until the juices run clear when the thigh is pierced with a skewer.

3 large onions, finely chopped

**500 g (1 lb 2 oz) fresh white
breadcrumbs**

Finely grated zest of 1 lemon

4 tablespoons chopped fresh sage

3 tablespoons chopped curly leaf parsley

1 large egg, beaten

FOR THE APPLE SAUCE:

4 Cox's apples, peeled, cored and sliced

120 ml (4 fl oz) water

7 When the goose is cooked, lift it onto a board, cover it with foil and leave it to rest for at least 20 minutes. Return the tin of potatoes to the oven and increase the oven temperature to 220°C/425°F/Gas Mark 7. Roast them for a further 20–25 minutes until crisp and golden. Remove and transfer to a serving dish. Set the roasting tin over a source of heat, add the giblet stock and deglaze the tin by rubbing the base with a wooden spoon. Season to taste and pass through a sieve into a gravy boat.

8 For the apple sauce, put the prepared apples and water into a pan and simmer for 12–15 minutes, stirring now and then, until soft and smooth. I like to serve it unseasoned. Keep warm.

9 Not being a very neat carver, I like to carve in the kitchen and take the slices of goose to the table on a large, warm plate. (Cut off the legs and cut each one in half, then carve the breast meat away from each side into long, thin slices.) I serve the stuffing, apple sauce and gravy separately, with some sprouts, the roast potatoes and the carrot and swede purée. I like a really hearty wine to go with goose, such as Barossa Shiraz from South Australia.

The Cornish Smoked Fish Company in Charlestown near St Austell (see page 185) has been supplying us with smoked mackerel, smoked sea trout and smoked duck breasts for all of the 27 years we've been open. Martin and Sarah Pumphrey have boundless enthusiasm for what they do in their little unit above that matchless harbour, which looks as though it's a film set for one of Patrick O'Brien's naval novels. In the early days Martin used to bring all kinds of smoked things for us to try, so much so that I thought of a slogan for him: 'If it moves, smoke it'. The duck breasts are pretty special, though, and this salad has been on the menu of one of our restaurants for about 20 years.

smoked duck breast with bitter leaves, lentils and new potatoes

SERVES 4

2 x 225–275 g (8–10 oz) smoked duck breasts

25 g (1 oz) Puy lentils

**8 small waxy new potatoes such as
Jersey Royal, scraped well**

**100 g (4 oz) (4 good handfuls) of
prepared frisée (curly endive)**

1 shallot, finely chopped

3 tablespoons chopped chives

Salt and freshly ground pepper

FOR THE MUSTARD VINAIGRETTE:

1 teaspoon Dijon mustard

1 teaspoon white wine vinegar

5 teaspoons sunflower oil

1 For the mustard vinaigrette, whisk together the mustard and vinegar and then whisk in the oil and some seasoning to taste.

2 Slice each of the duck breasts into thin slices – you'll get about 8–10 slices out of each breast.

3 Simmer the lentils in salted water for 20–25 minutes and boil the new potatoes in salted water until just tender. Drain both well, then cut the potatoes lengthways into wedges and mix the potatoes and lentils with the duck slices.

4 Toss the frisée and shallot with the dressing, then gently mix in the duck, lentils and potatoes. Divide the salad between 4 plates and sprinkle with the chopped chives.

I have long persevered with black pudding. It carries such an aura of 'best-of-British' about it that it seemed churlish to own up and say, 'Actually I don't really like this.' Yet it always seemed bland, and then I discovered the black puddings of George Stafford Ltd (see page 188) and everything changed. The secret is in the texture and quality of the pork-back fat and the graininess of the cereal. A British black pudding is a far less elaborate affair than a French boudin noir, but when made just as carefully it's almost more satisfying in its simplicity. Needless to say, good free-range chicken breasts and a simple, slightly sweet sauce like this are a perfect combination.

pan-fried chicken breasts with muscat wine and black pudding

SERVES 4

900 ml (1½ pints) *Roasted chicken stock* (see page 176)
4 large boneless chicken breasts
40 g (1½ oz) butter
1 x 225–250 g (8–9 oz) black pudding
175 ml (6 fl oz) sweet Muscat wine, such as a Muscat Beaumes de Venise
1½ teaspoons lemon juice
1½ teaspoons tarragon leaves
Salt and coarsely ground black pepper

1 Put the stock into a wide-based pan and boil it vigorously until it has reduced to 175 ml (6 fl oz).

2 Season the chicken breasts on both sides with salt and pepper. Heat a small knob of the butter in a large frying pan and, when it is foaming, add the chicken breasts, skin-side down, and cook over a medium heat for 6 minutes until the skin is crisp and richly golden. Turn the chicken breasts over and continue to cook them for 6–7 minutes until cooked through.

3 Thinly slice the black pudding into 16 or so slices. Remove the chicken from the pan and keep warm. Add the slices of black pudding to the pan and fry them for 1 minute on each side. Set them aside with the chicken.

4 Add the sweet wine to the pan and boil, scraping up all the browned bits from the bottom of the pan with a wooden spoon, until reduced to about 3 tablespoons. Add the reduced chicken stock and boil for 1–2 minutes. Whisk in the rest of the butter a small piece at a time, then add the lemon juice and some seasoning to taste.

5 To serve, slice the chicken breasts diagonally and at a slight angle and arrange the slices in the centre of each warmed plate with the black pudding. Stir the tarragon leaves into the sauce and spoon some of it over the chicken and a little around the outside edge of the plates.

What are the constituents of a great chicken pie? A good chicken, of course – free-range, but properly free-range, like those from The Ellel Free Range Poultry Co. (see page 185) – some ham, a velouté made with the chicken poaching liquor, and cream. Then there should be some flavouring vegetables like leeks, onions and button mushrooms. All should be cooked and mixed before the final baking under a light layer of buttery puff pastry. It's the equal to a good fish pie.

chicken pie

SERVES 6–8

1 x 1.5 kg (3½lb) chicken
The *Chicken stock* ingredients on page 176, for poaching
90 g (3½oz) butter
1 large leek, cleaned and sliced
1 medium onion, halved and thinly sliced
225 g (8 oz) button mushrooms, sliced
50 g (2 oz) plain flour
85 ml (3 fl oz) double cream
Juice of ¼ lemon
2 tablespoons chopped parsley
175 g (6 oz) cooked ham, thickly sliced and roughly chopped
450 g (1 lb) puff pastry
1 beaten egg, to glaze
Salt and freshly ground white pepper
Glazed spring carrots with tarragon and chives (see page 169) and *Steamed broccoli* (see page 170), to serve

1 Poach the chicken with the stock ingredients and 1 teaspoon of salt for 40 minutes.

2 Remove the chicken from the pan and leave to cool. Strain the stock into a clean pan and reduce the volume by rapid boiling to 600 ml (1 pint).

3 Remove the skin and bones from the chicken and break the meat into chunky pieces.

4 Melt 25 g (1 oz) butter in another pan, add the leek and onion and cook gently for 5 minutes until soft. Heat 15 g (½ oz) butter in a frying pan, add the mushrooms and cook over a high heat, stirring, until the excess liquid has cooked off. Season both to taste with salt and pepper.

5 Melt the remaining 50 g (2 oz) butter in a pan, stir in the flour and cook for 1 minute without colouring. Add the reduced stock one third at a time and stir vigorously with a wooden spoon until smooth and thick. Stir in the cream, lemon juice, parsley and season to taste with salt and white pepper. Stir in the chicken, vegetables and cooked ham.

6 Spoon the mixture into a 2.25 litre (4 pint) ovenproof dish and push a pie funnel or piping nozzle into the centre of the mixture. Cover and chill for 1 hour.

7 Preheat the oven to 200°C/400°F/Gas Mark 6. Roll out the pastry on a lightly floured surface until it is 2.5 cm (1 in) larger than the top of the pie dish. Cut off a thin strip from around the edge, brush it with a little beaten egg and press it onto the rim of the pie dish. Brush with more egg, cut a small cross into the centre of the larger piece of pastry and lay it over the dish, so that the funnel pokes through the cross. Press the edges together to seal and crimp them between your fingers to give it an attractive finish. Trim away the excess overhanging pastry, stack up the trimmings and roll them out again. Cut into 2.5 cm (1 in) wide strips and then cut each strip on the diagonal to form rudimentary leaves. Brush the top of the pie and the leaves with beaten egg and decorate around the pie funnel or nozzle with the leaves. Bake for about 40 minutes until the pastry is crisp and golden. Serve with the carrots and broccoli.

This is the sort of dish I remember from the 60s, when the idea of so much garlic was frightfully exotic. It reminds me of a bistro in Pavilion Road, Knightsbridge, which, naturally, had red-and-white checked tablecloths, candles in bottles on the tables, and the lovely, romantic yet daring scent of garlic. It was all very informal, and the red wine would presumably be thought undrinkable now.

sautéed chicken with forty cloves of garlic

SERVES 4

1 x 1.5–1.75 kg (3½–4 lb) chicken
15 g (½oz) butter
1 tablespoon olive oil
2 heads of garlic, broken into cloves
300 ml (10 fl oz) *Chicken stock*
(see page 176)
50 ml (2 fl oz) dry white wine
3 tablespoons double cream
1 tablespoon chopped curly leaf parsley
Salt and freshly ground black pepper
1 quantity of *Buttery rice pilaf*
(see page 175), to serve

1 Joint the chicken into 8 pieces. To do this, lay the bird breast-side up and pull a leg away from the body. Cut through the skin at the joint, then pull the leg further away, cutting the skin to free it as you go. Turn the bird over and feel along the backbone for the soft oysters of meat. Cut under the oysters with the tip of the knife and remove them with the legs. Cut the legs into 2 pieces at the thigh joint. Remove the breasts still on the bone from the carcase in 1 piece by cutting backwards from the point of the breast down towards the neck through the ribs. Don't forget to save the rest of the carcase for stock. Separate the breasts by cutting lengthways between them, and then cut each one in half on the diagonal so that each piece gets an equal amount of breast meat.

2 Heat the butter and oil in a shallow, heavy-based sauté pan. Season the chicken pieces well, add them to the pan with the garlic cloves and sauté them carefully over a medium heat until nicely browned all over – this will take about 15–20 minutes.

3 Add the stock and white wine to the pan and scrape up all the browned bits from the base with a wooden spoon. Cook for another 5 minutes or until the juices from the chicken run clear and the sauce has reduced and thickened slightly. Stir in the double cream. Scatter over the parsley and serve the chicken from the pan with the buttery rice pilaf.

This recipe really brings out the best in a free-range chicken. It really is the most satisfying of dishes. I first had it in Singapore where my then very young sons sat entranced by the number of lizards running across the walls in the restaurant. I love hot and cold food – here, the cold chicken and the hot rice. The secret of the success of this dish is in the cutting of the chicken. The pieces need to be on the bone and you can only cut it up cleanly when the chicken is quite cold and firm. The three dips and the crisp lettuce with coriander go towards making a fascinatingly complex combination of flavours – the best food ever, especially if you're on a diet!

chinese white-cooked chicken with ginger, spring onion and coriander

SERVES 4

2.75 litres (5 pints) water
5 cm (2 in) fresh root ginger, sliced
1 x 1.5 kg (3½lb) chicken
1 quantity of *Steamed rice* (see page 175), to serve

FOR THE SEASONINGS:
1 teaspoon Sichuan peppercorns
1 teaspoon black peppercorns
1 teaspoon Maldon sea salt flakes
4 spring onions, trimmed
1 slice of fresh ginger, peeled and finely chopped
3 tablespoons dark soy sauce
1 medium-hot red Dutch chilli, thinly sliced
1 teaspoon caster sugar
2 tablespoons rice wine or white wine vinegar

1 Put the water into a pan just large enough to take the chicken. Add the ginger and bring to the boil. Add the chicken, bring back to the boil and boil rapidly for 10 minutes. Then turn the heat right down and simmer very gently for 20 minutes. Remove from the heat and leave the chicken to go cold in the liquid. You can do this the day before if you wish and keep it cold, but don't refrigerate it.

2 Remove the chicken from the pan and cut it into 5 cm (2 in) pieces. You will need a large kitchen knife which is sharp enough to cut through chicken bones (and some poultry shears are also quite useful). Cut off the legs, cut them in 2 at the joint and then cut each thigh section in half. Now remove the breasts still on the bone from the carcase; cut horizontally just under the breasts from the cavity end of the chicken, through all the rib bones and down towards the wings. Separate the 2 breasts by cutting through the breast bone and then cut each breast into 3 pieces. Finally, cut off the wing bones. Arrange all the pieces attractively on a cold serving platter.

3 For the seasonings, heat a dry, heavy-based frying pan, add the Sichuan and black peppercorns and shake them around until they start to smell aromatic. Transfer to a mortar and coarsely grind with the pestle. Stir in the sea salt and transfer to one small dish. Thinly slice the spring

FOR THE SALAD:

½ **iceberg lettuce**

1 small bunch fresh coriander

onions and mix with the ginger and soy sauce in a second dish. Mix the chilli, sugar and vinegar together in a third dish.

4 Tear the iceberg lettuce into 5–7.5 cm (2–3 in) pieces. Pick small sprigs from the bunch of coriander and mix with the lettuce in a salad bowl. Take the chicken and salad to the table with the seasonings and serve with a bowl of steamed rice.

The basis of this recipe is from *Sally Clarke's Book – Recipes from a restaurant, shop and bakery*. It is a marvellously balanced idea: the poached fowl, the delicately flavoured root vegetables cooked with it, then the piquancy of the salsa verde and a tablespoon or two of nice soft, dark green Puy lentils to stir into the broth, made by reducing the stock in which you poached the guinea fowl. Lots of lovely flavours and very little fat, the sort of food which Sally, influenced by her early experiences of cooking in California with Alice Waters, does so well. I had a long discussion with my wine-merchant chum, Bill Baker, about the best wine to go with this. You need a fresh young red with little tannin, the sort of wine the French say should 'dance in the mouth', and we decided that it had to be a young village Burgundy, like a Cotes de Nuits Villages.

poached guinea fowl with winter vegetables, herbed lentils and salsa verde

SERVES 4

1 x 1.5 kg (3 lb) guinea fowl
4 medium-sized carrots, peeled
2 medium-sized leeks, cleaned and halved
2 small fennel bulbs, halved through the stalk, or 350 g (12 oz) baby fennel, trimmed
4 celery stalks, halved
Salt

FOR THE SALSA VERDE:
20 g (^{3}/$_4$ oz) flatleaf parsley leaves, very roughly chopped
10 g (^{1}/$_4$ oz) mint leaves, very roughly chopped
3 tablespoons capers in brine, drained and rinsed
6 anchovy fillets in olive oil, drained
1 garlic clove
1 teaspoon Dijon mustard
1^1/$_2$ tablespoons lemon juice
120 ml (4 fl oz) extra virgin olive oil

FOR THE HERBED LENTILS:
300 g (11 oz) Puy lentils
2 bay leaves

1 Put the guinea fowl into a large pan and cover with water so that the bird is completely submerged. Add 1 teaspoon of salt, bring to the boil, skimming any scum off the surface, and simmer for 40 minutes until the juices from the guinea fowl run clear when the thigh is pierced with a skewer.

2 Meanwhile, for the herbed lentils, put the lentils into a pan with the bay leaves and enough cold water to cover twice their depth. Bring to the boil slowly and simmer for 15 minutes until tender. Drain and return to the pan.

3 Cut the vegetables into neatly-shaped pieces – cut the carrots in half lengthways and then across into 2, cut the leeks into 2 or 3 shorter pieces, trim the baby fennel (or cut the fennel bulbs into 6 or 8 wedges, depending on their size) and halve the celery stalks.

4 Lift the guinea fowl onto a plate and leave until cool enough to handle. Bring the stock back to the boil, add the carrots, leeks, fennel and celery and cook for 6–7 minutes until tender. Lift out with a slotted spoon and set to one side. Strain the stock into a large, shallow pan and leave to boil rapidly until reduced to 450 ml (15 fl oz).

5 For the salsa verde, pile the parsley, mint, capers, anchovies and garlic onto a chopping board and chop together into a coarse paste. Transfer the mixture into a bowl and stir in the mustard, lemon juice, olive oil and ½ teaspoon of salt.

85 ml (3 fl oz) olive oil
1 garlic clove, crushed
1 medium-hot red Dutch chilli,
finely chopped
1 small handful of coriander leaves,
chopped
1 small handful of flatleaf parsley leaves,
chopped
1 tablespoon of chopped chives
½ teaspoon salt

6 To joint the guinea fowl, cut off the legs and remove the skin. Cut the legs in half at the joint and trim off and discard the ends of the drumsticks if still in place. Carefully remove the breast meat from the carcase in 2 whole pieces and cut each on the diagonal into 2.

7 Put the guinea fowl and vegetable pieces into a large, shallow pan and pour over the reduced stock. Simmer for 3–4 minutes until heated through.

8 Add the olive oil, garlic, chilli, coriander, parsley, chives and salt to the lentils and heat gently for a few minutes.

9 Arrange the vegetables in the base of 4 deep, bowl-like plates and put the pieces of guinea fowl on top. Ladle over some of the cooking liquor and serve with the herbed lentils and salsa verde.

5

meat and

THE DAY I WENT TO BOROUGH MARKET FOR THE FIRST TIME, I HAD BEEN READING AN ARTICLE IN *SLOW*, THE JOURNAL OF THE SLOW FOOD MOVEMENT, ON THE MCDONALDSIZATION OF SOCIETY. SLOW FOOD CAN BEST BE SUMMED UP BY SAYING THAT MOST OF ITS PRINCIPLES ARE THE OPPOSITE OF FAST FOOD, OF WHICH MCDONALDS IS PERHAPS THE BEST-KNOWN EXAMPLE. IN THE PIECE, GEORGE RITZER DESCRIBED THE COMPANY'S EMPHASIS ON EFFICIENCY, AND ON A CONSISTENT AND PREDICTABLE RATHER THAN HIGH-QUALITY PRODUCT. THIS LED TO THE REPLACEMENT OF SKILLED HUMAN BEINGS WITH NON-HUMAN TECHNOLOGY AND A DRIVE FOR EVER-FASTER SERVICE. REASONABLY, HE POINTED OUT THAT THIS WAS NOT ALL BAD.

offal

LEFT *When you see the contentment of animals such as the sheep owned by Griffith David Williams (BELOW) or the cows of Edward Hamer (RIGHT) you can tell that the meat they produce is going to be of the highest quality.*

He mentioned Starbucks as a case where a consistent product has benefited us all. Recalling the quality of coffee generally available in this country ten years ago I completely agree, and, remembering hamburgers in the 60s in Britain, McDonalds have certainly improved things.

But to find myself in that gloriously unpredictable market under the railway arches in Southwark (which was founded nearby in the fourteenth century because it was the closest place to the city of London, just across the Thames, where farmers could sell their cattle) was to seriously emphasize a point made later in the article, that the inexorable growth of massive food chains producing standardized food must lead to a decline in knowledge about how meat should really taste. No wonder one of my meat-producer heroes is called The Real Meat Company, and another (could this be slightly tongue in cheek?) West Country Well Hung Lamb. Will future generations judge quality by reference to a 4 oz disk of intensively reared minced beef . . . ?

Already I think that the Herdwick lamb of Andrew Sharp (who runs Farmer Sharp) or the Middle White pigs of Peter Gott of Sillfield Farm, not to mention the Welsh salt-marsh lamb or Black beef from a company like Edwards of Conwy, would not appeal to many because they have too strong a taste; there are signs everywhere that many people don't like a lot of flavour. Armed with an image of fluorescent lighting, bright primary colours, wash-down surfaces and the slightly trance-like feeling of déjà vu that chain restaurants induce in me, I have the remembrance of those two Cumbrian Farmers, stockily built and weather tanned in their tweed jackets, dressed for market looking like Beatrix Potter's next-door neighbours. I went to see them on their farms afterwards. I honestly think you wouldn't need to taste their produce to know it was going to be full of flavour. Whenever I call on these confident, committed producers you can see in the contentment of their stock that there is a real connection between farmers who rear their stock non-intensively and the flavour and quality of the meat produced. I went to see a farmer from Suffolk, Roger Clark of Weylands Farm, who made me feel very optimistic – what a source of hope and common sense. We stood in a small field and surveyed the hilly patchwork of grass pastures and woodlands and admired two of his Suffolk rams, one of which butted David, our director. It was farming on a small, human scale. 'An animal's got to be content to thrive,' he said.

The only way in which I've changed the basic hotpot recipe is to use best-end chops rather than middle neck, because they're not as fatty and add a couple of boned lamb shanks. I've also trimmed off some of the fat. The only drawback to this magnificent dish can sometimes be its richness. There are various possible additions to a hotpot: carrots, Worcestershire sauce, field mushrooms, sometimes even oysters, but I think chops, potatoes, onions and a few kidneys is the best combination, with the essential accompaniment of a good, well-flavoured and not harshly assertive pickled red cabbage.

lancashire hotpot with pickled red cabbage

SERVES 6

4 lambs' kidneys
1.5 kg (3 lb) floury potatoes, such as
Maris Piper, peeled and sliced
450 g (1 lb) onions, halved and thinly sliced
8 x best-end lamb chops, bony ends
cut off and trimmed of excessive fat
2 small boned lamb shanks, cut into
small chunks
2 teaspoons fresh thyme leaves
600 ml (1 pint) *Chicken stock*
(see page 176)
50 g (2 oz) butter, melted
Salt and freshly ground black pepper

FOR THE PICKLED RED CABBAGE:
450 g (1 lb) red cabbage
25 g (1 oz) Maldon sea salt flakes
300 ml (10 fl oz) balsamic vinegar
2 dried red chillies
2 cloves
1 teaspoon coriander seeds
1 teaspoon black peppercorns
2.5 cm (1 in) fresh root ginger,
peeled and bruised
½ teaspoon juniper berries
2 pieces of blade mace
2 teaspoons caster sugar

1 Make the pickled red cabbage 3–4 days beforehand. Remove the outside leaves of the cabbage, cut it into quarters and cut out the core. Slice it across very thinly and layer it in a large bowl with the salt. Weight the top of the cabbage with a plate and leave for 24 hours, turning the cabbage every now and then.

2 The next day, rinse the cabbage under running water and drain really well. Put the vinegar, chillies, cloves, coriander seeds, peppercorns, ginger, juniper berries, blade mace and sugar into a pan, bring to the boil and simmer for 5 minutes, then leave to cool. Pack the cabbage into large sterilized jars, strain over the vinegar and seal. Leave for 2–3 days.

3 For the hotpot, preheat the oven to 160°C/325°F/Gas Mark 3. Cut the lambs' kidneys in half and snip out the cores with scissors. Cut them into thin slices.

4 Put a layer of potatoes in the bottom of a lightly buttered 4.5 litre (8 pint) casserole dish. Scatter over some of the onions, half the chops and chunks of shank, some of the kidneys and a few thyme leaves, seasoning well between each layer. Repeat the layers once more, pour over the stock and finish with a neat layer of overlapping potato slices.

5 Brush the top of the potatoes with some of the butter and cover with a well-fitting lid. Bake the hotpot in the oven for 2 hours.

6 Remove the hotpot from the oven and increase the temperature to 220°C/425°F/Gas Mark 7. Remove the lid, brush the potatoes once more with the rest of the melted butter and return it to the oven for 30 minutes or until the potatoes are crisp and golden.

I had a great couple of days filming on Bredon Hill in Worcestershire a few summers ago for a TV series called *Fresh Food*. We were following up a story about a lost variety of perry pear called 'Early Treacle' which it was thought had been found in an old orchard. We filmed the blossoming of the first bud on the tree, but sadly it was not the fruit we hoped it would be. We repaired for consolation to Kevin Minchew's cider and perry shed, as it was he who had instigated the search. With us was Charles Martel, the maker of Stinking Bishop, a cheese which has a rind washed in perry. Many different barrels of single-variety perry and cider were tried: Rock, Gin, and several varieties of Huffcap, and of the ciders I recall Yarlington Mill and Kingston Black. I liked Rock best. The next day I cooked a leg of local Gloucester Old Spot ham in it in an old pear orchard. Kevin's perry and cider are listed in the back of the book (see page 194). Serve with braised red cabbage and baked potatoes.

In summertime on Bredon
The bells they sound so clear;
Round both the shires they ring them
In steeples far and near,
A happy noise to hear.

A.E. HOUSMAN

gammon poached in perry with braised red cabbage and baked potatoes

SERVES 10

1 x 2.75 kg (6 lb) unsmoked gammon,
boned and rolled
4 cloves
2 fresh bay leaves
¼ teaspoon dried chilli flakes
A large bottle of perry or dry cider
1 tablespoon Dijon mustard
50 g (2 oz) chilled unsalted butter,
cut into small pieces
2 tablespoons chopped curly leaf parsley
Freshly ground black pepper
Braised red cabbage (see page 170)
and *Baked potatoes* (see page 172),
to serve

1 Some gammon joints are more salty than others, so to check if it needs soaking overnight, cut off a slice and simmer it in water for 5 minutes, then taste it. If it's more salty than you like, cover it with plenty of cold water and leave it to soak for 12 hours.

2 Put the gammon in a large saucepan, add the cloves, bay leaves and chilli flakes and pour over the perry or cider and enough cold water to cover. Bring to the boil, skimming off any scum as it rises to the surface, lower the heat and cover. Leave it to simmer very gently for 20 minutes per lb – 2 hours for a 2.75 kg (6 lb) piece of gammon – then take the pan off the heat and set it aside.

3 For the sauce, strain 600 ml (1 pint) of the cooking liquor into a large, shallow pan and boil rapidly until reduced by three-quarters – keep tasting it just to check it's not getting too salty. Whisk in the mustard and then the pieces of butter, a few at a time, until you have a light, buttery sauce. Season with black pepper and stir in the parsley.

4 Carve the gammon into thin slices and serve with the sauce, together with the braised red cabbage and baked potatoes.

There is no better accompaniment to the pleasure of suet pastry than steak and kidney. This thought is derived from a remark made by Shaun Hill, the gifted but modest cook of The Merchant House restaurant in Ludlow (Tel: 01584 875438), who once said to me that the escalope of veal was the perfect vehicle for fried breadcrumbs. I also enjoy the fact that the simpler you make a steak and kidney pudding, the better it tastes. You don't even need to brown the meat because the finished sauce will have quite enough colour, although I have taken the highly unorthodox step of adding a little soy sauce. Could there ever be, I wonder, a better accompaniment to a glass of Pomerol.

steak and kidney pudding

SERVES 6

750 g (1½ lb) chuck steak
225 g (8 oz) ox kidney
2½ tablespoons plain flour
1 teaspoon of salt
1 teaspoon of cracked black pepper
1 medium onion, chopped
10 g (¼ oz) curly leaf parsley, chopped
The leaves from 2 sprigs of thyme
2 bay leaves
1 tablespoon dark soy sauce
Beef stock (see page 176)
Steamed Savoy cabbage (see page 170)
and Plain boiled potatoes
(see page 172), to serve

FOR THE SUET PASTRY:
350 g (12 oz) self-raising flour
175 g (6 oz) shredded suet
A large pinch of salt
250 ml (8 fl oz) cold water

1 Cut the steak into 2.5 cm (1 in) pieces. Cut the ox kidney into small pieces and snip out the white core with scissors. Put the steak and kidney into a bowl with the flour and seasoning and toss together well. Mix in the onion, parsley, thyme and bay leaves.

2 For the pastry, mix the flour, suet and salt with the water to form a soft dough. Turn out onto a lightly floured surface and knead briefly until smooth. Roll out, using a little more flour, into a 36 cm (14 in) circle and cut out a quarter of the circle. Set it aside for the lid and use the remainder to line the base and sides of a lightly buttered 1.75 litre (3 pint) pudding basin, overlapping the cut edges slightly, brushing them lightly with water and pressing them together well to seal.

3 Spoon the meat mixture into the basin and add the soy sauce and enough beef stock to come three-quarters of the way up the meat.

4 Roll the reserved piece of pastry into a circle about 1 cm (½ in) larger than the top of the basin. Brush the edge with water, press it firmly onto the top of the pudding and crimp the edges together well to make a good seal. Cover the basin with a floured pudding cloth and tie securely in place with string.

5 Put some sort of trivet into the base of a large saucepan, cover with about 5 cm (2 in) of water and bring it to the boil. Put the pudding into the pan, cover with a well-fitting lid and leave it to steam for 4 hours, topping up the water now and then from the kettle when necessary.

6 To serve, uncover the pudding and serve it straight from the basin with some steamed Savoy cabbage and boiled potatoes.

In this recipe, I have made the most of the melt-in-the-mouth quality of the best fillet steak by serving it extremely underdone but with a highly seared crust flavoured with sea salt, black pepper and Sichuan pepper. I serve it cold and thinly sliced with pickled chicory and a lemon and Thai fish sauce dressing. If you can get the red-tinged chicory that seems to be widely available now, it looks really good. The point of the chicory is the contrast between its bitterness and the heat of the chilli in the pickle.

sliced seared fillet steak salad with pickled chicory

SERVES 4

10 g (¼oz) Sichuan peppercorns
10 g (¼oz) black peppercorns
10 g (¼oz) Maldon sea salt flakes
350 g (12 oz) piece of thick beef fillet
2–3 tablespoons sunflower oil
25 g (1 oz) wild rocket leaves

FOR THE SALAD DRESSING:
1½ tablespoons Thai fish sauce
3 tablespoons water
½ teaspoon granulated sugar
½ teaspoon freshly squeezed lemon juice
¼ teaspoon arrowroot
5 cm (2 in) piece of spring onion,
very thinly sliced

FOR THE PICKLED CHICORY:
15 g (½oz) fresh ginger, peeled
¼ medium-hot Dutch red chilli, halved
lengthways and deseeded
40 g (1½oz) granulated sugar
150 ml (5 fl oz) white wine vinegar
1 head of red or green chicory
1 teaspoon salt

1 For the pickled chicory, cut the ginger and red chilli into 2.5 cm (1 in) long, thin matchsticks. Put them in a pan with the sugar and vinegar, bring to the boil and simmer for 5 minutes. Tip into a shallow plastic container and leave to cool. Meanwhile, break the chicory into leaves, then cut each leaf in half and thinly slice the core. Place in a colander set over a bowl and toss with the salt. Leave for 2 hours to soften. Stir the salted chicory into the cold spiced vinegar, stir well, cover and set aside in the refrigerator for 24 hours. Discard the salty liquor left behind in the bowl.

2 For the beef, put the Sichuan peppercorns and black peppercorns into a mortar and grind to a coarse powder. Add the salt and grind a little more. Set aside ½ a teaspoon of the mixture for the salad dressing and sprinkle the rest over the base of a large baking tray.

3 Brush the piece of beef fillet all over with the oil, then roll it in the salt and pepper mixture so that it takes on an even coating. Heat a char-grill, ridged cast-iron skillet or heavy-based frying pan until hot. Brush with a little more oil, then add the beef and sear it on one side for about 2 minutes. Give it a quarter turn and sear for another 2 minutes. Continue like this, turning maybe once or twice more, until it is richly browned all over but still very rare in the centre. Set aside to cool.

4 For the dressing, put the fish sauce, water, sugar, reserved salt and pepper mixture and lemon juice into a small pan and bring to the boil. Slake the arrowroot with a tiny amount of water, stir in and simmer for 1 minute. Pour into a small bowl and leave to cool.

5 To serve, carve the beef across into thin slices and arrange it on 4 large plates. Drain the pickling liquid from the chicory and place a small pile alongside the beef, together with a small pile of rocket leaves. Stir the spring onions into the dressing, spoon a little over the beef and a little more around the outside edge of each plate.

I'm much indebted to this dish. The first year we opened the Seafood Restaurant we had to stay open all through the winter as we were so short of money. I cooked and my friend Johnny looked after the restaurant, then we both did the dishes – not that we had many because most nights we were empty. I put this meat dish on, hoping that the locals would go for it as it wasn't fish, and they did a bit. We survived and I forgot about it, except for cooking it at home. It's magnificent and so easy, but it does need the very best loin pork chops.

sautéed pork chops with shallots, sage and cider

SERVES 4

4 x 2.5 cm (1 in) thick pork loin chops
3 shallots
A small handful of sage leaves
50 g (2 oz) softened butter
175 ml (6 fl oz) cider
2 teaspoons chopped curly leaf parsley
Salt and freshly ground black pepper
Steamed sprouting broccoli
(see page 170)
and *Sautéed potatoes* (see page 172),
to serve

1 Lightly score the surface of the chops on both sides in a criss-cross pattern, cutting them at 1 cm (½ in) intervals first one way and then the other.

2 Finely chop the shallots and sage together on a board and then mix with the butter and some salt and pepper. Spread the butter over each side of the chops, working it well down into the cuts with the tip of the knife.

3 Heat a large frying pan over a medium heat. Add the chops and sauté them gently for 3–4 minutes on each side until lightly browned.

4 Now sprinkle the cider around the edge of the pan, cover with a well-fitting lid and continue to cook for a further 5 or so minutes, until the chops are cooked through. Uncover the pan, remove the chops to a plate and keep them warm.

5 Boil the remaining juices until slightly reduced and well flavoured, then stir in the parsley and some seasoning to taste. Place the chops onto warmed plates and pour over some of the sauce. Serve with some sprouting broccoli and sautéed potatoes.

This mélange of dried flageolets and fresh peas, which is more of a sauce than an accompanying vegetable, is, I think, a perfect accompaniment to the fatty delicacy of a best-end of lamb, and is particularly appropriate with Welsh salt-marsh lamb which has a unique tenderness and sweetness.

roast rack of salt-marsh lamb with a stew of peas and flageolets, garlic, parsley and olive oil

SERVES 4

2 x 8 cutlet racks of Welsh salt-marsh lamb (see pages 187-90)
Salt and freshly ground black pepper

FOR THE PEAS AND FLAGEOLETS:
175 g (6 oz) dried flageolet beans, soaked overnight
1.2 litres (2 pints) water
1 carrot, peeled and halved
3 garlic cloves, finely chopped
1 shallot, finely chopped
1 thyme sprig
1 bay leaf
175 g (6 oz) fresh or frozen petit pois
2 tablespoons extra virgin olive oil
15 g (½ oz) butter
2 tablespoons coarsely chopped flatleaf parsley

1 Drain the flageolet beans and put them into a pan with the water, the carrot, two-thirds of the chopped garlic, the shallot, thyme and bay leaf. Simmer for 30 minutes or until the beans are soft – this can take anything up to 1½ hours, depending on how old they are. Remove the carrot after 15 minutes, cool slightly and then cut into small dice. Drain the beans, reserving the cooking liquor, and return them to the pan with the carrot. Discard the bay leaf and thyme stalks from the cooking liquor.

2 Preheat the oven to 230°C/450°F/Gas Mark 8. Season the racks of lamb with salt and pepper, put them into a small roasting tin and roast for 20 minutes. Transfer to a plate, cover with foil and leave to rest for 10 minutes.

3 Pour away the excess fat from the roasting tin and add 120 ml (4 fl oz) of the bean cooking liquor. Put the tin over a medium heat and rub all the juices from the base of the tin with a wooden spoon. Pour into the pan of beans and add the peas, the remaining chopped garlic, olive oil, butter, ½ a teaspoon of salt and some pepper. Stir over a low heat for 5 minutes until the peas are tender. Stir in the chopped parsley.

4 Carve the racks of lamb into cutlets and pour any juices from the plate into the beans. Spoon some of the beans and peas into the centre of 4 warmed, deep plates, rest the lamb on top and serve.

These days, most roasting joints of pork don't produce crackling. There's just not enough fat between the flesh and the skin to make the skin go crisp; there has to be a good layer to keep the water in the meat away from the skin and allow the skin to reach higher temperatures than that of boiling water to achieve crispness. Such is our apparent desire to eat ever-leaner meat, we seem to have foregone the delights of such things as crackling and really marbled steak. The Chinese esteem belly pork, I imagine this is because of its high fat content, from which comes succulent meat and crisp, crackly skin. Here, a square of belly pork is dry marinated with Chinese spice then slow-roasted to produce crisp and tender roast pork. Add some steamed Chinese greens in oyster sauce and steamed rice and, only my opinion of course, you can forget endless stir-fries; this is Chinese food at its best.

crisp chinese roast pork with steamed rice

SERVES 4–6

1 x 1.5 kg (3 lb) piece of thick belly pork
with the rind
1 tablespoon Sichuan peppercorns
1 teaspoon black peppercorns
2 tablespoons Maldon sea salt flakes
2 teaspoons five-spice powder
2 teaspoons caster sugar
1 quantity *Steamed Chinese greens in oyster sauce* (see page 171) and *Steamed rice* (see page 175),
to serve

1 Spike the skin of the pork with a fine skewer or a larding needle as many times as you can, going through into the fat but not so deep that you go into the flesh. Then pour a kettle full of hot water over the skin, leave it to drain and then dry it off well.

2 Heat a dry, heavy-based frying pan over a high heat. Add the Sichuan and black peppercorns and shake them around for a few seconds until they darken slightly and start to smell aromatic. Transfer them to a spice grinder and grind to a fine powder. Tip them into a bowl and stir in the sea salt, five-spice powder and sugar.

3 Turn the pork flesh-side up on a tray and rub the flesh all over with the spice mixture. Set it aside somewhere cool for 8 hours or overnight.

4 Preheat the oven to 200°C/400°F/Gas Mark 6. Turn the pork skin-side up and place it on a rack resting on top of a roasting tin of water. Roast the pork for 15 minutes, then lower the oven temperature to 180°C/350°F/Gas Mark 4 and roast it for a further 2 hours, topping up the water in the roasting tin now and then when necessary.

5 Increase the oven temperature once more to 230°C/450°F/Gas Mark 8 and continue to roast the pork for a further 15 minutes. Then remove it from the oven and leave it to cool. It is best served warm.

6 Cut the pork into bite-sized pieces and arrange them on a warmed platter. Serve with the Chinese greens in oyster sauce and steamed rice.

This is one of those recipes that I have to limit myself to cooking occasionally, otherwise I'd overdose on it, it's that good. But not only is it good, it seems to be the sort of food that everyone else likes, too: rough slices of pink lamb tinged with the flavour of the fire. The best time to eat new season's lamb is June and July, which is also the nicest time for barbecuing. There's something immensely satisfying about boning out a leg and cooking it with extreme care, on an early summer's evening with the odd glass of Beaujolais nearby. The new season's lamb bred for Easter tends to be tender yet disappointingly bland, but by June it is full of the taste of summer pastures.

barbecued butterflied lamb with lemon, garlic and thyme

SERVES 6

1 x 2.5 kg (5½ lb) leg of lamb
Olive oil chips (see pages 172–3)
and *Tomato, shallot and basil
salad* (see page 174),
to serve

FOR THE MARINADE:
2 large garlic cloves, chopped
1 medium-hot Dutch red chilli,
seeded and finely chopped
1 teaspoon chopped rosemary
The leaves from 6 thyme sprigs
1 fresh bay leaf, finely chopped
3 strips of pared lemon zest
Juice of ½ a lemon
1 teaspoon Maldon salt
½ teaspoon black pepper,
coarsely crushed
6 tablespoons olive oil

1 To butterfly the leg of lamb, find the place where the long bone running down the length of the leg appears to run quite close to the surface. Split open the meat along this bone and cut the meat away from either side. At the fatter end of the leg there is a group of smaller bones. Continue to cut the meat away from these until you have completely opened up the leg and can lift them all out. You should now have a piece of meat shaped like butterfly wings. Trim off any excess fat and open up any thicker areas of the meat so that it is all about 4–5 cm (1½–2 in) thick. If in doubt, get your butcher to do it.

2 Mix the marinade ingredients together in a shallow roasting tin. Add the lamb, turn it a few times until well coated, then turn skin-side up, cover and leave in the fridge for at least an hour.

3 If you are using a charcoal barbecue, light it 40 minutes before you want to start cooking. If you are using a gas barbecue, light it 10 minutes beforehand.

4 Because a leg of lamb contains a good deal of fat, you will need to be careful when barbecuing it, to avoid excessive flare-ups, which would cause the meat to burn. Place it on the bars of the barbecue grill and keep turning and moving it to different parts of the grill and cook for 10–12 minutes on each side. Alternatively, just barbecue the leg for 5–7 minutes on each side until well-coloured, then transfer it to a hot oven for 20–25 minutes.

5 Lift the lamb onto a board, cover with foil and leave to rest for 5 minutes. Then carve across into thick slices and serve with olive oil chips and the tomato, shallot and basil salad.

Vincenzo Borgonzolo used to come down to our place about 20 years ago with his wife Elaine and his daughter, Angela. He has a restaurant in London called Al San Vincenzo. I'd never met an Italian chef before but he seemed to cook like me, sort of feeling his way as he went along but with an instinctive enjoyment for what worked. He gave us this dish and it was on the menu for years. The heart of it is the Luganega sausages, a classic Italian mixture, the origin of which is uncertain. The sausages from Monza are said to be among the best. That being said, the long-established firm of Fratelli Camisa Ltd in London (see page 193) make utterly wonderful Luganega; it's the flavouring of fennel seeds and garlic that makes them so distinctive.

vincenzo's sausages with parmesan polenta

SERVES 4

2 tablespoons extra virgin olive oil
550 g (1¼ lb) Luganega sausages,
cut diagonally into 10 cm (4 in)
long pieces
(see Fratelli Camisa Ltd, page 193)
1 medium onion, finely chopped
2 garlic cloves, thinly sliced
A large pinch of dried chilli flakes
1 teaspoon picked thyme leaves
85 ml (3 fl oz) dry white wine
6 sun-dried tomatoes in olive oil, drained
and thinly sliced
2 teaspoons lemon juice
1 tablespoon finely shredded
flatleaf parsley
Salt and freshly ground black pepper

FOR THE PARMESAN POLENTA:
900 ml (1½ pints) water
120 g (4½ oz) polenta
40 g (1½ oz) butter
75 g (3 oz) Parmesan cheese,
finely grated

1 For the Parmesan polenta, bring the water to the boil in a medium-sized pan. Pour in the polenta in a slow, steady stream, stirring all the time, bring to a simmer and leave to cook, stirring frequently, for 20 minutes.

2 After the polenta has been cooking for about 10 minutes, start the sausages. Heat the olive oil in a deep sauté pan, add the sausages and lightly brown. Add the onion and garlic and cook briefly until soft but not browned. Add the chilli flakes and thyme and cook for 1 or 2 minutes, then add the wine, leave it to bubble up for a few seconds and add the sun-dried tomatoes and some salt and pepper. Cover and simmer for 5 minutes.

3 Uncover the sausages, increase the heat slightly and reduce the cooking juices a little. Then add the lemon juice, parsley and seasoning to taste.

4 Stir the butter, Parmesan cheese and some salt to taste into the polenta. Spoon it into 4 warmed, deep plates, spoon the sausages on top and serve.

I am looking for the taste of the fire here. The meat should be slightly burnt on the outside yet very rare in the centre, and the only way to do this is on a barbecue. Because this cut of meat, a côtes de boeuf, contains a lot of fat, it needs a great deal of attention, and unless you have quite a sophisticated barbecue, which can dampen down the effects of a lot of flaring fat, it's probably best to start cooking the ribs on the barbecue and then transfer them to your oven once they have taken on a good dark brown colour. You can buy ribs on the bone which have been trimmed right down to what is now called the rib eye. These are much more controllable on the barbecue, but I think something is missing if the outer fattier and tougher muscle of the rib is missing. In the winter, we always have a wood burning stove alight in the kitchen. I leave the wood to burn down to hot ash and then rest a simple cast-iron grill rack on the fire box. This is perfection: a char-grilled joint with a faint hint of wood smoke. Serve with Goose fat chips.

fore ribs of beef with béarnaise sauce and goose fat chips

SERVES 4

2 chined fore ribs of beef (separated)
Salt and freshly ground black pepper
1 x quantity of *Goose fat chips*
(see pages 172–3) and *Cheese-makers' salad* (see page 174),
to serve

FOR THE BÉARNAISE SAUCE:
1 tablespoon chopped tarragon
2 shallots, finely chopped
20 turns of the black pepper mill
50 ml (2 fl oz) white wine vinegar
3 tablespoons water
225 g (8 oz) unsalted butter
2 egg yolks
½ teaspoon salt

1 Preheat your barbecue to high. For the béarnaise sauce, put the tarragon, shallots, pepper, vinegar and 1 tablespoon of the water into a small pan and boil rapidly until it has reduced to 1 tablespoon. Clarify the butter in another small pan (see page 177) and set both aside.

2 Season the ribs well on both sides with salt and pepper. Cook them on the barbecue for 5 minutes on each side for rare or 6½ minutes on each side for medium-rare. Remove, cover and leave to rest for 15 minutes.

3 Meanwhile, finish the béarnaise sauce: put the egg yolks and remaining water into a bowl set over a pan of simmering water, making sure that the bowl is not touching the water, and whisk vigorously until the mixture is voluminous and creamy. Then remove the bowl from the pan and gradually whisk in the warm clarified butter. Stir in the tarragon and shallot reduction and salt.

4 To serve, cut off the bone and carve the meat across into long, thin slices. Serve with the béarnaise sauce, chips and salad.

I don't think we cook enough with beer in this country. Our beer, with its body and fragrant hoppiness, is ideal for cooking – particularly the Adnam's Suffolk ale (see page 193) which we filmed and sampled last September. You'd have thought that a carbonnade, though from Belgium, would be found in many a pub because a good British beer would be the obvious thing to drink with a carbonnade, but sadly it isn't. My carbonnade is made with slices of shin of beef. Though this requires long, slow cooking, the meat acquires a beguiling succulence in the process.

carbonnade of beef 'à la flamande'

SERVES 4

2 tablespoons sunflower oil
900 g (2 lb) sliced shin of beef
750 g (1½ lb) onions, thinly sliced
50 g (2 oz) butter
2 tablespoons flour
2½ tablespoons Worcestershire sauce
600 ml (1 pint) hoppy beer
600 ml (1 pint) *Beef stock* (see page 176)
A bouquet garni of 2 bay leaves, 2 thyme sprigs and a small bunch of parsley
Salt and freshly ground black pepper
Braised red cabbage (see page 170) or *Cabbage with shallots, garlic and flatleaf parsley* (see page 170) and *Baked potatoes* (see page 172), to serve

1 Preheat the oven to 160°C/325°F/Gas Mark 3. Heat the oil in a flameproof casserole, add the slices of shin and brown well on both sides. Lift them onto a plate, add the onions and butter to the casserole and cook over a low heat for 15 minutes, stirring often, until soft and well coloured.

2 Stir in the flour and cook for a minute or two. Return the shin of beef to the pan and lift some of the onions on top. Add the Worcestershire sauce, beer, stock, bouquet garni, 1 teaspoon of salt and 20 turns of the black pepper mill. Cover and cook in the oven for 2 hours. Serve with the braised red cabbage or cabbage with shallots, garlic and flatleaf parsley and baked potatoes.

Alan Davidson is one of my greatest food heroes. His two books, *North Atlantic Seafood* and *Mediterranean Seafood*, were, along with Jane Grigson's *Fish Cookery*, the books that set me up as a fish cook. So I've taken to his *Oxford Companion to Food* with great enthusiasm. It's a lovely mixture of fact and anecdote, where he quotes a poem by the Welsh poet Dewi Emrys on cawl (pronounced cowl):

With leeks and potatoes and stars on its face,
You'll see the cauldron on the tripod there
And the gorse blazing gaily beneath it.

It's a great dish in the tradition of Irish stew and Pot au Feu, dating back to a time before roasting ovens. I first tried it in Merthyr Tydfil at a little café in Cyfarthfa Castle, and I thought at the time that it is as good in its way as bouillabaisse. When you go to Marseilles you can't get away from bouillabaisse, so why doesn't cawl appear on the menu of every other pub in Cardiff?

welsh cawl

SERVES 8–10

750 g (1½ lb) piece of rolled
bacon collar
750 g (1½ lb) middle-neck of lamb
2 celery stalks, sliced
2 large carrots, peeled and sliced
1 medium onion, halved and sliced
1 teaspoon black peppercorns
4 cloves
2–3 small young turnips,
cut into quarters
A bouquet garni of parsley, thyme
and bay leaves
2–3 small leeks, cleaned
350 g (12 oz) baby carrots, frondy tops
trimmed and halved lengthways
225 g (8 oz) small, whole onions, peeled
450 g (1 lb) small new potatoes,
scraped clean
225 g (8 oz) shelled broad beans
225 g (8 oz) summer green cabbage,
sliced across into 2 cm (¾ in)
wide strips
Chopped curly leaf parsley, to garnish
Caerphilly cheese and fresh crusty bread,
to serve

1 Put the bacon, lamb, celery, carrots, onion, peppercorns, cloves, one of the turnips and the bouquet garni into a very large pan. Cover with 3.4 litres (6 pints) of water, bring to the boil, and leave to simmer very gently for 2 hours, skimming the scum and any fat off the surface now and then with a ladle during cooking. Very thinly slice the green part from the leeks and then cut the remaining white parts into 4 cm (1½ in) pieces.

2 Remove the bouquet garni and taste the stock for saltiness – this will depend on your bacon collar – and adjust if necessary. Add the rest of the turnips, baby carrots, small onions and the potatoes. Bring back to the boil, skim again and continue to simmer uncovered for 15 minutes. Add the white part of the leeks, the broad beans and cabbage and cook for a further 5 minutes.

3 To serve, remove the bacon, carve it into rough slices and return it to the soup. Ladle into large, deep soup plates. Sprinkle the top of the soup with the sliced green leek and chopped parsley and then scatter over some crumbled thin slices of Caerphilly cheese. Serve with fresh crusty bread.

The celeriac and mustard salad that is served with this dish is glorious and never better than when partnered with some good aromatic salt brisket. I say good because it's hard to buy brisket that appeals. I tried cooking two briskets and a silverside when testing this recipe and rejected them all as more like soaked floorboards than meat, until I got hold of some brisket from my favourite local butcher, Philip Warren of Tideford (see page 190), and the realization of a great combination gripped me. 'One for the café,' I exclaimed excitedly. The lesson is to buy from a butcher who turns the brisket over; otherwise it could sit in its salted and stable state on a shelf somewhere for many months.

poached salt beef with celeriac and mustard salad

SERVES 6

1.75 kg (4 lb) piece of rolled salt brisket
2 carrots, halved
2 celery stalks
2 onions, peeled and halved
2 plum tomatoes
2 bay leaves
1 thyme sprig
1 teaspoon black peppercorns
Plain boiled potatoes (see page 172), to serve

FOR THE CELERIAC AND MUSTARD SALAD:
1 tablespoon sunflower oil
1 tablespoon yellow mustard seeds
2 tablespoons Dijon mustard
1 teaspoon white wine vinegar
1 teaspoon lemon juice
50 g (2 oz) *Mayonnaise* (see page 177), made with sunflower oil
4 tablespoons soured cream
1 large celeriac, weighing about 750 g (1½ lb)
100 g (4 oz) gherkins, cut into long, thin matchsticks
1 tablespoon chopped flatleaf parsley
Salt and freshly ground black pepper

1 Soak the salt beef in cold water for 24 hours.

2 Put the piece of beef into a large pan with the carrots, celery, onions, tomatoes, bay leaves, thyme and peppercorns, bring to the boil and leave to simmer very gently (it should hardly bubble at all) for up to 3½ hours, topping up the water now and then so that the beef remains covered, until tender. A skewer should pass through the meat with very little resistance.

3 Shortly before the beef is ready, make the salad. Heat the oil in a small frying pan, add the mustard seeds and cover with a lid. Cook until they begin to pop, then take off the heat and as soon as the popping has subsided, uncover and pour the oil and all the seeds into a small bowl. Stir in the mustard, vinegar, lemon juice, mayonnaise, soured cream and some seasoning to taste.

4 Peel the celeriac and grate it into long, thin shreds on a mandolin or using a coleslaw blade on the food processor. You want to be left with about 350 g (12 oz). Stir into the dressing with the gherkins and parsley.

5 Carve the beef into thin slices and divide between 6 plates. Spoon some of the salad alongside and serve with some boiled potatoes.

Everywhere I went on my travels to find food heroes for this book, I longed for simply grilled lamb chops. I kept saying to myself, it's not too much to ask in a country well populated by sheep for a pub to turn out a chop, some mint sauce, potatoes and, say, green beans. But while I could find beef rendang, chicken creole and Thai green chicken curry, could I find a lamb chop? Never. And yet they are so nice to eat.

grilled lamb chops with a rosemary and mint jelly sauce

SERVES 4

8 loin lamb chops
Steamed broccoli (see page 170),
Plain boiled potatoes (see page 172),
or *Sautéed potatoes* (see page 172),
to serve

FOR THE ROSEMARY AND MINT
JELLY SAUCE:
300 ml (10 fl oz) *Chicken Stock*
(see page 176)
The leaves from 1 sprig of rosemary
2 garlic cloves, finely chopped
Juice of ¼ lemon
15 g (½ oz) butter
1 tablespoon mint jelly
Salt and freshly ground black pepper

1 For the rosemary and mint jelly sauce, put the chicken stock into a wide-based pan and boil it vigorously until reduced by half.

2 Season the chops on both sides with salt and lots of black pepper. Heat a heavy-based frying pan over a high heat, add the chops and cook them for 3–4 minutes on each side. Then turn them onto their fatty edges and cook for 1 minute more, until the fat is crisp and golden. Lift them onto a plate and keep warm.

3 Add the rosemary leaves, reduced chicken stock, garlic, lemon juice, butter and mint jelly to the pan and rub the base of the pan with a wooden spoon to release all the caramelized juices into the sauce. Leave it to vigorously bubble down to about 6 tablespoons of well-flavoured sauce, then pass through a sieve into a small, clean pan and season to taste with salt.

4 Arrange the lamb chops in the centre of 4 warmed plates and spoon some of the sauce over and around the chops. Serve with the steamed broccoli and boiled or sautéed potatoes.

Though the word 'navarin' just means a lamb casserole with vegetables, and can be made at any time of the year, 'navarin printanière' means lamb with spring vegetables, and surely must be made with spring lamb. Our spring vegetables come a little later in the year, and in early June our spring lamb has got just that little bit more flavour, particularly if you can get shoulder of salt-marsh lamb. If you're in a hurry this can be an everything-in-one-pot dish, but I like to remove the stewing vegetables before replacing them with the small carrots still with their tops on, just a few tiny mauve and white turnips, some peas, haricots vert and new potatoes. Not unnaturally, being a British 'navarin' (and this is an English word, too) I like to finish the whole dish with a little chopped mint and garlic.

navarin of lamb 'printanière'

SERVES 6

1 x boned shoulder of spring lamb
weighing about 1.5 kg (3 lb)
50 g (2 oz) butter
2 tablespoons sunflower oil
2 medium onions, thinly sliced
4 garlic cloves
1 large carrot, peeled and sliced
1 teaspoon sugar
2 tablespoons flour
1 tablespoon tomato purée
2 thyme sprigs
2 bay leaves
600 ml (1 pint) *Chicken stock*
(see page 176)
8 button onions or small shallots, peeled
8 spring carrots, tops trimmed and
then scraped
2 small turnips, cut into quarters
8 small new potatoes, scraped
50 g (2 oz) fresh peas
50 g (2 oz) French green beans, topped,
tailed and halved
8–10 mint leaves
Salt and freshly ground black pepper
Mashed potatoes (see page 172), to serve

1 The fat on a shoulder of spring lamb is not excessive and has a good flavour but you do need to trim most of it off – say about 70%. Then cut the meat into 50 g (2 oz) pieces.

2 Take a flameproof casserole, add a tablespoon of the butter and the oil, and when smoking add the meat in 2 batches and turn it over briskly until well browned. Lift onto a plate and pour off the excess oil. Add the rest of the butter and the onions, 3 of the garlic cloves, thinly sliced, the carrot and sugar and fry until the onions are golden brown.

3 Add the flour and tomato purée and fry for another couple of minutes, then return the lamb to the casserole and add the thyme, bay leaves, stock and 1½ teaspoons of salt. Bring to the boil, cover and simmer very gently for 40 minutes.

4 Meanwhile, cook the button onions, carrots, turnips and new potatoes separately in boiling, well-salted water until tender. Drain, cover and keep warm.

5 Remove the pieces of lamb from the casserole and strain the sauce through a sieve into a bowl, pressing the vegetables against the side of the sieve to extract as much flavour as possible. Discard the vegetables and return the lamb and the cooking liquid to the casserole. Add the peas and beans and simmer for 5 minutes, then gently stir in the other cooked vegetables and simmer for 2–3 minutes until they have warmed through.

6 Finely chop together the mint leaves with the remaining clove of garlic and stir into the stew. Serve from the casserole with the mashed potatoes.

Calves' liver is by far the nicest to eat. Unfortunately a lot of people don't like the way that veal is reared, so I was excited to find a producer in Newick, East Sussex, who not only produces excellent veal but also rears it humanely at Little Warren Farm (see page 189). Having said that, this dish is also very nice made with pigs' or lambs' liver.

pan-fried calves' liver and dry-cured bacon with balsamic caramelized onions

SERVES 2

15 g (½ oz) butter
1 large onion, halved and thinly sliced
A pinch of sugar
1½ teaspoons balsamic vinegar
6 rashers of thinly sliced dry-cured streaky bacon, rind removed
275–350 g (10–12 oz) calves' liver, very thinly sliced
15 g (½ oz) seasoned flour, for dusting
1 tablespoon sunflower oil
Salt and freshly ground black pepper
Mashed potatoes (see page 172), to serve

1 Preheat the grill to high. Melt the butter in a large frying pan and fry the onions and sugar over a medium heat, stirring frequently, for 7–8 minutes until nicely browned. Season with salt and pepper, add the balsamic vinegar and leave it to bubble up for a few seconds. Keep warm.

2 Grill the bacon until beginning to crisp at the edges. Keep warm.

3 Season the liver on both sides with salt and pepper and then coat lightly in the seasoned flour. Pat off the excess.

4 Heat another large frying pan over a high heat. Add the oil and then the slices of liver and cook them over a high heat for 30 seconds on each side, the object being to have the liver nicely browned on the outside, yet still pink and juicy on the inside.

5 Lift the liver onto warmed plates and serve with the bacon, onions, and, of course, some mashed potatoes.

A recent trip to Kirkgate Market in Leeds in search of local food specialities like tripe, pigs' cheek, savoury duck, faggots and brawn, was not quite as rewarding as I had hoped. The market is visually splendid, with Venetian domes, an Edwardian façade, art nouveau detail and cast-iron shop units. It's also very busy, but more and more with non-food stalls; evidence, I suspect, of the wasting effect that supermarkets are having on established food shops and stalls. Nevertheless, there's still some really interesting food to be had there: oven-bottom bread, which is our version of pitta bread and almost better, and a stall selling tripe, chitterlings and other rare offal. Not everyone's cup of tea, but Mrs Hey of the Tripe Dressers of Dewsbury (see page 189), who runs the stall, mentioned how much her Italian customers loved tripe and did much more interesting things with it than just stewing it in milk with onions. I recalled a very pleasant dish I had last year in Rome and here it is.

roman tripe with tomato, borlotti beans and parmesan

SERVES 4

75 g (3 oz) dried borlotti or cannellini beans, soaked overnight
900 g (2 lb) blanched tripe
50ml (2 fl oz) extra virgin olive oil
1 carrot, peeled and cut into small dice
1 celery stick, cut into small dice
1 medium onion, chopped
4 garlic cloves, thinly sliced
A large pinch of dried chilli flakes
150 ml (5 fl oz) dry white wine
300 ml (10 fl oz) *Chicken stock*, (see page 176)
250 g (9 oz) tomato passata
1 tablespoon fresh oregano, shredded
4 tablespoons Parmesan cheese, finely grated
Salt and freshly ground black pepper
Rustic white bread, such as ciabatta, to serve

1 Drain the beans, cover with cold water and simmer for 30–40 minutes or until tender. Drain and set aside. Cut the tripe into thin 7.5 cm (3 in) long strips.

2 Heat the oil in a large flameproof casserole. Add the carrot, celery, onion, garlic and chilli flakes and cook gently until just beginning to brown. Add the wine and cook until it has almost disappeared. Add the stock, passata, oregano, tripe, cooked beans and some salt and pepper and simmer for 30 minutes.

3 Stir in the Parmesan cheese and adjust the seasoning if necessary. Serve in warm, deep plates with the bread.

grilled, lightly smoked sirloin steak with chive and black peppercorn butter and pommes coq d'or

SERVES 4

4 x 225–275 g (8–10 oz) sirloin steaks
A large handful of wood chips or
hardwood sawdust, such as hickory,
oak or mesquite
Salt and freshly ground black pepper
Pommes Coq d'Or (see page 173) and the
White cabbage salad (see page 170),
to serve

FOR THE CHIVE AND BLACK
PEPPERCORN BUTTER:
2 tablespoons black peppercorns,
coarsely crushed
Juice of ½ a lemon
3 tablespoons chopped chives
½ teaspoon salt
100 g (4 oz) unsalted butter, softened

1 For the chive and black peppercorn butter, mix the peppercorns, lemon juice, chives and salt into the butter. Spoon it onto a sheet of cling film, shape it into a 2.5 cm (1 in) thick roll and wrap up tightly. Chill in the fridge or freezer until firm.

2 To smoke the steak, put the wood chips or sawdust into a large shallow pan such as a wok or deep sauté pan and rest a cooling rack over the top. Place the pan over a high heat until the wood chips or sawdust begin to smoke. Reduce the heat to low, put the steaks onto the cooling rack and cover with a lid (don't worry if it doesn't fit too well). Smoke the steaks for 2 minutes. Uncover and lift off the rack.

3 To cook, heat a ridged cast-iron griddle until smoking hot. Season the steaks on both sides with salt and pepper and cook for 2 minutes on each side for rare and 3 minutes on each side for medium. Then lift them up with a pair of tongs and sear the fatty edge on the grill until crisp and golden. Meanwhile, slice the butter into thin slices.

4 Transfer the steaks to warmed plates and put 2 slices of the butter on top of each (save the rest of the butter for next time). Serve with pommes Coq d'Or and the white cabbage salad.

My method of lightly smoking steak, giving it the taste of having been cooked at the hearth over a log fire, may seem as bogus as adding oak chips to Chardonnay, but it works. There's something so comforting about wood smoke, and a whiff of it in your steak is a delight. Buying top-quality sirloin by mail order is easy now, and well worth the extra cost. I regularly use Ormsary Farm in Argyllshire (see page 189) when cooking this. Serve with Pommes Coq d'Or; the potatoes, thinly sliced and baked in stock until crisp on top, come from the old Coq d'Or restaurant in Stratton Street in Mayfair, now Langan's Brasserie.

My brother in law, Shaun, rang me the other day from the Yorkshire Dales, where he now lives and which he enthuses greatly about after years in London working as a TV director. He'd been to the Karachi Restaurant in Bradford (Tel: 01274 732015) and was somewhat surprised to have seen a letter from me on the table by the kitchen asking Mumrez for his recipe for the karahi curry. It's not the most exclusive restaurant, with Formica tables, a kitchen area on view in an entirely unforced sort of way, a tandoor oven in the back turning out sublime naan bread, and local customers, some of whom have been going there since the 60s when it opened. They're very lucky, these customers; they probably think curries are always like this, but they're not. The lamb and spinach karahi was sensational, alive with coriander and cumin and fresh green chillies, and I drank far too much salted lassi, it was so good. It's the sort of place you hesitate to write about for fear of changing a place of great style. Shaun loved it, too; he was bought up in Sri Lanka.

mumrez khan's lamb and spinach karahi curry from the karachi restaurant

SERVES 6

250 g (9 oz) ghee (or *Clarified butter*, see page 177)
550 g (1¼ lb) onions, chopped
1 x 400 g (14 oz) can chopped tomatoes
120 ml (4 fl oz) of water
50 g (2 oz) fresh ginger, peeled and roughly chopped
65 g (2½ oz) garlic
900 g (2 lb) boneless leg or shoulder of lamb, cut into 4 cm (1½ in) pieces
1 tablespoon salt
1 tablespoon ground turmeric
1 tablespoon red chilli powder
1 tablespoon ground cumin
1 tablespoon paprika
1 tablespoon ground coriander
350 g (12 oz) fresh spinach, washed and large stalks removed
4 medium-sized green chillies, stalks removed and roughly chopped
3 tablespoons coriander, chopped
½ tablespoon garam masala
A pinch of ground cumin and freshly ground black pepper to garnish
Pilau rice (see page 175), to serve

1 Heat the ghee in a large, heavy-based pan. Add the onions and cook over a medium heat, stirring now and then, for 20–30 minutes until they are very soft and a light brown.

2 Put the tomatoes, water, ginger and garlic into a liquidizer and blend until smooth. Remove the fried onions with a slotted spoon, add them to the paste and blend briefly until smooth.

3 Return the purée to the ghee left in the pan and add the lamb and salt. Simmer for 30 minutes, by which time the lamb will be half cooked and the sauce will be well reduced. Stir in the turmeric, chilli powder, cumin, paprika and coriander and continue to cook for 30–45 minutes for shoulder, or 45 minutes–1 hour for leg, until the lamb is tender, adding a little water now and then if the sauce starts to stick.

4 Meanwhile, put 175 g (6 oz) of the spinach leaves into a large pan and cook until it has wilted down into the bottom of the pan. Cook for 1 minute, then transfer to the rinsed out liquidizer and blend to a smooth purée. Set aside. Rinse out the liquidizer again and add the green chillies and 2–3 tablespoons of water and blend until smooth. Set aside.

5 When the lamb is cooked, there should be a layer of ghee floating on the top of the curry. You can either skim it off or leave it there, whichever you prefer. Then stir in the spinach purée and the remaining leaf spinach and cook for 2 minutes.

6 Now taste the curry and add as much green chilli purée as you wish, according to how hot you like your curries. Simmer for 2 minutes.

7 Stir in the fresh coriander and garam masala. Transfer the curry to a serving dish and sprinkle with a little more ground cumin and some freshly ground black pepper just before you take it to the table. Serve with the pilau rice.

Ann Muller's stature as a pasty maker is fêted throughout Cornwall, but mostly on the Lizard Peninsula and in the town of the same name, where her bright yellow shop can be found (see page 194). Her pasties are the best I've ever tasted, and the secret of them is in a generous, but not absurd proportion, of meat to vegetables, sensitive seasoning and a pastry which will retain as much filling as possible. Like most good cooking it's attention to the basics which ensures success.

ann muller's cornish pasties

MAKES 4

450 g (1 lb) beef skirt or chuck steak
225–350 g (8–12 oz) swede
(known in Cornwall as turnip)
750 g (1½ lb) potatoes
225 g (8 oz) onion or shallot
1 beaten egg or milk, to glaze
Salt and freshly ground black pepper

FOR THE PASTY PASTRY:
100 g (4 oz) lard
100 g (4 oz) hard margarine
(such as Stork or Echo)
450 g (1 lb) strong plain flour,
(such as Doves organic)
A good pinch of salt
175 ml (6 fl oz) cold water

1 For the pastry, put the lard and margarine into the freezer and leave until very hard. Meanwhile, prepare the filling. Trim any gristle off the meat and cut it (with the fat) into 5 mm (¼ in) pieces. Chop the swede into similar-sized pieces. Peel and slice the potatoes and chop the onion.

2 Sift the flour and salt into a bowl and grate in the lard and margarine straight from the freezer. Gently mix through the flour and then stir in the water, 1 tablespoon at a time, with a round-bladed knife until the mixture comes together. Turn it out onto a lightly floured surface and knead briefly into a ball. Wrap in cling film and chill for 1 hour.

3 Preheat the oven to 180°C/350°F/Gas Mark 4. Cut the pastry into 4 even-sized pieces, shape each one into a ball and then roll out one piece into a 20–23 cm (8–9 in) circle. The pastry will now be the right thickness. Place an upturned plate over the pastry and cut out a neat round. Repeat with the rest of the pastry.

4 Put most of the swede and onion in a line across each pastry disc and season with salt and pepper. Cover with the meat, making sure it goes right to either end, season lightly, then top with most of the potato and the rest of the swede. Season again with salt and add the rest of the potato.

5 Very lightly brush half the circumference of the circle with water, then bring the edges together over the top of the pasty and press together. Working from right to left (or the other way if you're left-handed), fold over the corner and then fold over the edge, towards yourself, working from one end of the pasty to the other, creating a rope-like design to seal. Tuck in the other end well. Chill for 1 hour.

6 Make a small slit in the top of each pasty, then brush with beaten egg or milk and place on a greased and floured baking sheet, leaving 5 cm (2 in) between each one. Bake for 1 hour.

I buy the chorizos and butter beans for this from a company called Brindisa
(see page 193), which specializes in Spanish produce, but I know that you can get both at
many supermarkets, too. The quality of the chorizo is all-important and I would
recommend Brindisa's parrilla chorizo picante. The butter beans I use,
called Judion de la Granja, are also sensational.

chorizo and butter bean stew with garlic and thyme

SERVES 4

350 g (12 oz) dried Judion butter beans,
soaked overnight

225 g (8 oz) hot chorizo for cooking, such
as parrilla chorizo picante (see left)

50 ml (2 fl oz) olive oil

5 garlic cloves, thinly sliced

½ medium onion, finely chopped

175 ml (6 fl oz) red wine

1 x 400 g (14 oz) can chopped tomatoes

1 tablespoon thyme leaves

2 tablespoons chopped flatleaf parsley

Salt

1 Put the butter beans into a large pan with lots of water, bring to the boil and simmer for 1 hour or until tender. Drain and set aside.

2 Cut the chorizo sausages into thin slices. Put the olive oil and garlic into a pan and heat over a medium–high heat until the garlic begins to sizzle. Add the chorizo and cook until the slices are lightly browned on either side, then add the onion and continue to cook until it has softened.

3 Add the red wine and cook until it has reduced to almost nothing. Add the canned chopped tomatoes, thyme, butter beans and half a teaspoon of salt and simmer for 15 minutes.

4 Scatter over the parsley, spoon the stew into deep, warmed bowls and serve with some crusty fresh bread.

I hope Paul, Ian and Neil Hartland who make Mrs King's Pork Pies at Cropwell Butler in Nottinghamshire (see page 194) would pronounce this recipe a good one. Their pork pies are sublime. I expect it seems repetitive of me, but I am always charmed and excited by seeing people cook something very straightforward but doing it using the best ingredients and with real love. They like their rugby, too, real heart-of-England types. They make hand-raised pies, where the hot water pastry is shaped on a wooden mould, the filling is added, then the lid put on. The pies, or rather scores of them, are baked until dark brown and bubbling with savoury goodness, then the unctuous jelly is poured through a little hole in the top to set when cold. The advantage of hand-raised pies is that the crust is high baked, not being contained in a baking tin, and is therefore very crisp. My pastry is pretty crisp, though, and the filling is the stuff of picnics, as is the accompanying spicy apple and walnut chutney.

pork pie with spicy apple and walnut chutney

SERVES 10–12

FOR THE JELLY:

900 g (2 lb) pork bones and 1 pig's trotter
1 carrot
1 onion
A bouquet garni of celery, bay leaf, thyme and parsley
12 black peppercorns
4 cloves
Salt and freshly ground black pepper

FOR THE FILLING:

1.5 kg (2½ lb) boned pork shoulder
225 g (8 oz) lean diced bacon
1 tablespoon chopped fresh sage
½ teaspoon each of ground mace, freshly grated nutmeg and ground allspice
2 teaspoons anchovy essence
Sunflower oil, for frying

FOR THE PASTRY:

450 g (1 lb) plain flour
1 teaspoon salt
275 g (10 oz) chilled butter, cut into pieces
2 medium eggs
1 egg yolk
2–3 tablespoons cold water
1 beaten egg, to glaze

1 For the jelly, put all the ingredients into a large pan, cover with water and bring to the boil. Cover and simmer gently for 3 hours. Strain through a very fine sieve into a clean pan and boil vigorously until reduced to 600 ml (1 pint). Season to taste and leave to cool.

2 For the filling, cut the pork and bacon into 1 cm (½ in) pieces. Put half of the pork and 50 g (2 oz) of the bacon into a food processor and process using the pulse button until coarsely chopped. Scrape into a bowl and stir in the rest of the diced pork and bacon, the sage, spices, anchovy essence, 1 teaspoon of salt and some pepper. Fry a little piece of the mixture in sunflower oil, taste and adjust the flavourings if necessary.

3 For the pastry, sift the flour and salt into a food processor or mixing bowl. Rub in the butter until the mixture looks like fine breadcrumbs. Beat the whole eggs with the egg yolk and water and gradually stir into the dry ingredients to make a soft dough. Knead briefly until smooth then cut off one third of the mixture and set it aside for the lid. Roll out the larger piece and use to line the base and sides of a greased 20 cm (8 in) clip-sided cake tin, leaving the excess pastry overhanging the edges.

4 Preheat the oven to 200°C/400°F/Gas Mark 6. Spoon the pork filling into the tin and slightly round the top of the mixture to give the finished pie a nice shape. Brush the edge of the pastry with beaten egg. Roll out the remaining pastry and use to cover the top of the pie. Trim away the excess pastry and re-roll to make the decoration. Cut a small hole in the centre of the lid with a small pastry cutter, remove the plug of pastry and leave the cutter in place to retain the hole during baking. Brush with more beaten egg and decorate with a twisted rope of pastry and pastry leaves, made from the pastry trimmings. Brush the top with beaten egg.

Spicy apple and walnut chutney
(see page 175) **and** *Cherry tomatoes,*
spring onions and rocket
(see page 69), **to serve**

5 Bake the pie for 30 minutes, then lower the oven temperature to 180°C/350°F/Gas Mark 4 and continue to cook for a further 1½ hours, loosely covering the pie with a triple-thickness sheet of greaseproof paper once it is nicely browned.

6 Remove the pie from the oven and leave to cool for 2 hours. Warm the jelly through and pour into the pie through the hole in the top. Leave to go cold overnight. Cut into wedges and serve with the spicy apple and walnut chutney and cherry tomatoes, spring onions and rocket.

This is the sort of dish that you might think typifies how bland and boring British food is until you taste it cooked well. My conversion came at the Garrick Club in London, seated for lunch at the large communal table there and noting with great, but hidden excitement that Kingsley Amis was opposite – who was also eating mutton with caper sauce. It's sublime and no one enthused about it more than Johnny Noble, who founded Loch Fyne Oysters on the shores of the loch at Ardkinglas (see page 184). Johnny built up what is now a very successful seafood supplier, simply because he couldn't make his twelve thousand-acre-estate pay, there was no money in sheep; he turned to the munificence of the Loch as a way of paying the upkeep. But he loved his lamb and mutton. He died this year which is a sad loss; another hero gone. This is his recipe.

johnny noble's boiled gigot of mutton with caper sauce

SERVES 6

1 leg of mutton, or well-aged lamb, weighing about 1.75 kg (4 lb)
1.5 litres (2½ pints) water
4–6 medium onions, sliced
4 medium carrots, sliced
1 small sprig of rosemary
6 black peppercorns
Salt and freshly ground black pepper
Plain boiled potatoes (see page 172), to serve

FOR THE CAPER SAUCE:
2 tablespoons butter
2 tablespoons plain flour
600 ml (1 pint) of the mutton stock from above
3 tablespoons capers, drained and rinsed

1 Put the meat into a large pan and add the water, which should come about three-quarters of the way up the meat. Add the vegetables, rosemary, peppercorns and some seasoning. Bring to the boil, skimming off any scum as it rises to the surface, cover and simmer for 2 hours (30 minutes per 450 g/1 lb) or until the meat is tender. There should be little resistance when the meat is pierced with a skewer. Skim the fat from the top of the stock.

2 For the caper sauce, melt the butter in a pan, add the flour and cook gently for 1 minute. Gradually stir in the mutton stock and bring to the boil, stirring. Simmer for 5 minutes, then stir in the capers and some seasoning to taste.

3 Remove the mutton and carve it into slices. Serve with the caper sauce and the boiled potatoes.

6 furred and

I'M THINKING OF INTRODUCING A FEW GAME DISHES TO THE MENU AT THE SEAFOOD RESTAURANT. TRADITIONALLY, FISH RESTAURANTS ALSO SOLD GAME IN SEASON. IT MAKES SENSE: CHOOSING GOOD GAME IS ABOUT AS TRICKY AS GETTING THE BEST FISH, AND IT WOULD BE NICE TO HAVE A REPUTATION FOR BOTH. SELECTING GOOD GAME IS DIFFICULT BECAUSE, LIKE FISH, IT'S WILD FOOD, AND AGE AND CONDITION CANNOT BE PREDICTED AS ACCURATELY AS FOR FARMED STOCK. THERE IS ALSO CONSIDERABLE SKILL INVOLVED IN HANGING GAME FOR THE OPTIMUM TIME. THIS IS DONE TO TENDERIZE THE MEAT AND DEVELOP THE FLAVOUR.

feathered game

Take hare, for example. How do you assess its condition? How long do you hang it? Which of the two kinds of hare in this country, the brown or the blue, is the better for eating? The brown is better, larger and fortunately the one most game dealers will sell. But how do you tell the age? The answer is to buy your game from one of the dealers in this book, butchers who buy from known local shoots and hand-pick the produce.

There's a new buzz word in assessing the quality of food: traceability. This is the information that should come with all food, such as who caught it, raised it or grew it; where, how and when. I wish we didn't need such an assurance. I'm writing this on the island of Gozo next to Malta. I've just been into a fruit and vegetable shop where they're selling local capers and Gozo honey in recycled jam jars with just a hand-written label, but it's a small island where everyone knows everyone else. If I tried to do that in my deli I'd probably do some time at the Weights and Measures Board's behest – even though my produce is only available in my shop – so reliant have we become on additional information on labels about what our food really contains. Yet still the truth evades us because we also have the skilful verbal dexterity of advertisers to deal with. Sometimes it almost seems as though they are being economical with the truth: does wild mean wild anymore, and does game mean game? Is wild boar game or wild? It certainly used to be wild when hunted in the forests of Europe, but now it's reared like any domestic animal – albeit in our suppliers' case with plenty of land to roam in, but it's hardly game, which I take to mean hunted animals. Is a pheasant wild if reared in captivity, then set free a few weeks before the beginning of the shooting season? Any word or phrase to do with food that conjures up a satisfying image needs to come under close scrutiny. Free range often doesn't mean free to range; dry-cure bacon doesn't necessarily mean just cured with dry salt.

Wild rabbits and pigeons are fortunately not subject to the same degree of verbal gymnastics. They're not foods with mass appeal, but traceability is vital with them as they're so variable in quality. Old game is pure misery; dishes like *Rabbit pie with forcemeat balls* (see page 128) would be as disappointing as any of my fish recipes when made with stale fish if made with a wild, sinewy old rabbit. Pigeons too are hard-flying birds and can be amazingly tough. Trust in game dealers like Philip Warren in Launceston in Cornwall and Manor Farm at Chesham in Buckinghamshire who run their own shoots so all their game is immediately traceable, or Steadman's in Sedbergh who won't sell game that doesn't come from Cumbria, and you will blossom with the satisfaction of eating something quite special.

LEFT AND BELOW

Traceability is key

when buying game.

Tender, good-quality

meat is a real pleasure

to eat, but older game

can be very tough;

all the more reason to

buy from trusted game

dealers such as my

recommended

producers.

This was inspired by a day spent with Chris Green at Menheniott near Liskeard in Cornwall. Chris keeps the local farms relatively free from pigeons and rabbits, and reminded me of the bounty available from the countryside all the year round. I should bag the pigeons in my garden. They go for my purple-sprouting broccoli and I keep meaning to shoot them with one of my son's air rifles, but I like the sight of young pairs with soft feathers, cooing in the trees round our house in early summer and can't bring myself to do it. Interestingly, pigeons are now attracted by the sound of pigeon scarers going off, so presumably countrymen like Chris are in constant demand. I've rather modified this classic French dish to take account of the fact that pigeons are very cheap, and you might as well use just the breasts and make stock with the rest. The pigeons eat the peas, we eat the pigeons and the peas: that's how it is.

pigeon with peas

SERVES 4

1 tablespoon olive oil
12 button onions, peeled
100 g (4 oz) rindless smoked streaky
bacon, chopped
2 garlic cloves, chopped
8 prepared pigeon breasts
2 tablespoons cognac
175 ml (6 fl oz) red wine
175 ml (6 fl oz) *Roasted chicken stock*
(see page 176)
1 bay leaf
1 sprig of thyme
1 tablespoon *Beurre manié* (see page 177)
350 g (12 oz) fresh or frozen petit pois
Salt and freshly ground black pepper
Mashed potatoes (see page 172), to serve

1 Heat the oil in a shallow, heavy-based casserole or deep sauté pan, add the onions and fry them until they have taken on some colour. Add the bacon and garlic and cook gently until the bacon is lightly golden.

2 Push the onions and bacon to the side of the pan, add the pigeon breasts, skin-side down, and season well with salt and pepper. Cook them for 1 minute on each side.

3 Increase the heat slightly, sprinkle over the cognac and set it alight to burn off the alcohol. Add the red wine and let it boil for 3–4 minutes. Add the stock, bay leaf and thyme and simmer uncovered for another 2–3 minutes.

4 Remove the thyme and bay leaf if you wish, then stir in the beurre manié and simmer for 2 minutes. Add the peas and simmer for 3–4 minutes until the peas are well cooked but the pigeon breasts are still pink in the centre. Adjust the seasoning and serve with the mashed potatoes.

This Chinese method of cooking pork in a stew with soy and dried tangerine peel is a perfect way to cook Peter Gott's wild boar from Sillfield Farm in Cumbria (see page 191). It differs from Western stews in that the meat is first marinated in soy sauce to give it colour, then deep-fried. On the subject of red-cooked dishes, the great Chinese cook Ken Lo said, 'Soy sauce is probably the one single item which above all distinguishes Chinese cooking from Western cooking.' He then describes the soy and vegetable mixture in the recipe below and goes on, 'I suspect that a great many Western stews would be immeasurably improved by the addition of this basic soy herbal sauce.'

red-cooked wild boar with star anise and dried tangerine peel

SERVES 4

1.5 kg (3 lb) skinned
and boned leg of wild boar or pork
6 tablespoons dark soy sauce
300 ml (10 fl oz) sunflower oil
6 tablespoons water
2 teaspoons sugar
4 tablespoons Chinese rice wine or
dry sherry
25 g (1 oz) fresh ginger, peeled and
finely grated
2 medium onions, thinly sliced
4 garlic cloves, finely chopped
5–6 x 5 mm (¼in) pieces of Chinese
dried tangerine peel
2 star anise
2.5 cm (1 in) piece cinnamon stick
½ teaspoon Sichuan peppercorns,
dry roasted and ground
1 quantity of *Steamed rice*
(see page 175), to serve

1 Cut the wild boar into 4 cm (1½ in) pieces. Put them into a bowl with the soy sauce, mix well and set aside for 20 minutes to marinate.

2 Preheat the oven to 160°C/325°F/Gas Mark 3. Heat the oil in a medium-sized ovenproof casserole dish to 190°C/375°F. Lift the wild boar out of the soy sauce and pat dry on kitchen paper. Deep-fry it in batches, turning the pieces over halfway through, until nicely browned.

3 Discard the cooking oil, return the wild boar to the casserole dish and add the remaining soy sauce and all the other ingredients. Cover with a well-fitting lid and cook in the oven for 1½ hours until the meat is really tender. Serve with the steamed rice.

As with the pigeon dish on page 126, this was inspired by a day's shooting at harvest time near Liskeard. Much as I enjoy wild rabbits from the fields, it's worth pointing out that when buying a rabbit for this dish, you need to be able to ascertain how young it is. Like finding a good fishmonger, another milestone in culinary life is to find a good game dealer, which is why this recipe is dedicated to Manor Farm Game (page 190), whose knowledge of game is second to none. Old rabbits are not fun to eat so you need to buy one from someone you trust. Alternatively, French farmed rabbits are available here and are consistently good, if slightly lacking the gamey flavour of wild ones.

rabbit pie with forcemeat balls

SERVES 6

1 large rabbit, jointed into 6 pieces
35 g (1¼oz) seasoned plain flour
50 g (2 oz) butter, bacon fat or dripping
175 g (6 oz) thick-cut rindless streaky bacon, cut across into strips
1 large onion, chopped
225 g (8 oz) carrots, cut into small dice
The finely grated zest of 1 small lemon
4 sprigs of thyme
600 ml (1 pint) *Chicken stock* (see page 176)
1½ quantities *Basic shortcrust pastry* (see page 177)

1 Coat the pieces of rabbit in the seasoned flour and then pat off the excess. Heat the butter, bacon fat or dripping in a heavy-based pan, add the rabbit pieces and brown them lightly on both sides. Lift out onto a plate, add the bacon to the pan and when it is lightly coloured, add the onion and carrots and fry gently for a further 5 minutes.

2 Stir the remaining seasoned flour into the vegetables, followed by the lemon zest, thyme and stock. Return the rabbit to the pan, cover and simmer for 45 minutes–1 hour or until the rabbit is tender.

3 For the forcemeat balls, mix the breadcrumbs, suet, parsley, thyme leaves, lemon zest and bacon together lightly in a bowl. Stir in some seasoning and enough beaten egg to bind, then gently shape the mixture into balls about the size of walnuts.

1 egg, beaten to glaze
Salt and freshly ground black pepper
Plain boiled potatoes (see page 172) and
*Cabbage with shallots, garlic and
flatleaf parsley* (see page 170),
to serve

FOR THE FORCEMEAT BALLS:
100 g (4 oz) fresh white breadcrumbs
50 g (2 oz) shredded suet
1 tablespoon chopped curly leaf parsley
1 teaspoon thyme leaves
Finely grated zest of ¹⁄₂ small lemon
50 g (2 oz) rindless streaky bacon,
finely chopped
1 large egg, beaten

4 Lift the rabbit out of the pan and, when cool enough to handle, remove the bones, leaving the meat in big pieces. Return to the sauce, spoon into a shallow 1.2 litre (2 pint) pie dish and leave to cool. Then arrange the forcemeat balls over the top so that they will support the pastry lid.

5 Roll out the pastry on a lightly floured surface until it is about 2.5 cm (1in) larger than the top of the pie dish. Cut off a thin strip of pastry from around the edge, brush it lightly with water and press it onto the rim of the dish. Brush once more with water, lift on the larger piece of pastry and press the edges together to seal. Crimp the edge between your fingers to give an attractive finish. Cut a small cross in the centre of the lid and decorate with a few leaves made from the pastry trimmings. Chill for 30 minutes.

6 Preheat the oven to 220°C/425°F/Gas Mark 7. Brush the top of the pie with beaten egg and bake for 25–30 minutes until the pastry is nicely coloured. Serve from the pie dish with the boiled potatoes and cabbage with shallots, garlic and parsley.

Both 'jugged hare' and the French civet de lievre are dishes that call for the sauce to be thickened with the blood of the hare. Much as I like sticking to tradition, I find this tends to give the dish an overpoweringly livery taste. Instead, this ragoût has plenty of red wine for flavour. I've specified a bottle but more would be better. One of the advantages of having a restaurant is that one is always given samples of wine by merchants eager to get a slice of the action. Generally a glass will suffice to tell me what I need to know, unless it is especially good. The rest I simmer gently with a couple of tablespoons of sugar per bottle and reduce in volume by about 90%. I then have a fantastic deep red sauce base which keeps in the fridge for ever. I do the same with white wine, too. Incidentally, you can buy a highly reduced Italian grape-must called saba which has the same quality.

ragoût of hare with red wine from the loire

SERVES 6–8

1 x 1.75–2.25 kg (4–5 lb) hare
2 tablespoons vegetable oil
55 g (2 oz) butter
225 g (8 oz) dry-cured streaky bacon,
rind removed and cut across into
thin strips
2 medium red onions, sliced
2 garlic cloves, crushed
2 tablespoons plain flour
1 bottle of red wine
600 ml (1 pint) *Roasted chicken stock*
(see page 176)
2 teaspoons dark soy sauce
A bouquet garni of 2 bay leaves, 2 thyme
sprigs and a small bunch of parsley
½ teaspoon ground allspice
550 g (1¼ lb) shallots, peeled
A good pinch of sugar
24 small chestnut mushrooms, wiped clean
1 quantity *Persillade* (see page 16)
Salt and freshly ground black pepper
Parsnip and potato mash (see page 172),
to serve

FOR THE CROÛTES:
3 slices of white bread, each cut into
4 triangles
2 tablespooons olive oil

1 If your hare is unjointed, joint it as follows some time before making the ragoût so you can add the trimmings to the chicken stock. Leave the kidneys if they are still attached but remove the liver and gall bladder. Lay the hare flat on a chopping board. Remove the front legs by pulling each leg away from the body and cutting through the connective tissue joining the leg and body. Cut each one into 2 at the joint between the thigh and leg. Next remove the hind quarters by cutting across the body at the point where the hind quarters join the saddle. Cut the 2 hind quarters in 2, lengthwise, to separate the legs, cutting to one side of the backbone or the other. Cut the 2 rear legs into 2 at the thigh/leg joint. Divide the saddle into 2 pieces; the kidneys can be cooked in the ragoût. The ribcage will normally contain the heart and lungs. All can be added to the roasted chicken stock. The liver, minus the gall bladder, can be thinly sliced and tossed in butter and scattered on the finished ragoût with the shallots and mushrooms at the end.

2 Preheat the oven to 180°C/350°F/Gas Mark 4. Heat the oil in a flameproof casserole, add the hare joints and brown lightly on all sides. Lift them onto a plate, add 15 g (½ oz) butter and the bacon, onion and garlic and fry until lightly browned.

3 Sprinkle in the flour and cook until the flour has lightly browned. Return the hare to the casserole with the red wine, stock, soy sauce, bouquet garni, allspice, 1 teaspoon of salt and 1 teaspoon of freshly ground black pepper. Cover and cook in the oven for 45 minutes, then uncover and return to the oven for a further 20 minutes.

4 Meanwhile, melt another 15 g (½ oz) butter in a large pan. Add the shallots and sugar and fry over a medium–high heat until nicely browned. Season with ¼ teaspoon of salt, add 100 ml (4 fl oz) water, cover and cook gently until the liquid has reduced to a glaze and the shallots are tender. Remove to a plate. Cut the mushrooms in half if large. Melt the remaining 25 g (1 oz) of butter in the pan, add the mushrooms and fry for 2–3 minutes until soft. Season with salt and pepper and set them aside with the shallots.

5 For the croûtes, shallow-fry the bread triangles in the oil until crisp and golden on both sides. Drain briefly on kitchen paper and keep warm.

6 To serve, lift the pieces of hare into a warmed deep serving dish and scatter over the shallots, mushrooms, and liver if using. Return the casserole to the heat and boil the sauce rapidly until it has reduced to a good sauce consistency. Strain the sauce back over the hare and sprinkle with the persillade. Tuck the croûtes in around the edge of the dish and serve with the parsnip and potato mash.

Pheasant tends towards leanness and needs nurturing with bacon; I also think it is best suited to pot-roasting. It seems pedantic, but using a special bacon like the dry-cured middle cuts from Ramsay of Carluke, in Ayrshire (see page 191) makes all the difference. I love to serve this dish with some braised sauerkraut and plainly boiled potatoes – oh, and a Gewürztraminer.

pot-roasted pheasant with bacon, fennel, leeks and carrots

SERVES 4

1 brace of prepared pheasants
4 rashers Ayrshire bacon, rind removed
50 g (2 oz) butter
1 fennel bulb, cut lengthways into 8 wedges
1 leek, cleaned, halved and cut into 5 cm (2 in) pieces
2 carrots, peeled, cut in half lengthways and then thinly sliced on the diagonal
2 celery stalks, thinly sliced
2 fresh bay leaves
1 sprig of thyme
6 juniper berries
150 ml (5 fl oz) *Chicken stock* (see page 176)
Salt and freshly ground black pepper
Plain boiled potatoes (see page 172) and *Braised sauerkraut* (see page 171), to serve

1 Preheat the oven to 160°C/325°F/Gas Mark 3. Cover each of the pheasants with 2 of the bacon rashers and tie them in place with string.

2 Melt the butter in a large flameproof casserole dish, add the prepared vegetables, herbs, juniper berries, ½ a teaspoon of salt and 10 turns of the black pepper mill. Turn them over once or twice, cover and sweat gently over a low heat for 20 minutes until the vegetables are tender.

3 Rest the pheasants on top of the vegetables, re-cover and transfer the casserole to the oven for 45 minutes. Then uncover the casserole, increase the oven temperature to 200°C/400°F/Gas Mark 6 and continue to cook the pheasants for 15–20 minutes until the bacon is crisp and golden and the pheasants are cooked through.

4 Lift the birds onto a plate, cover and keep warm. Add the stock to the vegetables and simmer until reduced to a good sauce consistency. Remove the bay leaves and thyme and adjust the seasoning if necessary.

5 Lift the pheasants onto a board, cut off the string and then lift off the bacon. Cut off the legs and cut each one in 2 at the joint. Then cut the breast meat away from the carcase in 2 whole pieces and cut the meat diagonally into slices.

6 To serve, spoon some of the vegetables and sauce into each warmed plate and place a piece of thigh meat on top. Put the sliced breast meat on top of that and rest a drumstick alongside. Serve with the potatoes and sauerkraut.

warm salad of pan-fried pheasant breasts with watercress, potatoes and sherry vinegar and walnut-oil dressing

SERVES 4

225 g (8 oz) small floury potatoes,
such as Maris Piper
15 g (½ oz) butter
3 tablespoons olive oil
2 x 175–225 g (6–8 oz)
pheasant breasts
75 g (3 oz) watercress sprigs
½ small red onion, thinly sliced
1 tablespoon chopped chives
Salt and freshly ground black pepper

FOR THE DRESSING:

1 small shallot, finely chopped
½ garlic clove, finely chopped
2 tablespoons sherry vinegar
2 teaspoons walnut oil
2 tablespoons olive oil
1 teaspoon chopped chives

1 Peel the potatoes and cut them in half lengthways, and then each half across into 5 mm (¼ inch) thick slices. Drop them into a pan of boiling salted water and cook for 2–3 minutes until just tender. Drain well.

2 Heat the butter and 1 tablespoon of the olive oil in a heavy-based frying pan, add the potato pieces and sauté until golden brown and sandy on the outside. Season with some salt and pepper, remove from the pan and keep warm.

3 Brush the pheasant breasts on both sides with the remaining olive oil and season with some salt and pepper. Heat the cleaned frying pan over a high heat. Add the pheasant breasts, skin-side down, sear briefly on both sides until they have taken on a good colour, then lower the heat to medium, cover and cook gently for 5–6 minutes on each side until just cooked through. Lift onto a plate, cover and leave to rest for 5 minutes.

4 For the dressing, add the shallot and garlic to the pan and fry for just a few seconds, then add the vinegar and rub all the caramelized juices from the base of the pan with a wooden spoon. Tip the mixture into a small bowl and whisk in the walnut oil, olive oil, chives, ½ teaspoon of salt and some black pepper. Lift the pheasant breasts onto a board and carve each one diagonally across into thin slices.

5 To assemble the salad, place a few sprigs of watercress and some slices of onion into the centre of 4 plates. Add a few slices of the pheasant and a few sautéed potatoes. Scatter over some more watercress and onion, drizzle over the dressing and sprinkle with some chopped chives. Serve immediately.

The particularly peppery tang of watercress is what makes this salad such a pleasure; that and the use of pheasant breasts. It's possibly a little unrealistic to expect everyone to stock them, but a good game butcher should be able to supply them – certainly the ones in the back of this book will. Interestingly, I found some pheasant breasts on sale in a supermarket, albeit with a frightful sauce in a little pouch to go with it. I used the breasts and jettisoned the sauce. Pheasants are so cheap in the shooting season that it is not a travesty to remove the breasts, but use the thighs as well – it is easy to remove the bone from the thighs and sauté them, too. The legs are too sinewy and are best used for stock.

The head chef at The Seafood Restaurant, Stéphane Delorme, brought this recipe with him when he arrived three years ago. What excited me about it was the sautéed spätzle with roasted hazelnuts, garlic and parsley, and the sauce, which was a basic red wine and stock reduction with cranberry sauce and sour morello cherries. I find that venison needs a slightly sour yet sweet, fruity sauce to counteract its rather bloody flavour and then the combination becomes very pleasant indeed.

medallions of venison with red wine and morello cherries with roasted hazelnut spätzle

SERVES 4

FOR THE RED WINE REDUCTION:
600 ml (1 pint) *Beef stock* (see page 176)
300 ml (10 fl oz) red wine
1 teaspoon sugar

FOR THE ROASTED HAZELNUT SPÄTZLE:
125 g (5 oz) plain flour
3 medium eggs
120 ml (4 fl oz) milk
1 garlic clove
25 g (1 oz) lightly toasted hazelnuts
1 tablespoon chopped flatleaf parsley
25 g (1 oz) butter

FOR THE VENISON:
750 g (1½ lb) venison fillet (i.e. the eye of the loin)
1 tablespoon sunflower oil

FOR THE SAUCE:
2 shallots, finely chopped
The red wine reduction (see above)
1 tablespoon cranberry sauce
25 g (1 oz) butter
16 tinned morello cherries
Salt and freshly ground black pepper

1 For the red wine reduction, put the beef stock, red wine and sugar into a wide-based pan and boil rapidly until reduced by three-quarters.

2 For the spätzle, put the flour into a bowl, make a well in the centre and add the eggs. Gradually beat the flour into the eggs, adding the milk bit by bit until you have a smooth batter. Bring a large pan of salted water to the boil. You need to pour the batter through a colander to create short lengths of pasta in the boiling water, so hold the colander over the pan and pour in the batter. Have a wooden spoon nearby to push the last of the batter through. Cook for 1 minute, lift out with a slotted spoon onto a clean tea towel and leave to drain.

3 Coarsely chop the garlic, hazelnuts and parsley together on a board. Melt the butter in a large pan, add the spätzle and fry them until pale yellow, turning frequently. Take the pan off the heat and stir in the hazelnut and parsley mixture and a little salt to taste. Keep warm.

4 Cut the venison loin into 4 even-sized pieces and season with salt and pepper. Heat the oil in a heavy-based frying pan and sear the venison over a high heat for 3 minutes on each side. Lift onto a warm plate.

5 For the sauce, add the shallots to the pan in which the venison was cooked and fry briskly. Add the red wine reduction and rub all the caramelized juices off the bottom of the pan with a wooden spoon. Boil rapidly until the sauce is syrupy and concentrated in flavour – there should be about 175 ml (6 fl oz) left. Whisk in the cranberry sauce and butter and season to taste with salt and 10 turns of the black pepper mill. Stir in the cherries.

6 To serve, slice the fillet steaks into medallions about 1 cm (½ in) thick, slightly on the diagonal so that they lay on the plate neatly. Lift them onto 4 warmed plates and spoon the sauce over the meat. Spoon the hazelnut spätzle alongside.

I always think of grouse as the perfect analogy to a sought after fish, like turbot. They're both rare and it is all too easy to waste a great deal of money on them unless you know what to look for. Buying game from the producers in the back of this book should guarantee you an exceptionally well-flavoured bird, but it's as well to have a bit of information about them. For roasting, the birds should be young, less than a year old. Grouse are at their best between August 12th when the season starts, and the end of October. Though the season lasts till December 10th, the birds are getting tougher all the time. Older birds can be successfully cooked using recipes such as the one for *Pot-roasted pheasant with bacon, fennel, leeks and carrots* on page 131. A degree of hanging is essential to bring out the unique flavour gained from a diet of heather – two days in warm weather and four when cold. I'm assuming that you will be buying oven-ready game and so much of the information about the age of the dressed bird when alive and since death will be lost. It should appear dry and plump, it shouldn't have too many blotches caused by shotgun pellets. It should smell gamey but not high – similar to ripe cheese and in no way unappetizing. I would not recommend buying birds that have been frozen unless you know they have only been frozen for a short time. The average dressed weight of a grouse is 12 oz (300 g). All of us have our little ways of varying the traditional accompaniments to roast game birds like grouse, partridge, woodcock and wild duck. I have my own method for making bread sauce, for example and I can't be bothered with fried breadcrumbs or game chips. I think *Pommes Anna* (see page 171) go exceptionally well with roast feathered game, as do crisped bacon, a simple gravy and my *Soft green lettuce salad with an olive oil and garlic dressing* (see page 174). If you don't like the idea of a salad the *Steamed savoy cabbage* on page 170 would be a good choice.

roast grouse with bread sauce and all the trimmings

SERVES 4

4 young grouse, cleaned
50 g (2 oz) butter
4 rashers rindless streaky bacon
300 ml (10 fl oz) *Chicken stock* (see page 176)
Salt and freshly ground black pepper
Pommes Anna (see page 171) and *Soft green lettuce salad with an olive oil and garlic dressing* (see page 174), to serve

FOR THE BREAD SAUCE:
15 g (½oz) butter
1 large shallot, finely chopped
2 cloves
600 ml (1 pint) full cream milk
100 g (4 oz) fresh white breadcrumbs
4 tablespoons double cream

1 Preheat the oven to 190°C/375°F/Gas Mark 5. Season the cavity of each bird with salt. Rub the birds with butter and season with salt and freshly ground black pepper, then lay a piece of streaky bacon over the breasts of each. Put the grouse into a large roasting tin and roast for 25–30 minutes, removing the bacon 10 minutes before the end of cooking so that the skin can brown.

2 Meanwhile, for the bread sauce, melt the butter in a small pan, add the shallot and cloves and cook gently until the shallot is soft but not coloured. Add the milk and the breadcrumbs and leave to simmer for 10 minutes. Mash the bread a little to break it up, then stir in the cream and some salt and pepper to your taste. I like the sauce quite hot with fresh pepper.

3 Remove the grouse to a warm serving plate, cover with foil and leave them to rest in a warm place for at least 10 minutes. To make the gravy, heat the roasting tin, add the chicken stock and any juices that have run out of the grouse. Rub up all the caremelized juices from the base of the tin with a wooden spoon and pour through a sieve into a serving jug.

4 Serve the grouse with the bread sauce, gravy, pommes Anna and the soft green lettuce salad. I like to accompany this with a bottle of old Pomerol, the farmyard flavour of which will echo that of the grouse.

7 fruit desserts,

I WAS UNENTHUSIASTICALLY TOYING WITH A
SOUTH-EAST-ASIAN DESSERT OF PAPAYA AND
SWEET STICKY RICE THE OTHER DAY AND
CONSIDERING THE SOPHISTICATION OF BRITISH
PUDDINGS. AM I ALONE IN FINDING RIPE
PAPAYAS PRETTY BORING? GREEN ONES IN THE
MORTAR-POUNDED SALADS WITH CHILLI,
CORIANDER, PEANUTS AND LIME JUICE THAT
YOU BUY ON EVERY STREET IN THAILAND ARE
A DIFFERENT MATTER, BUT RIPE ONES ARE NOT
FOR ME; THE ONLY WAY YOU CAN GET ANY
FLAVOUR FROM THEM IS BY SQUEEZING FRESH
LIME JUICE OVER THEM.

cakes and bread

ABOVE *The mild, damp climate of Britain makes it the perfect place to grow a whole range of fruits such as apples, raspberries and currants.*
RIGHT AND FAR RIGHT *Jennifer and David Trehane of The Dorset Blueberry Company grow many varieties of blueberry at their farm in Dorset.*

Give me a punnet of Tayside raspberries, the finest in the world, from a grower like Bankhead of Kinloch any day. I would want nothing more than some pouring cream and plenty of caster sugar, though for a special occasion *Raspberry cranachan* (see page 151), the Scottish mess of whipped cream stirred with honey, a little malt whisky, toasted oats and raspberries, is magnificent. But consider other marvellous puddings like *Sussex pond pudding* (see page 141), which I've finally learnt how to make well:

such a perfect combination of the richness of steamed suet paste and the bitterness and sourness of lemons alleviated by proper Demerara sugar from Billingtons of Liverpool. Or a simple *Blackcurrant fool* (see page 144) is something to really look forward to at the end of lunch, or *Rhubarb crumble* (see page 150), the best pudding in the world; these are dishes to be proud of.

I went to Ashfield House in the village of Carlton, just outside Wakefield in Yorkshire to see the forcing sheds for the pale red and pink stems of rhubarb grown from December through to April before the outdoor crop arrives. The owners, Janet Oldroyd-Hulme and Neil Hulme, talked rhubarb with restrained passion. Their life spent growing rhubarb was quite as serious to them as a fisherman's life on the sea. I enjoyed the thought of the cartoon that my children loved, *Roobarb and Custard* – Roobarb the dog and

the voice of Richard Briers. I can't think of the word rhubarb without a smile, but they had an admirable quiet dignity when talking about their livelihood. The forcing shed had a low roof to conserve energy. It was dark and damp and lit only by candles because the plants would photosynthesize under bright electric lights, go green and lose their delicate skin. The rhubarb on either side of the dirt path down the centre of the shed was like a ghostly host in the dim yellow light, a quiet presence of listeners whose growth could be heard as the new shoots forced themselves through the diaphanous membranes at the top of the crown. They pack the red stems in bright yellow and blue boxes and the price is double that of the outdoor crop. Some say this sweeter and less acidic produce, which has names such as Timperley Early and Queen Victoria, is not as good for rhubarb crumble as the main crop, but it seems pretty good to me and can be used in those long winter months when there's no other local fruit around.

This is an Australian dish named after the Russian ballerina, Anna Pavlova, who danced there in the late 1920s. Though it's long been associated with strawberries, it is far nicer when made with this more appropriate local fruit. The meringue is marshmallow-like in the centre and the whole thing is a triumph of fragility, created by the addition of cornflour and vinegar to the egg white. The recipe comes from the home economist who works with me on all my books, Debbie Major. She's a bit of a food hero to me, mostly for helping me translate my wild restaurant ideas into servings for two or four people, but also because she feels the same as me about trying to locate the best produce. She's also a very good cook. Here's to all those unsung heroes, the home economists, who quietly make the disorganized work of chefs like me possible.

pavlova with cream and passion fruit

SERVES 8

6 egg whites
350 g (12 oz) caster sugar
2 teaspoons cornflour
1 teaspoon white wine vinegar
A pinch of salt
600 ml (1 pint) double cream, to serve
8 passion fruit, to serve

1 Preheat the oven to 140°C/275°F/Gas Mark 1. Lightly grease 1 large or 2 smaller baking trays and line with non-stick baking paper.

2 In a large bowl, whisk the egg whites with a pinch of salt into stiff peaks. Gradually whisk in the sugar to make a very stiff and shiny meringue. Whisk in the cornflour and vinegar.

3 Drop 8 large spoonfuls of the mixture onto the baking sheet(s) and spread each one into a 10 cm (4 in) round. Bake for 45 minutes until pale in colour and marshmallow-like in the centre. Turn off the oven, leave the door ajar and leave them to cool.

4 To serve, whip the cream into soft peaks. Spoon some into the centre of each pavlova and spread it out very slightly. Halve the passion fruit and spoon the pulp over the cream. Serve within 5 minutes.

I must confess to a resistance to Sussex pond pudding. I had always found the presence of pieces of lemon and pith in the centre to be unpleasantly bitter, and it makes the sauce cloudy as well. A whole lemon is different, though; and it helps to hold the pastry up. The secret is to buy a large, thin-skinned lemon, one with a minimum layer of pith, and then the recipe is a delight. Spearing the lemon all over ensures that the juice runs into the sauce during the long steaming and gives it a marvellous tartness.

sussex pond pudding

SERVES 6

1 large, thin-skinned lemon
100 g (4 oz) unsalted butter, plus extra
for greasing
100 g (4 oz) demerara sugar

FOR THE PASTRY:
225 g (8 oz) self-raising flour
100 g (4 oz) shredded suet
A pinch of salt
150 ml (5 fl oz) cold water

1 Lavishly grease a 900 ml (1½ pint) pudding basin with butter. For the pastry, mix the flour, suet and salt with the water to make a soft dough. Turn out onto a lightly floured surface and knead briefly until smooth. Roll out, using a little more flour, into a 36 cm (14 in) circle and cut out a quarter of the circle. Set it aside for the lid and use the remainder to line the base and sides of the basin, brushing the cut edges with a little water, overlapping them slightly and pressing them together well to seal.

2 Prick the lemon all over so that you go right into the flesh. Cut the butter into small pieces and mix it with the demerara sugar. Put half of the butter and sugar mixture into the base and slightly up the sides of the basin, add the lemon and surround it with the rest of the butter and sugar mixture.

3 Roll the reserved piece of pastry into a circle about 1 cm (½ in) larger than the top of the basin, brush the edge with water and press it firmly onto the top of the pudding. Crimp the edges together well to make a good seal. Cover the basin with a pleated, buttered sheet of foil and tie it securely in place with string.

4 Put some sort of trivet into the base of a large saucepan, add 5 cm (2 in) or so of water and bring to the boil. Put the pudding into the pan, cover with a well-fitting lid and leave it to steam for 4 hours, topping up the water now and then.

5 To serve, uncover the pudding and run a round-bladed knife around the pudding to release it from the basin. Invert it onto a serving plate and serve, cut into wedges, making sure each person gets some of the lemon along with the pastry and buttery sauce.

This is in memory of a troubled food hero. He had worked in most major London restaurants when he came to us, and he lorded it over us just a little bit as a result – this provincial restaurant in Cornwall. He had a vast motorbike, a Kawasaki with fat tyres, and strode around Padstow in leathers. He was always being stopped for speeding on his frequent runs to London. He was uncommunicative but skilled; some of the girls loved him, others thought he was impossible, but he was a totally driven pastry cook whose real love was baking bread. He had recently lost a baby daughter and his marriage had broken up through the grief that followed. He fled to Vietnam and learnt how to bake great French bread from the Vietnamese bakers there. He came to us difficult, uncompromising, but highly intelligent and gifted, and he fashioned the most fabulous sweets. This is one of them.

apple and frangipane band with warm caramel sauce

SERVES 8

250 g (9 oz) chilled puff pastry
2 Cox's apples
2 tablespoons apricot jam
1 tablespoon water

1 Roll out the pastry on a lightly floured surface into a 13 x 38 cm (5 x 15 in) strip. Put onto a greased baking sheet and chill for 20–30 minutes.

2 Preheat the oven to 200°C/400°F/Gas Mark 6. For the frangipane, beat the butter and sugar together until pale and fluffy. Gradually beat in the egg, then fold in the ground almonds and plain flour. Spread the mixture over the pastry, leaving a 2.5 cm (1 in) border all around the edge.

FOR THE FRANGIPANE:

50 g (2 oz) butter, at room temperature

50 g (2 oz) caster sugar

1 medium egg, beaten

50 g (2 oz) ground almonds

15 g (½oz) plain flour

FOR THE CARAMEL SAUCE:

100 g (4 oz) white sugar

4 tablespoons water

150 ml (5 fl oz) double cream

15 g (½oz) unsalted butter

A large pinch of salt

3 Core the apples, peel them and then cut them in half. Lay each half flat and slice into very thin, half-moon slices. The object with this dessert is to create quite a thick layer of apple on top of the frangipane, so overlap the slices tightly down the centre of the 'band'. Bake in the oven for 35–40 minutes, covering it with a sheet of greaseproof paper if it starts to get too brown.

4 For the caramel sauce, put the sugar and water into a pan and leave to dissolve over a low heat. Then boil rapidly until it has turned to a rich amber-coloured caramel. Remove the pan from the heat and add the cream, then the butter and the salt. Return the pan to a low heat and stir until all the caramel has dissolved into the sauce. Leave to cool slightly.

5 Put the apricot jam and water into a small pan and warm through gently. Press through a fine sieve into a bowl, then brush over the top of the tart to glaze.

6 Cut the band across into slices and lift them into the centre of each warmed plate. Pour some of the warm caramel sauce around each slice and serve.

Of all fools, I like blackcurrant best. I think the acidic and leafy flavour blends with whipped cream perfectly. Some people like to make fools with proper custard, but I think cream and fruit are all that's needed. I often think that something like a blackcurrant fool or a rhubarb crumble is as far as you need to go with a pudding: rhubarb crumble in the winter, and blackcurrant fool in the summer; no one can say that our British fruit puddings aren't a joy.

blackcurrant fool with lightly toasted sponge cake

SERVES 8

450 g (1 lb) blackcurrants, stripped from
their stalks
175 g (6 oz) caster sugar
2 small, young blackcurrant leaves
450 ml (15 fl oz) double cream
Icing sugar, for dusting

FOR THE SPONGE CAKE:
3 medium eggs, at room temperature
90 g (3½oz) caster sugar
90 g (3½oz) plain flour
40 g (1½oz) butter, melted

1 For the sponge cake, preheat the oven to 190°C/375°F/Gas Mark 5. Lightly grease a deep, 20 cm (8 in) sandwich tin with butter, then base-line with greaseproof paper and grease once more. Add 1 teaspoon each of caster sugar and flour and shake them around to lightly coat the inside of the tin. Tap out the excess.

2 Break the eggs into a large heatproof bowl, add the sugar and rest the bowl over a pan of just simmering water. Whisk (by hand or with a hand-held electric whisk) until the mixture is very thick and moussey and leaves a trail behind when drizzled over the surface. Lift the bowl off the pan and whisk for a further 3–4 minutes, to cool the mixture slightly.

3 Sift the flour into the bowl and then gently fold it in with a large metal spoon. Fold in the melted butter. Pour the mixture into the prepared tin and bake for 20–25 minutes or until a skewer inserted into the cake comes out clean. Remove from the oven and leave to cool for 5 minutes, then turn out onto a wire rack and leave to go cold.

4 Put the blackcurrants, sugar and blackcurrant leaves into a pan and cook over a gentle heat for 5 minutes until the berries just burst. Leave to cool, remove and discard the leaves and then purée three-quarters of the fruit and stir the purée back into the remaining currants.

5 Put the cream into a large serving bowl and whip it into soft peaks. Gently fold in the blackcurrant purée so that the cream and fruit are only just mixed together and the fool still has a marbled effect. Cover and chill.

6 Preheat the grill to high. Cut the sponge cake into small, thin wedges and lightly toast them on each cut side until golden. Dust with a little icing sugar and serve with the fool.

An orchard full of blueberries… I am someone who has enjoyed raiding kitchen gardens from an early age. At Jennifer Trehane and her son David's orchard at Hampreston in Dorset (see The Dorset Blueberry Company, page 192), there were eight different types of blueberries to try, from early Dukes to large and acidic Darrows. Some were sweet, some large, some tart, but all had a blue satin skin and juicy chubbiness which prompted me at the time to remark that they had to be of American origin, because they were so generously abundant and easy to pick and eat. They make a fantastic compote, of course (and the slightly tart ice cream is the perfect accompaniment). It is worth recording that I favoured the Herbert variety above all, and Marks and Spencer sell most of the varieties with a label that shows the name of each one.

blueberry compote with yogurt ice cream

SERVES 6–8

550 g (1¼ lb) blueberries
300 ml (10 fl oz) water
75 g (3 oz) caster sugar
Pared zest of ½ a small orange
Juice of 2 limes
4 teaspoons arrowroot

FOR THE ICE CREAM:
300 ml (10 fl oz) double cream
4 egg yolks
150 g (5 oz) caster sugar
300 ml (10 fl oz) wholemilk natural yogurt

1 For the ice cream, bring the cream to the boil in a non-stick pan. Meanwhile, cream the egg yolks and sugar together in a bowl. Gradually beat in the hot cream, return the mixture to the pan and cook over a low heat, stirring constantly, until the custard mixture thickens and lightly coats the back of the wooden spoon. Do not let the mixture boil. Transfer to a bowl and leave to cool.

2 Stir the yogurt into the cooled custard and churn in an ice cream maker, then transfer to a container and freeze until required. Alternatively, just buy a tub of frozen yogurt ice cream.

3 For the blueberry compote, put the berries into a pan with the water, sugar, orange zest and lime juice. Bring to a simmer. Slake the arrowroot with a little water and immediately stir it in. Simmer for 1 minute until the sauce has slightly thickened and the berries are just tender, then transfer to a bowl and leave to cool. Cover and chill until you are ready to serve.

4 To serve, remove the ice cream from the freezer and leave it at room temperature for 20 minutes, to allow it to soften slightly. Put 2 scoops of ice cream into a large bowl-like plate and spoon some of the blueberry compote on either side. Serve immediately.

I dreamt this up after a lively trip to the jam-making firm of Wilkin & Sons at Tiptree in Essex (see page 193). This family firm is still going strong in an age of consolidation. On the day we visited, the mulberries were being picked by a group of very young Ukrainian students who, perhaps not unsurprisingly, were pretty much like students everywhere. Some tried hard, others didn't bother too much, but I certainly got the feeling they were all having a pretty idyllic time in rural Essex, chatting up the local girls and enjoying drinking at the village pubs in the summer. The mulberries were difficult to pick; the trees were old and many-branched, requiring very long step ladders, and the branches were very brittle so only a little pressure would bring one crashing down. Mulberries don't have the tartness of similar fruit like loganberries, but they have a rich sweetness and a deep crimson colour. Loganberries are a good substitute here, but actually a jar of Wilkin's Mulberry jam, warmed in a small pan then passed through a sieve, is pretty nice, too.

poached pears with mulberries and mascarpone ice cream

SERVES 6

FOR THE PEARS:
300 ml (10 fl oz) water
300 ml (10 fl oz) white wine
350 g (12 oz) white sugar
Pared zest and juice of 1 lemon
1 vanilla pod
7.5 cm (3 in) piece of cinnamon stick
2 cloves
6 conference pears

FOR THE MASCARPONE ICE CREAM:
1 vanilla pod
600 ml (1 pint) full cream milk
6 egg yolks
75 g (3 oz) caster sugar
250 g (9 oz) mascarpone cheese
300 ml (10 fl oz) double cream

FOR THE MULBERRY SAUCE:
300 g (10 oz) mulberries
50 g (2 oz) icing sugar

1 For the ice cream, split open the vanilla pod and scrape out the seeds with the tip of a sharp knife. Put the milk, vanilla pod and seeds into a pan and bring to the boil. Meanwhile, cream the egg yolks and sugar together in a bowl. Remove the vanilla pod from the milk and gradually beat the milk into the yolks and sugar. Return the mixture to the pan and cook over a low heat, stirring constantly, until the custard thickens and lightly coats the back of the wooden spoon. Do not let the mixture boil. Transfer to a bowl and leave to cool.

2 Put the mascarpone cheese into a bowl and gradually beat in the cooled custard. Whisk the cream into soft peaks in another bowl, gently fold into the mixture and then churn in an ice-cream maker. Transfer to a container and freeze until required.

3 For the pears, put the water, wine, sugar, lemon zest and juice, vanilla pod, cinnamon stick and cloves into a pan large enough to take the pears and leave it over a low heat until the sugar has dissolved. Then increase the heat slightly and leave it to simmer for 5 minutes. Peel the pears, leaving their stalks in place, add them to the syrup and simmer for 6–8 minutes or until just tender when pierced with the tip of a knife. This will depend on how ripe your pears are. Lift them out of the syrup to a bowl and set aside. Boil the remaining syrup until reduced by about three-quarters, leave to cool and then strain back over the pears. Cover and chill.

4 For the mulberry sauce, put the berries and icing sugar into a liquidizer and blend briefly until smooth. Press through a fine sieve into a bowl.

5 Stand one pear up in each bowl-like plate and spoon over a little of the syrup. Add 2 scoops of ice cream, spoon over a little of the mulberry sauce and serve.

This is almost always on the menu at The Seafood Restaurant. What makes it so special is the quality of the Valrhona chocolate we use in the sauce (see page 165). That, and getting the right amount of cinnamon to go with the sugar. Sweets like this are where my heart really lies – uncomplicated, yet requiring the best materials: free-range eggs for the choux paste, fresh oil, and good dark chocolate. Even something as apparently unvariable as ground cinnamon wants attention. There's a vast difference in taste between freshly bought cinnamon and the stuff that's been in the cupboard far too long and is like dust. Every time I go through my drawers and cupboards and look at the dates on spice jars, I'm amazed how time nips along nicely. I hang on to things. There's a lovely idea in one of Anne Tyler's books, *A Patchwork Planet*, where the central character's job is cleaning out people's attics, removing the things they want to but can't get rid of.

beignets soufflés in cinnamon sugar with hot chocolate sauce

SERVES 6

75 g (3 oz) butter
225 ml (7½ fl oz) cold water
95 g (3¾ oz) plain flour, well sifted
3 large eggs, beaten
Sunflower oil, for deep-frying
50 g (2 oz) caster sugar
¾ teaspoon ground cinnamon

FOR THE CHOCOLATE SAUCE:
200 ml (7 fl oz) double cream
90 g (3½ oz) good-quality plain chocolate, broken into small pieces

1 For the chocolate sauce, put the cream and chocolate pieces into a small pan and stir over a low heat until the chocolate has melted and the sauce is silky smooth. Keep warm over a very low heat.

2 For the beignets, put the butter and water into a pan and leave over a low heat until the butter has melted. Turn up the heat, bring to the boil and then add the flour and beat vigorously until the mixture is smooth and leaves the sides of the pan. Leave to cool slightly and then gradually beat in the eggs to make a smooth, glossy choux pastry.

3 Heat a large pan of oil for deep-frying to 190°C/375°F. Drop about 6–8 heaped teaspoons of the choux pastry into the oil, taking care not to overcrowd the pan, and cook for 5 minutes, turning them over now and then, until they are puffed up, crisp and golden. Don't be tempted to lift them out too soon – they will continue to expand in size as they cook for the full 5 minutes, which allows sufficient time for the choux pastry in the centre to cook. Lift them out with a slotted spoon onto a tray lined with kitchen paper and drain briefly, then keep hot in a low oven while you cook the rest.

4 Mix the caster sugar and cinnamon together in a shallow dish, add the beignets a few at a time, and toss them gently until they are well coated.

5 To serve, arrange 4 of the beignets in the centre of large, warm plates and drizzle some of the chocolate sauce over and around them. Serve immediately while still warm.

My mother used to make a pudding very like this but she called it Apple Charlotte. She didn't use a charlotte mould or line the dish with fingers of buttered bread, but the result was a vivid memory of apple, lemon and buttery toasted bread. This is my attempt to recreate it and I've used demerara instead of caster sugar with the bread. It's a sort of deconstructed Apple Charlotte, all the flavours being there, but designed to be made in any old dish. In fact we make this in small Spanish terracotta dishes at the Bistro and serve it with a jug of double cream.

apple betty

SERVES 4

450 g (1 lb) peeled, cored
and thinly sliced cooking apples
Finely grated zest of ½ lemon
50 g (2 oz) caster sugar
100 g (4 oz) butter
175 g (6 oz) crustless white bread,
cut into 1 cm (½ in) cubes
100 g (4 oz) demerara sugar

1 Preheat the oven to 180°C/350°F/Gas Mark 4. Toss the sliced apples with the lemon zest and sugar and spoon them into the base of 1 large or 4 smaller ovenproof dishes.

2 Melt the butter in a large pan, add the bread cubes and turn them over gently until they are coated in butter. Then sprinkle over the demerara sugar and turn them over once more to coat in sugar.

3 Roughly pile the bread cubes over the top of the apples and bake in the oven for 40 minutes until crisp and golden brown.

Rhubarb crumble, the light-brown crust splitting and darkening round the edge of the dish with the rhubarb bubbling up from below, the smell of butter and baked flour with the sour tang of the rhubarb – a pudding which is about as close to the heart of British cooking as you can get. Yet why is it so often disappointing? Usually it's the crumble that's wrong: it's too lean so that it is rather dry and everlasting to eat, or it's undercooked so that it has the pasty flavour of uncooked flour. The rhubarb is usually less of a problem, though getting the balance of sugar right is critical; it should be tart but not so as to pucker the mouth. This last point is dependent on the variety of rhubarb chosen. I enjoy the early forced rhubarb that appears in long rectangular boxes in January and February, with its pale pink and delicate skin. This is surprisingly sweet, not having received much of the teeth-biting oxalic acid present in greener rhubarb stalks and in poisonous quantities in the leaves. So who's the hero here? Well, my mother; it's her recipe and she never got it wrong.

rhubarb crumble

SERVES 6–8

225 g (8 oz) plain flour,
plus 3 tablespoons
175 g (6 oz) chilled butter
275 g (10 oz) caster sugar
900 g (2 lb) rhubarb, trimmed and
wiped clean
Clotted cream, to serve

1 Preheat the oven to 190°C/375°F/Gas Mark 5. For the topping, put the flour and butter into a food processor or bowl and work together until the mixture looks like coarse breadcrumbs. Stir in 100 g (4 oz) of the sugar.

2 Cut the rhubarb into 2.5 cm (1 in) pieces, put into a mixing bowl and add the rest of the caster sugar and the remaining 3 tablespoons of flour. Mix together well and set aside for 15–20 minutes, stirring now and then, until slightly moistened.

3 Spread the fruit over the base of a shallow ovenproof dish and sprinkle over the topping. Bake for 45–50 minutes until the rhubarb is tender and the top is golden brown. Serve with some clotted cream.

I was asked to cook dinner for the Queen and the Duke of Edinburgh at 10 Downing Street last April as part of the Golden Jubilee celebrations. I was, however, somewhat stumped by the request for one of the courses to have a golden theme. Dourade Royale perhaps, gilt-headed bream, or something with gold leaf in it? Not really me, I felt. Then I remembered the Scottish whipped cream, oatmeal and honey dessert called cranachan which often has a little touch of whisky in it, and so I thought to use Chivas Regal and then make it with golden raspberries. It's equally good made with ordinary red raspberries and a drop of single malt like Springbank.

raspberry cranachan

SERVES 4

50 g (2 oz) medium oatmeal
300 ml (10 fl oz) double cream
3 tablespoons clear honey,
heather if possible
2 tablespoons whisky
350 g (12 oz) raspberries

1 Preheat the grill to medium. Spread the oatmeal on a grilling tray and toast, turning occasionally, until golden brown. Remove and leave to cool.

2 Whip the cream in a large bowl until it begins to thicken, then whisk in the honey and whisky until the mixture forms soft peaks. Fold in most of the oatmeal and then lightly fold in most of the raspberries, so that some of them still show through the cream.

3 Spoon the mixture into the centre of 4 large dessert plates and then sprinkle with a little more oatmeal and a scattering of raspberries. Serve immediately.

What an unlikely food hero you might think Billington's are (see page 192). Sugar-makers? Surely sugar is a mere commodity? The piece of information that follows is a perfect example of the message behind the whole book: buy the best materials. The recipe for butterscotch sauce here and the recipe for *Apple Betty* on page 150 both call for demerara sugar. Most of the demerara you can buy (also known as London demerara) just consists of large granules of white sugar with molasses added. Billington's demerara is the real thing, however: unrefined sugar which contains the natural molasses of the sugar cane, which gives it a much more rich and aromatic flavour. I've added some of their light muscovado sugar and black treacle to my steamed sponge, too, which gives it an incomparable flavour and colour.

steamed treacle sponge with butterscotch sauce and custard

SERVES 8

175 g (6 oz) softened butter, plus a little extra for greasing
175 g (6 oz) light muscovado sugar
1 tablespoon black treacle
3 large eggs
175 g (6 oz) self-raising flour

FOR THE BUTTERSCOTCH SAUCE:
50 g (2 oz) butter
75 g (3 oz) light muscovado sugar
25 g (1 oz) demerara sugar
150 g (5 oz) golden syrup
150 ml (5 fl oz) double cream

FOR THE CUSTARD:
1 vanilla pod
600 ml (1 pint) full cream milk
4 egg yolks
3 tablespoons caster sugar
4 teaspoons cornflour

1 Generously grease a 1.2 litre (2 pint) pudding basin with some butter. Cream the butter in a bowl until light and creamy. Add the muscovado sugar and beat vigorously until the mixture is pale and fluffy, then beat in the black treacle. Beat in the eggs one at a time, adding a large spoonful of the flour with the last egg, and then gently fold in the rest of the flour.

2 Spoon the mixture into the pudding basin and lightly level the top of the mixture. Cover the bowl with a pleated sheet of buttered foil and tie in place with string.

3 Bring 5 cm (2 in) of water to the boil in a large pan containing some sort of shallow trivet in the base. Add the pudding, cover and steam for 2 hours.

4 Meanwhile, make the butterscotch sauce. Put the butter, muscovado and demerara sugar and golden syrup into a pan and leave over a low heat, stirring now and then, until the sugars have dissolved. Stir in the double cream and keep warm.

5 For the custard, slit open the vanilla pod and scrape out the seeds with the tip of a sharp knife. Put the milk, vanilla pod and seeds into a non-stick pan and bring to the boil. Remove the pan from the heat and set aside for 20 minutes or so to allow the flavour of vanilla to infuse the milk. Cream the egg yolks, sugar and cornflour together in a bowl until smooth. Bring the milk back to the boil, remove the vanilla pod and gradually beat the milk into the egg yolk mixture. Return to the pan and cook over a medium heat, stirring constantly, until the custard thickens, but don't let the mixture boil.

6 To serve, uncover the pudding and carefully run a knife around the edge of the basin. Cover with an inverted plate and turn it out. Pour over some of the hot butterscotch sauce and serve cut into wedges with the custard and the rest of the sauce.

I'd forgotten the charm of these little hearts of cream cheese, which I used to make in the 70s and 80s, until I went to the Stilton factory in Colston Bassett (see page 180) last year and renewed my sense of wonder at the way curds and whey separate with the addition of so little rennet. The making of your own cream cheese is a source of great satisfaction, I think; something to be proud of when it's turned out of the muslin-lined, perforated, heart-shaped moulds, covered with cream and sugar, and served with just a handful of perfect raspberries. One addition I used to make back then was to pare the zest off a couple of lemons and grind it with lots of sugar, in a coffee grinder kept especially for this purpose, into a lemon-flavoured icing sugar for sprinkling over the hearts.

coeur à la crème

SERVES 4

600 ml (1 pint) full cream milk
1 tablespoon rennet
½ teaspoon salt
150 ml (5 fl oz) double cream
15 g (½oz) caster sugar
Single cream and fresh raspberries,
to serve

1 Put the milk into a pan and bring it up to 37°C (98°F). Pour it into a bowl, stir in the rennet and set it aside somewhere cool, but not in the fridge, until set.

2 When the mixture is firm, break it up into pieces and stir in the salt. Pour it into a large, muslin-lined sieve set over a bowl, cover and leave somewhere cool to drain for 8 hours or overnight, but again, do not refrigerate.

3 Tip the cheese-like mixture out of the muslin cloth into the sieve and press it through into a clean bowl. Lightly whip the cream and sugar together in another bowl into soft peaks and gently fold it into the cheese-like mixture.

4 Line 4 coeur à la crème moulds with small squares of damp muslin. Spoon in the mixture and lightly level the tops. Cover and chill in the fridge for 2–3 hours.

5 Turn them out onto small plates and pile some raspberries alongside. Sprinkle over some sugar, pour around a little cream, and serve.

When my sons were little we used to go to Molesworth Manor just outside Wadebridge to a 'pick your own fruit' farm, or in our case 'pick and eat your own fruit'. However, what little did come back I used to turn into this summer pudding – a tribute to a fantastic walled garden and a great British tradition. The traditional fruits for a summer pudding are raspberries and black, red and white currants, but you can also use loganberries, tayberries or mulberries, although not strawberries which are not concentrated or acidic enough in flavour. I've suggested below a mix of fruits that suits me, but use whatever you choose. Just make sure you don't overpower everything else with too many blackcurrants. An equally pleasant pudding is autumn pudding, based on blackberries, autumn raspberries and lightly poached tart plums.

summer pudding

SERVES 8

225 g (8 oz) caster sugar
150 ml (5 fl oz) water
Pared zest of 1 small lemon
450 g (1 lb) raspberries
225 g (8 oz) red currants
175 g (6 oz) blackcurrants
50 g (2 oz) white currants (or more red currants if you can't get white)
8–9 thin slices of white bread from a large loaf, crusts removed
Double cream, to serve

1 Put the sugar and water into a pan and leave over a low heat until the sugar has dissolved. Add the pared lemon zest, bring to the boil and simmer for 5 minutes. Remove the zest and blend 3 tablespoons of the syrup with 100 g (4 oz) of the raspberries. Press through a sieve to remove the seeds. Add the currants to the remaining syrup and simmer for 2 minutes. Remove from the heat and stir in the remaining 350 g (12 oz) of raspberries and the sieved raspberry sauce.

2 Tip the fruit into a sieve set over a bowl to collect the syrup. Dip the slices of bread briefly into the syrup and set 2 aside for the lid. Use the others to line the base and sides of a 1.2 litre (2 pint) pudding basin, overlapping the slices slightly to make sure there are no gaps.

3 Spoon in the fruit and 2–3 tablespoons of the remaining syrup and then cover neatly with the rest of the syrup-dipped bread. Cover the top of the pudding with cling film and then a plate that fits just inside the rim. Weight it down, sit it on a plate and chill overnight, along with any remaining syrup.

4 To serve, carefully run a knife around the edge of the pudding basin. Invert the pudding onto a serving plate and spoon over any remaining syrup. Cut into wedges and serve with pouring cream.

While hotter climates produce more succulent fruit than Britain's damp islands, not everything is better. Tayside in Scotland produces the best raspberries in the world. The long northern summer day, which is not too hot, leads to exactly the right degree of delicate, sweet acidity in the fruit. Our pastry chef, Anita, came up with this recipe for me a few years ago for a TV programme in which we were trying to match beer to food. This was to go with one of those fruit beers from Belgium, but ultimately I don't think it worked; it was too bitter. I would far sooner go for something like a sweet white Jurançon wine, like Domaine Cauhope.

fresh raspberry tart in coconut and hazelnut pastry

SERVES 8

FOR THE HAZELNUT AND
COCONUT PASTRY:
25 g (1 oz) toasted hazelnuts
25 g (1 oz) dessicated coconut
175 g (6 oz) plain flour
A pinch of salt
175 g (6 oz) butter, softened
65 g (2½ oz) caster sugar
1 medium egg, beaten

FOR THE FILLING:
2 egg yolks
50 g (2 oz) caster sugar
20 g (¾ oz) cornflour
20 g (¾ oz) plain flour
300 ml (10 fl oz) milk
1 teaspoon vanilla extract
15 g (½ oz) unsalted butter
50 ml (2 fl oz) double cream
225 g (8 oz) fresh raspberries
Icing sugar, for dusting

1 For the hazelnut and coconut pastry, put the toasted hazelnuts and dessicated coconut into a food processor and grind using the pulse button until finely chopped. Then add 25 g (1 oz) of the flour and grind to a fine mixture, but don't grind it for too long or it will start to go oily. Mix with the rest of the plain flour and salt and set to one side. Cream the butter and sugar together briefly until smooth. Beat in half of the beaten egg, followed by the flour mixture and enough of the remaining beaten egg to bind the mixture together. Knead briefly until smooth, wrap in cling film and chill for 20 minutes.

2 Preheat the oven to 190°C/375°F/Gas Mark 5. Carefully roll out the pastry between 2 sheets of greaseproof paper or cling film and use to line a greased 20 cm (8 in) loose-bottomed flan tin. Prick the base here and there with a fork and chill for 30 minutes. Line the pastry case with greaseproof paper and baking beans and bake blind for 15 minutes, then remove the paper and beans and bake for a further 5–7 minutes until crisp and golden. Remove and leave to cool.

3 For the filling, mix the egg yolks with the sugar, cornflour, plain flour and 2 tablespoons of the milk in a mixing bowl until smooth. Bring the rest of the milk to the boil in a non-stick pan. Gradually beat the hot milk into the creamed egg yolks, return the mixture to the pan and cook over a medium heat, stirring, until thick and smooth. Simmer gently for 2 minutes to cook out the flour, then stir in the vanilla extract and butter, transfer to a bowl and press a sheet of cling film onto the surface to prevent a skin forming. Leave to cool and then chill until needed.

4 Shortly before serving, whip the cream into soft peaks and fold it into the pastry cream. Spread the mixture into the base of the pastry case and cover with a single layer of the raspberries. Sprinkle with a light dusting of icing sugar and serve cut into wedges.

I'm one of those people who infinitely prefer a little fruit and cream in a restaurant to anything more filling. There's nothing much to this dessert, just boiled cream and sugar lightly curdled with lemon juice. The recipe comes from our Executive Chef Roy Brett, who is a bit of a hero. It's such a pleasure to work with people who really care about good cooking, who think nothing of putting in a seven-day week every now and then, if it's necessary, and who admit that they don't want to go straight home after a service, they just want to sit around and chat about food.

lemon posset with grilled figs

SERVES 6

FOR THE POSSET:
450 ml (15 fl oz) double cream
100 g (4 oz) caster sugar
Finely grated zest and juice of
2 small lemons

FOR THE GRILLED FIGS:
5 fresh figs, quartered
2–3 tablespoons caster sugar

1 For the posset, put the cream, sugar, lemon zest and juice into a pan and bring to the boil. Whisk well then pour into small tea cups or ramekins, cover and chill for 8 hours or overnight.

2 Meanwhile, preheat the grill to high. Lay the figs cut-side up on a baking tray and sprinkle them with the sugar. Slide them under the grill, as close to the heat as you can, and grill them for 3–4 minutes until the sugar has caramelized and given them a rich colour. Remove and leave to cool to room temperature.

3 Put a few pieces of fig on top of each posset and serve.

This is a fascinating recipe, a bit like Bakewell tart but much more interesting due to the tannin taste of walnuts in the background. You can make it perfectly successfully with a packet of supermarket walnuts, but if you are lucky enough to be able to buy the walnuts from Loaves and Fishes of Woodbridge in Suffolk (see page 184), the difference will be immeasurable.

walnut tart

SERVES 10–12

1 quantity of *Rich shortcrust pastry*
(see page 177)
3 tablespoons raspberry jam
225 g (8 oz) walnut pieces
50 g (2 oz) plain flour
225 g (8 oz) softened butter
225 g (8 oz) caster sugar
3 medium eggs, beaten
1 teaspoon vanilla extract
Icing sugar, for dusting
Crème fraîche, to serve

1 Roll out the pastry on a lightly floured surface and use to line a 4 cm (1½ in) deep, 25 cm (10 in) loose-bottomed flan tin. Spread the base of the case with the jam and chill for 30 minutes.

2 Preheat the oven to 180°C/350°F/Gas Mark 4. Put the walnuts into a food processor and grind briefly until chopped. Then add the flour and blend briefly once more into a fine mixture, but don't overdo it or the walnuts will go oily.

3 Cream the butter and the sugar together until pale and fluffy. Gradually beat in the beaten eggs, add the vanilla extract and then gently fold in the walnut mixture. Spread it into the pastry case, taking the mixture right up to the edges, and bake in the oven for 50–55 minutes or until springy to the touch and when a skewer, pushed into the centre, comes out clean. Cover with a double sheet of greaseproof paper towards the end of cooking if it starts to get too brown. Remove from the oven and leave to cool.

4 Remove the tart from the tin and dust it with icing sugar. Cut it into wedges and serve with some crème fraîche.

Middle Eastern Food by Claudia Roden was one of those books that opened my eyes to food. It came out in the late 60s, at a time when I had no idea that the flavours of the eastern Mediterranean round to North Africa could be so exotically different. I suppose it's the legacy of my first visit to Egypt in 1966 when, en route to Australia on a ship, I spent an afternoon in Port Said appalled at the teeming life there, the food shops and the flies. The diary I wrote at the time tells the story of a rather sheltered 19-year-old suddenly subjected to the sights and smells of the East, but now I can't get enough of such richness. The whole book – falafels, baba ghanoush, tabbouleh, hummus bi tahina – was a source of such excitement, featuring dishes which have now passed into my repertoire and that of many others, too, including this delightful Passover cake.

moist orange cake with citrus cheesecake cream

SERVES 8–10

2 oranges
6 medium eggs
225 g (8 oz) caster sugar
225 g (8 oz) ground almonds
1 teaspoon baking powder
Icing sugar, for dusting

FOR THE CITRUS CHEESECAKE CREAM:
200 g (7 oz) Philadelphia cream cheese
50 g (2 oz) caster sugar
Finely grated zest of 1 lemon and
1 small orange
Juice of 1 large lemon
(about 4 tablespoons)
300 ml (10 fl oz) double cream

1 Put the whole oranges into a small pan and cover with lots of water. Bring to the boil, cover and boil for 3 hours, topping up the water now and then when necessary. Drain, leave to cool, then break them open and remove the little stalks and any seeds. Put the flesh into a food processor and blend into a smooth purée. Set aside.

2 Preheat the oven to 180°C/350°F/Gas Mark 4. Grease and line a 23 cm (9 in) clip-sided cake tin with baking paper.

3 Whisk the eggs and sugar together in a large bowl until thick and moussey – the mixture should leave a trail over the surface. Gently fold in the ground almonds, baking powder and orange purée. Pour the mixture into the prepared tin and bake for 55 minutes to 1 hour or until a skewer, inserted into the very centre of the cake, comes out clean. Remove and leave to cool.

4 For the citrus cheesecake cream, beat the cream cheese with the sugar, lemon zest, orange zest and lemon juice. Whisk the cream into soft peaks and gently fold in.

5 Remove the cake from the tin and carefully remove the paper. Cut it into wedges, lightly dust with icing sugar and serve with a spoonful of the citrus cheesecake cream.

Michael Pearce's shop, The Bakery (see page 191), is in Kelly Bray, a village on the back road between Launceston and Callington in Cornwall. He makes pasties, bread and cakes, but the star attraction is the saffron cake. It's always the same when you find something that's being made with passion: it's flying out of the door. Michael has a sort of quiet confidence which comes with doing something really well. The shop looks just right, it must have been unchanged for 50 years – well, certainly the exterior – but it's what you'd expect, the windows painted with a nice bright green and the interior clean and tidy but not modern, and filled with the heavy, floral scent of saffron. The cakes are different because he uses butter, cream and eggs as well as the best saffron from Spain; he opened an enormous tin of it for us to savour and it was quite intoxicating. He wouldn't give me his recipe for saffron cake – it's secret, like successful fish and chip shops won't give you their recipe for batter – but he sent me a recipe which he said worked well. It only had a small amount of butter, no cream or eggs, so I've added them in the quantities I guess he'd use. I hope he doesn't mind.

saffron cake

MAKES 2 CAKES

A big pinch of saffron strands
Approx. 2 tablespoons milk
2 tablespoons single cream
25 g (1 oz) fresh yeast or 15 g (½oz) dried yeast (but not easy-blend)
75 g (3 oz) cold salted butter
350 g (12 oz) plain flour
A good pinch of salt
50 g (2 oz) granulated sugar
300 g (11 oz) currants
25 g (1 oz) mixed chopped peel

1 Soak the saffron in a couple of tablespoons of warm water for 10 minutes.

2 To make a ferment, warm the milk and cream to 36°C (98°F). Pour into a bowl and whisk in the crumbled fresh yeast or dried yeast and 1 tablespoon of the flour. Leave to ferment for 10 minutes until frothy. Meanwhile, work the butter into the rest of the flour and the salt, by hand or in a food processor, until the mixture resembles fine breadcrumbs. Stir in the sugar.

3 Add the saffron liquid and the ferment to the flour and knead well until the dough is soft and pliable. Add the currants and mixed peel and work in well. Cover the bowl with a cloth and leave in a warm place for 50 minutes until doubled in size.

4 Turn out the dough onto a lightly floured surface and punch out the air. Kead for 5 minutes until smooth, return to the bowl and recover. Leave for a further 20 minutes.

5 Divide the dough into two and drop into 2 warmed, greased and lined 450 g (1 lb) loaf tins. Leave to rise for 10 minutes. Meanwhile, preheat the oven to 200°C/400°F/Gas Mark 6.

6 Bake the cakes for approximately 50 minutes. Remove and leave in the tins for a few minutes, before turning out onto a cooling rack and leaving to cool.

This is a hymn of praise to the best chocolate in the world: Valrhona. You have to make this cake with Valrhona Noir Gastronomie. It comes in 250 g (9 oz) bars and has 61% cocoa paste content. The cake contains almost no flour, the bulk being made up with ground almonds, and it has an enticing way of sinking and cracking as it comes out of the oven. I like it served just warm, with nothing more than some ice-cold pouring cream. To my mind, it is the perfect way to enjoy the subtlety of great chocolate. (For stockists of Valrhona chocolate, see pages 192–3.)

sunken chocolate cake

SERVES 8

225 g (8 oz) butter
225 g (8 oz) good-quality plain chocolate, broken into pieces
50 g (2 oz) ground almonds
60 g (2¼ oz) plain flour
6 medium eggs, at room temperature
50 g (2 oz) light soft brown sugar
175 g (6 oz) caster sugar
Icing sugar, for dusting
Double cream, to serve

1 Preheat the oven to 180°C/350°F/Gas Mark 4. Grease and line a 20 cm (8 in) clip-sided cake tin with baking paper.

2 Put the butter and chocolate into a heatproof bowl and rest it over a pan of barely simmering water. Leave until melted, then stir until smooth. Remove and leave to cool slightly.

3 Sift together the ground almonds and flour. Separate the eggs into 2 large bowls. Add the light brown sugar to the egg yolks and whisk until pale and creamy. Gently fold in the melted chocolate mixture, followed by the almond and flour mixture.

4 Whisk the egg whites into soft peaks and then whisk in the caster sugar, a little at a time, to make a soft meringue. If it's too stiff you will find it difficult to fold into the rest of the cake mixture. Fold it in with a large metal spoon, pour the mixture into the prepared tin and bake for 50 minutes or until a skewer, inserted into the cake, still comes out a bit wet. This cake is best if slightly undercooked. Remove from the oven and leave to cool.

5 Carefully remove from the tin and pull off the paper. Cut into wedges, dust with icing sugar and serve with some pouring cream.

I find cheesecakes with biscuit bottoms and chilled fillings insipid, too sweet and a bit greasy, but a baked cheesecake with a great-quality fresh curd cheese like Crowdie is a different matter; it comes out grainy and slightly sour from the cheese. Crowdie, incidentally, is one of the oldest cheeses in the country and reputed in the north of Scotland to counter the effects of whisky – a good stomach liner before heading off to a *Local Hero* type of ceilidh.

baked highland crowdie cheesecake with allspice and raisins

SERVES 6–8

½ quantity *Basic shortcrust pastry*
(see page 177)
400 g (14 oz) Crowdie cheese
(see page 180, for stockists)
50 g (2 oz) caster sugar
2 tablespoons cornflour
50 ml (2 fl oz) double cream
3 large eggs
Finely grated zest of 1 lemon
½ teaspoon ground allspice
1 teaspoon vanilla extract
100 g (4 oz) raisins
Icing sugar, for dusting

1 Preheat the oven to 200°C/400°F/Gas Mark 6. Lightly grease the base of an 18 cm (7 in) clip-sided cake tin with a little butter. Roll out the pastry on a lightly floured surface into a 20 cm (8 in) disc and use to line the base and very slightly up the sides of the tin. Prick with a fork, cover with a layer of greaseproof paper and baking beans and bake blind for 15 minutes. Remove the paper and beans and return to the oven for 5 minutes, then remove and leave to cool. Lower the oven temperature to 180°C/350°F/Gas Mark 4.

2 Separate 2 of the eggs and put the whites into a large bowl. Put the Crowdie cheese, sugar, cornflour, cream, the egg yolks and remaining whole egg, lemon zest, allspice and vanilla extract into a food processor and blend until the mixture is smooth. Tip the mixture into a bowl and stir in the raisins. Whisk the remaining egg whites to soft peaks and gently fold in to the mixture.

3 Grease the sides of the tin with more butter, pour in the mixture and bake in the centre of the oven for 45–50 minutes until set around the edges but still with a little bit of a wobble in the centre. Turn off the oven, leave the door ajar and leave the cheesecake to cool inside.

4 Carefully run a knife around the outside of the cheesecake to release it from the tin. Transfer it to a plate, cut into wedges, then dust with icing sugar and serve.

The base of this bread is called the Grant Loaf and was invented
in the Second World War by a famous nutritionist, Doris Grant.
It comes from a book called *Your Daily Food: Recipe for Survival*.
It was designed to be easy to make – it only requires proving in
the tin – and to be very nutritious, containing 100% wholemeal
flour. I have added some walnuts and sesame seeds to the basic
recipe. It's not the easiest bread to get right because the flour
lacks the gluten content of strong white bread flour, and at its
worst it can be heavy, like cake. A lot depends on the quality of
flour used and how fresh it is. I find the wholemeal flour from
Shipton Mill (see page 193) makes a very good Grant Loaf. At its
besl it has a lovely nutty flavour and makes great toast, conjuring

memories for me of cooking breakfasts at the restaurant – walnut bread, sausages, tomatoes and bacon
under the grill and a pan of field mushrooms and another of eggs on the stove; the smell of freshly
ground coffee and an early delivery of salmon from Jim McOwen who'd been out fishing all night,
complaining about a seal stealing his fish from the net and threatening to shoot it, though he never did.

walnut bread

MAKES 2 X 450 G (1 LB) LOAVES

1 tablespoon dried yeast
1 tablespoon dark soft brown sugar
450 ml (15 fl oz) lukewarm water
600 g (1 lb 6 oz) wholemeal flour
2 teaspoons salt
20 g (¾oz) butter, melted
40 g (1½oz) walnut pieces
2 teaspoons sesame seeds

1 To make a ferment, whisk the yeast and 1 teaspoon of the sugar
in 150 ml (5 fl oz) of the lukewarm water. Leave in a warm place until
the surface has about 2 cm (¾ in) of froth on it. This will take about
15 minutes.

2 Put the flour, remaining sugar and salt in a large bowl or the bowl of
a mixer. Pour on the yeast ferment, the remaining water and melted
butter, mix together and form into a soft, rather sloppy dough which
should be kneaded manually or mechanically for 3 minutes, adding the
walnuts right at the end.

3 Cut the dough in half and form into 2 fat sausage shapes. Put them
into 2 buttered 450 g (1 lb) loaf tins. Cover each with cling film or put in
a large plastic bag and leave in a warm place for 45 minutes, until the
dough has risen to the top.

4 Preheat the oven to 230°C/450°F/Gas Mark 8. Sprinkle some
sesame seeds over the loaves and bake in the centre of the oven
for 25–30 minutes. Remove the loaves from their tins and return them
to the oven for a further 5 minutes to crisp up. Leave to cool on a
wire rack.

accompaniments and basic recipes

grilled mediterranean vegetables with marjoram

This is a vegetable accompaniment to a main course. However, if you are lucky enough to be able to buy the sort of vegetables that come via a box scheme, like those from Coleshill Organics near Swindon, it's worth celebrating them as a first course. I use marjoram here in a small quantity. I'm very fond of the taste, but only in a restrained way.

Preheat the oven to 180°C/350°F/Gas Mark 4. Cut half a large aubergine into 5 mm (¼ in) slices. Slice one 100 g (4 oz) courgette diagonally into 5 mm (¼ in) slices. Cut one medium red onion into 6 wedges through the root. Slice one small fennel bulb lengthways through the root into 5 mm (¼ in) slices. Halve one red pepper and remove and discard the stalk and seeds. Cut the flesh lengthways into 2.5 cm (1 in) wide strips. Put all the vegetables into a large roasting tin or bowl with 5 tablespoons of extra virgin olive oil and the leaves from about 5 sprigs of marjoram, ½ teaspoon of salt and 10 turns of the black pepper mill and mix together carefully so that all the vegetables are well coated in oil. Try to avoid breaking up the fennel and onion slices. Heat a ridged cast-iron griddle over a high heat until smoking hot. Add a single layer of vegetables and sear until nicely marked by the ridges, then turn over and repeat. Grill the fennel, red peppers and onions first, as they will take longer than the aubergines and courgettes. When all the vegetables have been char-grilled, transfer them to a shallow roasting tin and bake them in the oven for 5 minutes. Pile them onto a large plate and sprinkle with some Maldon sea salt flakes, a little more freshly ground black pepper and a little more olive oil.

glazed spring carrots with tarragon and chives

Scrub 450 g (1 lb) of small spring carrots and trim down their tops. Put them into a wide, shallow pan with 600 ml (1 pint) of water to barely cover and add ½ a teaspoon of white sugar, ½ a teaspoon of salt and 15 g (½ oz) of butter. Cover with a tight-fitting lid and simmer until just tender. Uncover the pan, increase the heat and boil rapidly to reduce the liquor, shaking the pan now and then, until just before the carrots start to catch on the base of the pan. They should just be allowed to colour very slightly here and there. Add ½ a teaspoon each of chopped tarragon and chives, toss well, and serve.

warm runner beans with summer savory

Run a potato peeler down either side of 450 g (1 lb) of runner beans, then shred them finely by hand or using a bean shredder. Drop them into a pan of boiling salted water, bring back to the boil and cook for 1 minute. Drain well. Whisk together 2 tablespoons of olive oil, 1 teaspoon of lemon juice, a good pinch of crushed garlic, 1 teaspoon of finely chopped summer savory and some salt and pepper to taste. Add to the warm beans, toss together gently, and serve straight away.

buttered leeks with mint

Trim 450 g (1 lb) of leeks, cut them in half lengthways and wash them well. Cut them in half once more if large and then into 1 cm (½ in) triangles by cutting across the leeks in alternating directions. Drop them into a pan of boiling salted water and simmer until tender but still al dente. Drain well. Melt 50 g (2 oz) of butter in a pan, add the leeks and sweat gently to drive off the excess moisture, and when they are all buttery, stir in 4 teaspoons of chopped mint.

courgettes with chervil and chives

If you can get hold of very small (and just picked) courgettes, all the better. Slice 350 g (12 oz) of young courgettes across into thin discs. Melt 25 g (1 oz) of butter in a large sauté pan. Add the courgettes and fry them gently over a low heat until they are just tender, sprinkling them with about 1 tablespoon each of chopped chervil and chives and a little salt and freshly ground black pepper about 1 minute after they have started cooking.

french beans with tomatoes and thyme

Trim the stalk ends off 350 g (12 oz) of French beans and cook them in boiling, well-salted water for about 2 minutes until just tender. Drain well and return to the pan with 2 tablespoons of extra-virgin olive oil, 2 seeded and diced vine tomatoes, 1 finely chopped garlic clove, ½ a teaspoon of picked thyme leaves and some salt and pepper. Toss together briefly over the heat and serve.

cavolo nero with fennel seeds and garlic

Take 450 g (1 lb) of cavolo nero, the younger the better. If the leaves are large, strip the green part away from the stems with a large, sharp knife. They get quite woody as they get older. Otherwise, just bunch them together and cut them across into 3. Cook them in 2.5–5 cm (1–2 in) of boiling salted water, turning them over regularly, for 4 minutes or until slightly undercooked. Drain and refresh in cold water, then spread them over a clean tea towel and leave to drain. Put 3 tablespoons of olive oil and 1 sliced garlic clove into a large pan and set over a medium–high heat. As soon as the garlic starts to sizzle, add a good pinch of lightly crushed

fennel seeds and cook gently without colouring for 1 minute. Add the cavolo nero leaves and stir-fry for 1–1½ minutes until heated through. Season well with salt and pepper and serve.

cabbage with shallots, garlic and flatleaf parsley

Serves 6
Put 900 g (2 lb) of thinly sliced white cabbage, 3 chopped garlic cloves, 5 sliced shallots, 4 tablespoons of sunflower oil, 2 teaspoons of salt and 10 turns of the black pepper mill into a large, heavy-based pan. Cover with a well-fitting lid, place over a low heat and cook gently for 10–12 minutes, stirring occasionally, until the cabbage is just tender. Stir in 20 g (¾ oz) of chopped flatleaf parsley and serve.

steamed savoy cabbage, sprouting broccoli, sprouts or broccoli

In this recipe the vegetables are steamed rather than boiled. I find this gives them a less watery taste and, if you are serving them with a roast, the cooking water makes a very fresh-tasting gravy.

Allow 1 large Savoy cabbage or 550 g (1¼ lb) of the other vegetables for 4 people. Cut the cabbage into quarters, remove the core and cut each piece lengthways into 1 cm (½ in) thick slices. Trim the base from the broccoli and break it into smaller florets. Trim the base of the sprouting broccoli. Remove the first 2 or 3 leaves from each sprout. Put 1 cm (½ in) of water into the base of a large pan, bring to the boil and add 1 teaspoon of salt and the vegetable. Cook over a vigorous heat, turning over now and then, for 3–4 minutes or until they are just cooked through but still slightly crisp.

white cabbage salad

Remove the outer leaves from ½ a small white cabbage, cut it in ½ and cut out the thick central core. Slice the rest across as thinly as possible, on a mandolin if you have one. Very thinly slice 1 medium onion and peel, core and chop 1 Cox's apple. Crush 1 clove of garlic on a board with a little salt under the blade of a large knife until smooth. Put the cabbage, onion and apple in a salad bowl and mix together. Scrape the garlic into a small bowl and add 50 ml (2 fl oz) of sunflower oil, 1½ tablespoons of white wine vinegar, 2 teaspoons of *Mayonnaise* (see page 177), 1 teaspoon of English mustard, ½ a teaspoon of caster sugar, ½ a teaspoon of salt and 5 turns of the black pepper mill. Whisk together well, stir into the salad with 1 small bunch of chopped flatleaf parsley, and serve immediately.

braised red cabbage

Serves 6
Preheat the oven to 150°C/300°F/Gas Mark 2. Remove the outer leaves from a red cabbage weighing about 900 g (2 lb), cut it into quarters and cut

out the core. Thinly slice the rest of the cabbage, preferably on a mandolin, and put it into a large ovenproof casserole with 2 thinly sliced onions, 450 g (1 lb) of peeled, cored and sliced cooking apples, 3 tablespoons of white wine vinegar, 3 tablespoons of dark muscovado sugar, 25 g (1 oz) of butter, 1 teaspoon of salt and 20 turns of the black pepper mill. You can also add a few ground spices if you like – about ½ a teaspoon of mixed ground cloves, grated nutmeg and ground cinnamon. Cover and cook for 3 hours, stirring once or twice during cooking.

braised sauerkraut

Serves 6

The best ready-fermented sauerkraut I know is called Wagner. Some prefer to rinse the sauerkraut in water before cooking, others say it doesn't smell the same if you do. I prefer it unrinsed, but if you want it milder, tip 1 x 500 g (1 lb 2 oz) jar of sauerkraut into a colander and rinse with cold water. Press out the excess liquid and cook as follows.

Melt 40 g (1½ oz) of butter or goose fat in a pan. Add 1 sliced medium onion, 1 thinly sliced carrot, 6 crushed juniper berries, 2 bay leaves, 3 cloves and 3 chopped cloves of garlic and cook gently for 3–4 minutes until soft but not coloured. Add the sauerkraut, 600 ml (1 pint) of *Chicken stock* (see page 176) and a wine glass (about 120 ml/4 fl oz) of dry white wine. Cover and simmer very gently for 1 hour.

steamed chinese greens in oyster sauce

Serves 4–6

Cut 8–12 small heads of pak choi lengthways into quarters and put them onto an opened-out petal steamer. Lower them into a shallow pan containing about 1 cm (½ in) of simmering water, cover and steam for 3–4 minutes or until tender. Meanwhile, mix together 2 teaspoons of sunflower oil, 1 teaspoon of sesame oil, 4 tablespoons of oyster sauce and 1 tablespoon of dark soy sauce in a small pan and leave to warm through over a low heat. Transfer the pak choi to a warmed serving plate, spoon over the sauce and serve.

steamed spinach

Serves 4–6

Wash 900 g (2 lb) of fresh spinach and remove and discard any large stalks. Dry well (in a salad spinner if you have one). Drop the spinach, a large handful at a time, into a large, hot pan, adding another as each one wilts down. When all the spinach has been added, cook for 1 minute, then tip into a colander and lightly press out the excess liquid. Melt 25 g (1 oz) of butter in the pan, add the spinach, and season with a little freshly grated nutmeg and some salt and pepper. Toss briefly over a high heat and serve immediately.

a purée of swede, carrot and potato with rocket

Cut 225 g (8 oz) each of peeled swede, carrots and floury potatoes into chunks. Cook in well-salted boiling water for 20 minutes until tender. Drain well and leave until the steam has died down. Then transfer them to a food processor with 25 g (1 oz) of butter and blend briefly into a smooth purée. Return to the pan and leave to cook over a gentle heat, stirring now and then, until the mixture has dried out. Add a large handful of roughly chopped rocket, season with ½ a teaspoon of salt and 5 turns of the black pepper mill and serve.

pommes anna

Pommes Anna, one of my favourite potato dishes, is a thick potato pancake flavoured only with butter, salt and pepper, held together by the starch in the potatoes. You will need a sloping-sided, heavy-based pan with a base measurement of 20 cm (8 in), so a tarte tatin mould or an ovenproof frying pan would be ideal. You start cooking it on the hob, so that the butter caramelizes and crisps up the bottom layer of the potato – a bit like when you make a tarte tatin – so that when you invert the finished pancake onto a plate to serve, you have a lovely crisp, brown top.

Serves 6

Preheat the oven to 220°C/425°F/Gas Mark 7. Peel 1.25 kg (2½ lb) of floury potatoes such as Maris Piper and thinly slice them on a mandolin or by hand. Heat the mould or ovenproof frying pan over a medium heat, add 25 g (1 oz) of butter, and then take some trouble to get the first layer of potatoes neatly overlapped in the base as this is what you will see when it's turned out. Layer in the rest of the potatoes, seasoning each layer with some salt and pepper, and top with another 25 g (1 oz) of butter pieces. Transfer the frying pan to the oven and bake for 1 hour. To serve, invert onto a warm serving plate and cut into wedges.

mashed potatoes

Cut 900 g (2 lb) of peeled floury potatoes into chunks and put them into a pan of well-salted water (1 teaspoon of salt per 600 ml/1 pint of water). Bring to the boil and cook for 15–20 minutes until tender. Drain and leave until the steam has died down. Pass them through a potato ricer back into the pan and fold in 50 g (2 oz) of butter, some salt and white pepper to taste, and enough milk to give you a smooth, creamy mash.

parsnip and potato mash

Cut 450 g (1 lb) of peeled floury potatoes and 450 g (1 lb) of peeled parsnips into large chunks. Put them into a large pan of well-salted water (1 teaspoon of salt per 600 ml/1 pint of water), bring to the boil and cook for 20 minutes. Drain well, leave until the steam has died down, and then pass the potatoes through a potato ricer back into the pan. Purée the parsnips in a food processor until smooth and then stir into the potatoes with 50 g (2 oz) of butter and a little milk. Season to taste with salt and pepper and serve.

celeriac and potato mash

Cut 450 g (1 lb) of peeled floury potatoes and 450 g (1 lb) of peeled celeriac into chunks. Put them into separate pans of well-salted water (1 teaspoon of salt to 600 ml/1 pint of water) and add 2 lemon slices to the pan of celeriac to stop it from discolouring. Bring to the boil and cook for 20 minutes until tender. Drain both well, discarding the lemon slices from the celeriac, and pass them both through a potato ricer back into one pan. Stir in 50 g (2 oz) of butter, 1 crushed garlic clove and some salt and pepper to taste.

baked potatoes

Preheat the oven to 220°C/425°F/Gas Mark 7. Scrub clean 4 x 250–275 g (9–10 oz) floury baking potatoes like King Edward or Maris Piper. Even if they come pre-washed, wet them to make the seasoning stick. Pierce each one on either side with the tip of a knife, and sprinkle with a little salt and freshly ground black pepper. Put them directly onto the rack at the top of the oven and bake for 1¼ hours. Remove, cut in half and squeeze gently to break open the potato. Dot each half with a small knob of butter and serve.

sautéed potatoes

Cut 750 g (1½ lb) of peeled floury potatoes into 4 cm (1½ in) pieces. Put them into a pan of well-salted water (1 teaspoon of salt per 600 ml/1 pint of water), bring to the boil and simmer until tender – about 7 minutes. Drain well and leave until the steam has died down. Heat 40 g (1½ oz) of butter and 3 tablespoons of oil in a large, heavy-based frying pan. It's important not to overcrowd the pan, so if you don't have a really large pan, use 2 smaller ones. Add the potatoes and fry them over a medium heat for about 10 minutes, turning them over as they brown, until they are crisp,

golden brown and sandy – the outside of the potatoes should break off a little as you sauté them to give them a nice crumbly, crunchy crust. Season with a little salt and freshly ground black pepper and serve immediately.

crushed potatoes with olive oil and watercress

Cook 750 g (1½ lb) of scrubbed new potatoes in well-salted boiling water (1 teaspoon of salt per 600 ml/1 pint of water) for about 15 minutes until tender. Drain well, return them to the pan with 85 ml (3 fl oz) of extra virgin olive oil and gently crush each potato with the back of a fork against the side of the pan until it just bursts open. Season with some sea salt flakes and black pepper and then stir in 50 g (2 oz) of roughly chopped watercress. Turn over gently until the watercress is well mixed in and serve.

plain boiled potatoes

Allow 900 g (2 lb) of potatoes for 4 people. Choose a slightly waxy potato that won't break up too much in the water. I like La Ratte (also known as Cornichon or Asparges), Belle de Fontenay, Charlotte, Pink Fur Apple, Jersey Royals and a red-skinned potato called Roseval. Rub or scrape off the skins and put them into a large pan of cold, well-salted water (1 teaspoon of salt per 600 ml/1 pint of water). Add a good sprig of mint to new potatoes. Bring to the boil and simmer until tender – about 15–20 minutes – until there is no resistance when pierced with the tip of a knife. Drain them well and serve immediately.

roast potatoes

Preheat the oven to 220°C/425°F/Gas Mark 7. Cut 900 g (2 lb) of peeled floury potatoes like Maris Piper or King Edward into 5 x 2.5 cm (2 x 1in) pieces. Put into a pan of well-salted water (1 teaspoon of salt per 600 ml/1 pint of water), bring to the boil and cook for 7 minutes until soft on the outside but still slightly hard in the centre. Drain and leave for the steam to die down, then return them to the pan, cover with a lid and shake gently to rough up the edges a little. Heat a layer of sunflower oil in a large roasting tin, add the potatoes and turn them over once or twice until well coated in the oil. Drain off any surplus oil and roast them in the top of the oven, turning them over halfway through, for 1 hour, until crisp and richly golden.

chips

Maris Piper potatoes make the best chips, but all recently dug new potatoes will make good chips. If you're using over-wintered potatoes the secret is to use ones that have been delicately handled and kept at a stable temperature (at about 5°C). If not, the starch in the potatoes turns into sugar and leads to dark and greasy chips caused by caramelization. If you're planning any sort of deep-fried potato for something special, it's always a good idea to fry a couple and, if they are not perfect, buy a different bag. See pages 182–3 for good chip-potato stockists.

Peel 550 g (1¼ lb) of medium-sized potatoes. These are the shapes I like: for thin chips, cut them into 1 cm (¼ in) thick slices and then lengthways into chips; for roughly cut chips, cut the potatoes into wedges; and for goose fat chips (see below), cut them into 1 cm (½ in) thick slices and then lengthways into 2 cm (¾ in) wide, flatter chips. Quickly rinse them under cold water to remove the starch and dry them well on a clean tea towel.

I like to cook most chips in groundnut oil as it is more stable at higher temperatures, but sunflower or vegetable oils are fine, too. Chips are also fantastic cooked in olive oil for certain dishes – just ordinary olive oil, not extra virgin. For goose fat chips you will need to empty about 2 x 350 g (12 oz) cans of goose fat into a medium-sized pan, so that when it has melted you have a sufficient depth in which to cook the chips – the pan should not be more than one-third full. Heat the oil or goose fat to 120°C/250°F/Gas Mark ½. Drop a large handful of the chips into a chip basket and cook them in batches until they are tender when pierced with the tip of a knife, but have not taken on any colour – about 5 minutes. Lift out and drain. To finish, heat the oil or fat to 190°C/375°F and cook them in batches until crisp and golden – about 2 minutes. Lift them onto kitchen paper, drain and then sprinkle with salt. Serve immediately.

pommes coq d'or

Preheat the oven to 180°C/350°F/Gas Mark 4. Boil 900 ml (1½ pints) of *Chicken stock* (see page 176) until reduced to 175 ml (6 fl oz) and then leave to cool slightly. Mash 2 garlic cloves with a little salt under the blade of a knife into a smooth paste and stir into the stock with 1 teaspoon of salt and 20 turns of the black pepper mill. Peel and thinly slice 750 g (1½ lb) of floury potatoes, on a mandolin if you have one. Liberally butter the inside of a large cast-iron gratin dish. Layer the potatoes in the dish, overlapping the slices slightly as you go, starting on the outside and working inwards. The potatoes should only be a maximum of three layers thick. Add the chicken stock, which should come just below the top layer of potatoes, and dot the top with another 25 g (1 oz) of butter. Cook for 1 hour.

quick dauphinoise potatoes

Serves 6
Preheat the oven to 200°C/400°F/Gas Mark 6. Peel 900 g (2 lb) of potatoes and slice them very thinly by hand, on a mandolin or in a food processor. Put 300 ml (10 fl oz) of double cream, 300 ml (10 fl oz) of milk, 1 crushed garlic clove and plenty of seasoning into a large non-stick saucepan. Add the potatoes and simmer for 10 minutes, stirring them very gently now and then so as not to break the slices, until they are just tender when pierced with the tip of a small, sharp knife. Stir in some freshly grated nutmeg and some seasoning to taste. Spoon them into a lightly buttered 1.5 litre (2½ pint) shallow ovenproof dish. Overlap the top layer of potatoes neatly if you wish. Bake in the oven for 30 minutes or until golden and bubbling.

jansson's temptation

Serves 6
Tip a 50 g (2 oz) can of good-quality anchovies and their oil into a frying pan. Add 2 thinly sliced onions and fry over a medium–high heat for 5 minutes until soft and lightly browned. Meanwhile, cut 900 g (2 lb) of peeled floury potatoes into 5 mm (¼ in) thick slices and then across into short batons. Add 175 ml (6 fl oz) of milk and 175 ml (6 fl oz) of double cream to the anchovies and onions and bring to the boil. Season to taste with salt and pepper and then stir in the potatoes and mix well so that the onions are evenly distributed. Pour the mixture into a lightly buttered, shallow ovenproof baking dish and bake at 190°C/375°F/Gas Mark 5 for 45 minutes until the potatoes are tender and nicely browned on top.

bitter leaf salad with mustard dressing

Serves 4–6
Remove the pale green central leaves from 1 small frisée (curly endive) and break them into small sprigs. Separate 2 heads of chicory into leaves. Toss them together in a bowl with a large handful of wild rocket, washed dandelion leaves (if you can get them) and baby spinach leaves. Whisk together 1 tablespoon of Dijon mustard and 1 tablespoon of white wine vinegar and then gradually whisk in 5 tablespoons of extra virgin olive oil and some salt and freshly ground black pepper. Toss just enough of this through the leaves to coat them lightly before serving.

fine leaf or herb salad with lemon oil dressing

Use a mixture of baby salad leaves and herb sprigs such as flatleaf parsley, tarragon, chervil, chives, fennel herb and dill. Simply drizzle over a little lemon olive oil or extra virgin olive oil and some salt and toss together until all the leaves are lightly coated. This doesn't need any vinegar or pepper.

patricia wells' 'cheese-makers' salad'

Put 2 thinly sliced shallots, separated into rings, and 1 tablespoon of good red wine vinegar into a large, shallow salad bowl. Toss them together and set aside for at least 20 minutes to soften the shallots. When you are ready to serve, add the washed and dried leaves from 1 mild, delicately flavoured green lettuce such as a butterhead or hothouse lettuce. Season with some salt, add 2–3 tablespoons of double cream and toss together very gently to coat all the leaves. Serve straight away.

soft green lettuce salad with an olive oil and garlic dressing

Break any soft lettuce such as hothouse lettuce, Tom Thumb or Little Gem into leaves, wash them well and dry them off in a salad spinner. Just before serving, whisk together 1 tablespoon of white wine vinegar, 4 tablespoons of olive oil, ¼ of a teaspoon of caster sugar and a large pinch of garlic salt. Drizzle this over the leaves, toss together very gently and serve.

italian radicchio, rocket and carrot salad

Break 1 radicchio lettuce into small pieces and put them into a bowl with 100 g (4 oz) of wild rocket leaves. Peel 1 large carrot and then cut it into long fine shreds, preferably on a mandolin. Mix with ½ a teaspoon of salt and set aside for 5 minutes for the carrots to absorb the salt. Whisk together 3 tablespoons of extra virgin olive oil, 2 tablespoons of good red wine vinegar, such as Cabernet Sauvignon vinegar from Brindisa (see page 193) and some seasoning to taste. Rinse the salt off the shredded carrot and toss it through the salad leaves with the dressing.

tomato, shallot and basil salad

Serves 4–6

Whisk together 4 tablespoons of extra virgin olive oil, 1 tablespoon of sherry vinegar, ¼ of a teaspoon of caster sugar, ½ a teaspoon of salt and some freshly ground black pepper. Thinly slice 3 beef tomatoes and lay them in a single layer over the base of a large serving plate. Sprinkle with 1 very thinly sliced shallot, the dressing and then 6–8 finely shredded basil leaves. Finish with a little more coarsely ground black pepper and serve immediately.

other side dishes and salads:

Cherry tomatoes, spring onions and rocket (see page 69)

Petit pois à la française (see page 73)

Rosemary and olive oil potatoes (see page 72)

Herbed lentils (see page 84)

Pickled red cabbage (see page 90)

A stew of peas and flageolets (see page 97)

Roasted hazelnut spätzle (see page 134)

steamed rice

Rinse 350 g (12 oz) of long grain or basmati rice in cold water until the water runs relatively clear. Drain, tip into a 20 cm (8 in) heavy-based saucepan and add ½ a teaspoon of salt and 600 ml (1 pint) of boiling water. Quickly bring to the boil, stir once, cover with a tight-fitting lid and reduce the heat to low. Cook the basmati rice for 10 minutes and the long grain rice for 15 minutes. Uncover, fluff up the grains with a fork, and serve.

pilau rice

Heat 2 tablespoons of sunflower oil in a 20 cm (8 in) heavy-based saucepan, add 3 cloves, 3 cracked green cardamom pods, a 5 cm (2 in) piece of cinnamon stick and a bay leaf and cook gently over a low heat for 2–3 minutes until they start to smell aromatic. Stir in 350 g (12 oz) of basmati rice and fry gently for 1 minute. Add 600 ml (1 pint) of boiling water and ½ a teaspoon of salt and quickly bring to the boil. Stir once, cover with a tight-fitting lid and cook over a low heat for 10 minutes. Remove the rice from the heat and leave undisturbed for 5 minutes. Uncover, fluff up the grains with a fork, and serve.

buttery rice pilaf

Cover a large pinch of saffron with 2 teaspoons of hot water and leave it to soak for 5 minutes. Melt 15 g (½ oz) of butter in a 20 cm (8 in) heavy-based saucepan, add 2 finely chopped shallots and cook gently until soft but not browned. Stir in a bay leaf and 350 g (12 oz) of long grain rice and fry gently for 1 minute. Add 600 ml (1 pint) of *Chicken stock* (see page 176), the saffron and its water and 1 teaspoon of salt and quickly bring to

the boil. Stir once, cover with a tight-fitting lid and cook over a low heat for 15 minutes. Uncover, remove the bay leaf and fluff up the grains with a fork before serving.

spicy apple and walnut chutney

Makes 7 x 450 g (1 lb) jars

Put 1.75 litres (3 pints) of malt vinegar and 900 g (2 lb) of light soft brown sugar into a large pan or preserving pan and bring to the boil. Add 1.75 kg (4 lb) of peeled, cored and roughly chopped cooking apples, 900 g (2 lb) of chopped onions, 450 g (1 lb) of raisins, 50 g (2 oz) of English mustard powder, 50 g (2 oz) of ground ginger, 4 teaspoons of yellow mustard seeds, 4 teaspoons of curry powder, 2 teaspoons of cayenne pepper and 50 g (2 oz) of salt. Bring back to the boil and cook, stirring more regularly as it gets thicker, until it is well reduced — remember that it will thicken even more once cold. Meanwhile, prepare the jars: wash them in hot, soapy water, rinse well and put them into an oven preheated to 160°C/325°F/Gas Mark 3. Leave until you are ready to use them. Stir 225 g (8 oz) of walnut pieces into the chutney, spoon it into the warm, sterilized jars and seal with vinegar-proof lids. It will keep for up to 1 year.

bread and butter pickles

Makes 4 x 450 g (1 lb) jars

Thinly slice 750 g (1½ lb) of small cucumbers, 450 g (1 lb) of onions and 1 green pepper. Mix together in a large bowl with 50 g (2 oz) of salt, cover and set aside for 3 hours. Put 350 g (12 oz) of light soft brown sugar, ½ a teaspoon of turmeric powder, ¼ of a teaspoon of ground cloves, 1 tablespoon of yellow mustard seeds, ½ a teaspoon of celery seed and 475 ml (16 fl oz) of cider vinegar into a large pan and slowly bring to the boil, stirring now and then to dissolve the sugar. Boil for 5 minutes and then set aside. Meanwhile, prepare the jars. Wash them in hot, soapy water, rinse well and put them into an oven preheated to 160°C/325°F/Gas Mark 3. Leave until you are ready to use them. Drain the vegetables and rinse them well under cold running water. Leave them to drain, then add them to the hot syrup and heat slowly to just below boiling point, stirring now and then. Spoon the pickle into the warm, sterilized jars, seal with vinegar-proof lids and leave to cool. This pickle is ready to eat immediately and will keep for up to 1 year.

basic recipes

The stocks below will be much intensified if the strained stock is then simmered with 225–450 g (8 oz–1 lb) of fish or chicken fillet in the case of fish and chicken stock respectively, or shin of beef for beef stock. We quite often combine chicken stock with fish stock for stronger flavoured fish sauces.

fish stock (fumet)

Makes approx. 1.2 litres (2 pints)

1 kg (2¼ lb) flat fish bones, such as lemon sole,
   brill and plaice
2.25 litres (4 pints) water
1 onion, chopped
1 fennel bulb, chopped
100 g (4 oz) celery, sliced
100 g (4 oz) carrot, chopped
25 g (1 oz) button mushrooms, sliced
1 sprig of thyme

Put the fish bones and water into a large pan, bring just to the boil and simmer very gently for 20 minutes.

Strain through a sieve into a clean pan, add the vegetables and the thyme and bring back to the boil. Simmer for 35 minutes or until reduced to about 1.2 litres (2 pints). Strain once more and use or store as required.

chicken stock

Makes approx. 1.75 litres (3 pints)

Bones from a 1.5 kg (3–3½ lb) uncooked chicken or 450 g (1 lb)
   chicken wings or drumsticks
1 large carrot, chopped
2 celery sticks, sliced
2 leeks, cleaned and sliced
2 fresh or dried bay leaves
2 sprigs of thyme
2.25 litres (4 pints) water

Put all the ingredients into a large pan and bring just to the boil, skimming off any scum from the surface as it appears. Leave to simmer very gently for 2 hours – it is important not to let it boil as this will force the fat from even the leanest chicken and make the stock cloudy.

Strain the stock through a sieve and use as required. If not using immediately, leave to cool, then chill and refrigerate or freeze for later use.

roasted chicken stock

Makes approx. 1.75 litres (3 pints)

450 g (1 lb) chicken wings or drumsticks
2 tablespoons sunflower oil
1 large carrot, chopped
2 celery sticks, sliced
2 leeks, cleaned and sliced
2 bay leaves
2 sprigs of thyme
2.25 litres (4 pints) water

Preheat the oven to 200°C/400°F/Gas Mark 6. Put the chicken wings into a roasting tin and roast them for 45 minutes or until crisp and richly golden. Meanwhile, heat the oil in a large pan, add the carrot, celery and leeks and lightly brown. Transfer the pieces of roasted chicken to the pan and add the herbs. Add some of the water to the roasting tin and place it over a medium heat on top of the stove. Bring to a simmer, rubbing all the caramelized juices from the base of the tin with a wooden spoon, then add to the pan with the rest of the water and leave to simmer very gently for 2 hours.

Strain the stock through a fine sieve and use as required. If not using immediately, leave to cool, then chill and refrigerate or freeze for later use.

beef stock

Makes approx. 1.75 litres (3 pints)

1 kg (2¼ lb) beef marrow bones
1 tablespoon tomato purée
2 tablespoons sunflower oil
2 unpeeled onions, sliced
2 carrots, sliced
2 celery sticks, sliced
2 leeks, cleaned and sliced
1 bay leaf
1 thyme sprig
12 black peppercorns

Preheat the oven to 200°C/400°F/Gas Mark 6. Put the beef bones and tomato purée into a roasting tin and roast them for 45 minutes until well browned.

Meanwhile, heat the oil in a large pan, add the onions, carrot, celery and leeks and lightly brown. Transfer the beef bones to the pan and add the herbs and peppercorns. Add some of the water to the roasting tin and place it over a medium heat on top of the stove. Bring to a simmer, rubbing all the caramelized juices from the base of the tin with a wooden spoon, then add to the pan with the rest of the water and leave to simmer very gently for 4 hours.

Strain the stock through a fine sieve and use as required. If not using immediately, leave to cool, then chill and refrigerate or freeze for later use.

mayonnaise

This recipe includes instructions for making mayonnaise in a liquidizer or by hand. It is lighter when made mechanically because the process uses a whole egg, whereas hand-made mayonnaise is softer and richer. You can use either sunflower oil, olive oil or a mixture of the two if you prefer. It will keep in the fridge for up to 1 week.

Makes 300 ml (10 fl oz)

2 egg yolks (by hand) or 1 egg (liquidizer)
2 teaspoons white wine vinegar
$\frac{1}{2}$ teaspoon salt
1 tablespoon of mustard (optional)
300 ml (10 fl oz) sunflower oil or olive oil

To make the mayonnaise by hand:
Make sure all the ingredients are at room temperature before you start. Put the egg yolks, vinegar, salt and mustard, if using, into a mixing bowl and then rest the bowl on a cloth to stop it slipping. Lightly whisk to break the yolks.

Using a wire whisk, beat the oil into the egg mixture a few drops at a time until you have incorporated it all. Once you have added the same volume of oil as the original mixture of egg yolks and vinegar, you can add the oil a little more quickly.

To make the mayonnaise in a liquidizer:
Put the whole egg, vinegar, salt and mustard, if using, into a liquidizer. Turn on the machine and then slowly add the oil through the hole in the lid until you have a thick emulsion.

clarified butter

Place the required quantity of butter in a small pan and leave it over a very low heat until it has melted. Then skim off any scum from the surface and pour off the clear (clarified) butter into a bowl, leaving behind the milky white solids that will have settled on the bottom of the pan.

beurre manié

Blend equal quantities of softened butter and plain flour together into a smooth paste. Cover and keep in the fridge until needed. It will keep for the same period of time as butter.

roasted red peppers

Roast the pepper in an oven preheated to 220°C/425°F/Gas Mark 7 for 20 minutes, turning once until the skin is black. Seal the pepper in a plastic bag and leave to cool. Then break it in half and remove the stalk, skin and seeds. The flesh is now ready to use.

basic shortcrust pastry

225 g (8 oz) plain flour
$\frac{1}{2}$ teaspoon salt
50g (2 oz) chilled butter, cut into pieces
50g (2 oz) chilled lard, cut into small pieces
$1\frac{1}{2}$–2 tablespoons cold water

rich shortcrust pastry

225 g (8 oz) plain flour
$\frac{1}{2}$ teaspoon salt
65 g ($2\frac{1}{2}$ oz) chilled butter, cut into pieces
65 g ($2\frac{1}{2}$ oz) chilled lard, cut into pieces
$1\frac{1}{2}$–2 tablespoons cold water

For each type of pastry, sift the flour and salt into a food processor or a mixing bowl. Add the pieces of chilled butter and lard and work together until the mixture looks like fine breadcrumbs.

Stir in the water with a round bladed knife until the mixture comes together into a ball, turn out onto a lightly floured work surface and knead briefly until smooth. Roll out on a little more flour and use as required.

directories of producers

A note about the list of producers

This is not a comprehensive guide to all producers and suppliers of good food. The first filter that we applied was that the product should be relevant to the recipes in the book. We have sifted through a list of names and addresses and judged who should be included by reference to the following criteria.

Eggs and cheese Eggs had to be truly free-range, preferably Freedom Foods-accredited, and traditional breeds of hen were a nice bonus. The cheese section was based on the maker or supplier's passion for cheese. If a supplier had a really wide range, or unusual kinds of cheese, or their own maturing rooms, so much the better.

Vegetables and fruit Many – but not all – of the entries are organic producers. The criteria laid down by the Soil Association for certification as an organic producer are sensible rules for producing crops with a better flavour, but I'm not insistent on these. I'm looking for fruit and vegetables from rich, clean soil produced without much recourse to pesticides or chemicals. The suppliers listed are all interested in the varieties they grow, and many experiment endlessly to achieve better and better flavour. Seasonality is important: these people don't try to force things out of the land that won't grow naturally.

Fish The good fishmongers tend to buy from day boats whenever possible. for freshness. They know which boats they like to buy from – they have built relationships with the best fishermen. A lot of the best fish shops hand pick the fish themselves each day, instead of relying on buyers. This does tend to mean that when you talk to an inland fish shop they seem to have less of a connection with the fish they are selling, though this is by no means always the case – Steve Hatt in the Essex Road in North London being a case in point.
I greatly favour undyed smoked fish, mainly because it's much easier to judge quality without the concealing effect of the dye. All the suppliers had a good selection of this.

Poultry and meat I looked for small producers, rearing rare or traditional breeds, with an emphasis on traceability, i.e. information which accompanies the product on where it came from and how and when it was produced and slaughtered, the latter hopefully using local abattoirs. Free-range animals that are slowly matured, without growth promoters, fed on natural feed and hung properly on the bone, produce the best flavour. As with the fruit and vegetables, many listed are organic farmers.

Game I have listed butchers and licensed game dealers who buy from known local shoots and hand pick the produce – again, traceability is the key. People who were vague about the source of their game were rejected.

Special ingredients Here are mail-order companies and delicatessens, chosen either for their range of produce and the fact that many of them stock exciting and unusual food, or because what they sell is otherwise very difficult to find, or has a real regional slant.

CHEESE AND EGGS

Cheese

The Cambridge Cheese Company
All Saints Passage
Cambridge
Cambridgeshire
CB2 3LS
Tel: 01223 565577/328672
Fax: 01223 506177
Website:
www.cheeseshop.co.uk
E-mail:
questions@cheeseshop.co.uk

A cheese shop/deli with a good range of artisan cheeses, Italian deli products and aged vinegars. Mail order available.

The Cheese Shop
116 Northgate Street
Chester
CH1 2HT
Tel: 01244 346240
Fax: 01244 314659

British cheese specialists stocking over 150 different British cheeses. Mail order available.

The Cheese Society
1 St Martins Lane
Lincoln
LN1 2HY
Tel: 01522 511003
Fax: 01522 512114
Website:
www.thecheesesociety.co.uk
E-mail:
cheese@thecheesesociety.co.uk

Huge selection of cheeses available, including Colston Bassett, Yarg, Blue Vinny, Mrs Kirkham's, Stinking Bishop, English Parmesan and Buffalo cheeses. Very informative website. Mail order available.

The Cheesemonger (Iain Mellis)
30a Victoria Street
Edinburgh
EH1 2JW
Tel/Fax: 0131 226 6215

British and Continental cheeses, ripened in Iain Mellis's own maturing rooms. Four branches in Scotland; call for details. Mail order available.

Colston Bassett Dairy Ltd
Harby Lane
Colston Bassett
Nottingham
NG12 3FN
Tel: 01949 81322
Fax: 01949 81132
Website:
www.colstonbassettdairy.com
E-mail:
stilton@colstonbassettdairy.com

Makers of Colston Bassett Stilton. Mail order available.

Cropwell Bishop Creamery
Nottingham Road
Cropwell Bishop
Nottingham
NG12 3BQ
Tel: 0115 989 2350
Fax: 0115 989 9046
Website:
www.cropwellbishopstilton.com
E-mail:
cropwellbishopcreamery@crop
wellbishop.fsnet.co.uk

Award-winning blue Stilton and blue Shropshire cheeses. Cropwell Bishop has won a British Cheese Award every year since 1995. Mail order available.

David Gray
Lynher Farms and Dairy
Netherton
Upton Cross
Liskeard
Cornwall
PL14 5BD
Tel: 01579 363128
Fax: 01579 362666
Website:
www.cornishyarg.co.uk
E-mail:
sales@lynherdairies.co.uk

Cornish yarg and other Cornish soft cheeses by mail order.

Dorset Blue Cheese Co.
Woodbridge Farm
Stock Gaylard
Sturminster Newton
Dorset
DT10 2BD
Tel: 01963 23216
Fax: 01963 23063
Email:
davies.woodbridge@virgin.net

Makers of Dorset Blue Vinny. Mail order available.

The Fine Cheese Co.
29 & 31 Walcot Street
Bath
BA1 5BN
Tel/Fax: 01225 448748
Website: www.finecheese.co.uk
E-mail:
sales@finecheeseco.demon.co.uk

Their product range reads like the list of British Cheese Awards winners. A good range of British cheeses, with some European. The Fine Cheese Co. also sells wines, crackers, biscuits and chocolate. Mail order available.

La Fromagerie
30 Highbury Park
London
N5 2AA
Tel/Fax: 020 7359 7440
Website: www.lafromagerie.co.uk
E-mail: info@lafromagerie.co.uk

British and European cheeses, including Yarg, Colston Bassett, Mrs Kirkham's, and many other artisan cheeses. A good selection of oils, pasta and chocolate. Free deliveries in London for orders over £30; charges vary for overnight delivery to addresses outside London.

Le Grand Fromage
8 East Street
Shoreham by Sea
West Sussex
BN43 5ZE
Tel: 01273 440337
Fax: 01273 440729
Website:
www.legrandefromage.co.uk
E-mail:
sales@legrandfromage.co.uk

British and European cheeses, including Blue Vinny, Colston Bassett, Stinking Bishop; also

Pecorino and Provolone. Mail order available.

Highland Fine Cheese Ltd
Blarliath Farm
Shore Road
Tain
Ross-shire
IV19 1EB
Tel: 01862 892034
Fax: 01862 894289

Suppliers of Crowdie cheese, and other Scottish cheeses. Mail order available, by phone only.

The Horsham Cheese Shop
20 Carfax
Horsham
West Sussex
RH12 1EB
Tel/Fax: 01403 254272
Website:
www.horshamcheeseshop.co.uk
E-mail:
sales@horshamcheeseshop.co.uk

Stocks Blue Vinny, Colston Bassett, Cornish Yarg and many other British cheeses. Mail order available.

The House of Cheese
Church Street
Tetbury
Gloucestershire
GL8 8JG
Tel/Fax: 01666 502865
Website:
www.houseofcheese.co.uk
E-mail:
enquiry@houseofcheese.co.uk

Good range of British and European cheeses, including Cornish Yarg and Dorset Blue Vinny. Mail order available.

Huge Cheese Direct
A37-42,
New Covent Garden Market
Nine Elms Lane
London
SW8 5EE
Tel: 020 7819 6099
Fax: 020 7720 2144
Website:
www.hugecheesedirect.co.uk
E-mail:
adrian.beal@hugecheese.co.uk

Not a huge range of cheeses, but some interesting and unusual

ones. A good range of oils and vinegars, and Valrhona chocolate. Mail order available.

Mousetrap Cheese
Monkland Cheese Dairy
The Pleck
Monkland
Leominster
Herefordshire
HR6 9DB
Tel: 01568 720307
Fax: 01568 720134
Website:
www.mousetrapcheese.co.uk
E-mail:
enquiries@mousetrapcheese.
co.uk

Extensive range of British cheeses. Mail order available, but only for set selections. You can, however, state what value you want your order to be.

Mrs Kirkham's Lancashire Cheese
Beesley Farm
Mill Lane
Goosnargh
Preston
Lancashire

Farm-gate sales available. Also available on-line from many of the suppliers listed.

Neal's Yard Dairy
6 Park Street
Borough Market
London SE1 9AB
Tel: 020 7645 3555
Fax: 020 7645 3564
E-mail:
mailorder@nealsyarddairy.co.uk

Interesting range of cheeses, many from small artisan producers, ripened in their own maturing rooms. Mail order available, but only for set selections of cheeses, from around £30.

Paxton & Whitfield
6 Fosseway Business Park
Moreton in Marsh
Gloucestershire
GL56 9NQ
Tel: 01608 652090
Fax: 01608 650660
Website:
www.cheesemongers.co.uk

# of produce

E-mail:
sales@cheesemongers.co.uk

Small selection of cheese available to buy on-line; much larger selection available in the shops. Mail order available. Paxton & Whitfield shops are located at:

93 Jermyn St
London
SW1Y 6JE
Tel: 020 7930 0259

13 Wood St
Stratford upon Avon
Warwickshire
CV37 6JF
Tel: 01789 415544

1 John St
Bath
Somerset
BA1 2JL
Tel: 01225 466403

Ribblesdale Cheesemakers
Ashes Farm
Settle
North Yorkshire
BD24 0JB
Tel: 01254 820222

Handmade mozzarella from British buffalo milk, available nationwide from September. Phone Adrian on the above number for details of nearest outlet.

Shepherd's Purse Cheeses Ltd
Leachfield Grange
Newsham
Thirsk
North Yorkshire
YO7 4DJ
Tel: 01845 587220
Fax: 01845 587717
Website:
www.shepherdspurse.co.uk
Email:
justin@shepherdspurse.co.uk

Makers of a variety of unusual blue cheeses, using cow, ewe and buffalo milk. Mail order available.

The Teddington Cheese
42 Station Road
Teddington
Middlesex
TW11 9AA
Tel: 020 8940 1944
Fax: 020 8940 2944

Website:
www.teddingtoncheese.co.uk
E-mail:
dougandtony@teddingtoncheese.co.uk

Good range of small-scale production, artisan cheeses, including Mrs Kirkham's. Only sells British cheese. Incredibly knowledgeable and enthusiastic staff. Mail order available.

Eggs

Bank Farm Produce
Bank Farm
Bank Road
Aldington. Ashford
Kent
TN25 7DF
Tel: 0800 5874999
Fax: 01233 721510
Website:
www.bankfarmproduce.co.uk
E-mail:
freerangehens@aol.com

Hens' eggs; also quail, duck and goose eggs, from free-range birds. Accredited by the RSPCA. Suppliers from Bank Farm attend farmers' markets and make delivery rounds in Kent and London. The eggs can also be bought from the farm itself. Suppliers to Michelin-starred restaurants in London.

Clarence Court Ltd
PO Box 37
Broadway
WR12 7YG
Tel: 01386 858007
Website:
www.clarencecourt.co.uk
E-mail:
info@clarencecourt.co.uk

Large commercial supplier, but with a very high level of animal welfare. The traditional British breed hens (Old Cotswold Legbar and Mabel Pearman Burford Brown) are truly free-range, with acres of pasture in which to roam. Accredited by the RSPCA Freedom Foods scheme, and by the Vegetarian Society. Clarence Court aims to revive old British

breeds; breeds that lay large, well-flavoured, interestingly coloured eggs. The eggs arc high density, low water content, and great for baking. Available from Tesco, Waitrose, and Sainsbury.

Clive Fruit Farm
Willingsworth Farmhouse
Upper Hook Road
Upton upon Severn
Worcestershire
WR8 0SA
Tel: 01684 592664

Gather your own free-range eggs! Chickens are free to roam outside, while customers can 'pick their own' eggs from the hen houses, for ultimate freshness. The farm also has a range of pick your own fruit, including apples, pears, plums and soft fruits.

Corrie Mains Farm
Mauchline
Ayrshire
KA5 5DT
Tel: 01290 550338

Isa Brown hens' eggs, and quail, goose and duck eggs, all free-range. Available at Ayr, Edinburgh, Larg, Kilmarnock, Glasgow and Paisley farmers' markets.

Higher Redwood Farm
Golberdon Road
Pensilva
Nr Liskeard
Cornwall
PL14 5RL
Tel/Fax: 01579 363275

Eggs from free-range Black Rock and Speckledy hens in small flocks. Available direct from the farm.

Holmansbridge Farm
Townlittleworth Road
Cooksbridge
Nr Lewes
East Sussex
BN8 4TD
Tel: 01273 400679

Free-range eggs that are RSPCA-accredited and lion coded. Available from the farm shop, or various local outlets; call for details.

Holt Vale Farm Shop
Holt Vale Farm
Holt

Wimborne
Dorset
BH21 7DL
Tel: 01202 881 525.

A farm shop selling only produce from Holt Vale Farm, including eggs from free-range hens. Farm-gate sales only.

Hopyard Farm
Bourne Road
Defford
Worcestershire
WR8 9BS
Tel: 01386 750902
Fax: 01386 751389
Website:
www.hopyardfarm.co.uk
E-mail: philip-earl@hopyardfarm.co.uk

Eggs from small flocks of hens allowed to roam outdoors all day, and fed a natural diet with no hormones or animal by-products. Thirteen local outlets – call or see website for details.

Kintaline Farm Plant & Poultry Centre
Benderloch
Oban
Argyll
PA37 1QS
Tel: 01631 720223
Fax: 01631 720759
Website: www.kintaline.co.uk
E-mail: farm@kintaline.co.uk

Eggs from Black Rock hens allowed to roam outside all day on permanent pasture. Very high level of animal welfare; birds are allowed natural resting and moulting periods. Feed is free from hormones and animal by-products, and is not high in protein (which can taint the eggs with a fishy taste). Also duck eggs and fresh herbs. Available from Fort William and Oban farmers' markets, and farm-gate sales.

The Lakes Free-range Eggs Co.
Stainton
Penrith
Cumbria
CA11 0EE
Tel: 01768 890460
Fax: 01768 892468

RSPCA-accredited, free-range hens' eggs. Available direct from the farm or from local outlets; call for details.

Milton Haugh Farm Shop
Carmyllie
Arbroath
Angus
Tel: 01241 875 364

Free-range hens' and duck eggs. Farm-gate sales only.

Sunny Side Up
Poplar Farm
Tealby Road
Market Rasen
Lincolnshire
LN8 3UL
Tel: 01673 844736
Fax: 01673 849227
E-mail: hammonds@poplar-farm.fsnet.co.uk

Free-range eggs available direct from the farm. The hens can be seen wandering the hillside as you go to buy their eggs.

Wynne's of Dinmore
Hope-under-Dinmore
Herefordshire
HR6 0PX
Tel/Fax: 01568 797314
Website: www.wynnes.co.uk
E-mail: info@wynnes.co.uk

RSPCA-accredited, the hens are allowed to roam freely outside from morning till dusk. Available from Leominster and Hereford farmers' markets, and local outlets; call or see website for details.

Yorkshire Farmhouse Freedom Eggs Ltd
Village Farm
Catton
Thirsk
North Yorkshire
Tel: 01845 577355
Fax: 01845 578666

Eggs from hens that roam freely outside. Available from Yorkshire branches of Sainsbury, Tesco and Morrison (branded as Yorkshire Farmhouse Freedom Eggs).

VEGETABLES, HERBS AND SALADS

Abbey Parks Asparagus
Park Farm
East Heckington,
Boston
Lincolnshire PE20 3QG
Tel: 01205 820722
Website:
www.abbeyparksasparagus.co.uk
E-mail:
info@abbeyparksasparagus.
co.uk

Asparagus and rhubarb, available via mail order and shipped on the day of harvest for ultimate freshness.

The Bell and Bird Table
Runnington
Wellington
Somerset
TA21 0QW
Tel: 01823 663080

47 varieties of tomato – and also soft fruit – grown organically (although not certified by the Soil Association). The tomatoes are old varieties from around the world that are rarely grown – you will find no examples in supermarkets of the 47 varieties grown here. The owner gets seeds from the Henry Doubleday Research Centre and equivalent institutions around the world. Every year in September a tomato tasting is held. This is a tiny smallholding, so call before visiting. Farm-gate sales only.

Borough Market
8 Southwark
London
SE1 1TL
Tel: 020 7407 1002
Fax: 020 7403 9162

Brickyard Farm Shop
Badsworth
Nr Pontefract
West Yorkshire
WF9 1AX
Tel: 01977 617327

Organic home-produced fruit and vegetables, with a range of over 40 different varieties of vegetables, all picked fresh every day. The owner happily admits to being old-fashioned in his farming methods. Farm sales and a box scheme delivering around West Yorkshire.

Chatsworth Farm Shops
Stud Farm
Pilsley
Bakewell
Derbyshire
DE45 1UF
Tel: 01246 583392
Fax: 01246 582514

also:
Elizabeth Street
Belgravia
London SW1 9BP
Tel: 020 7730 3033
Fax: 020 7730 3188
Website: www.chatsworth.org
E-mail:
farmshop@chatsworth.org

These shops sell fresh produce from the Chatsworth estate.

Church Farm Organics
Church Lane
Thurstaston
Merseyside
CH61 0HW
Tel: 0151 648 7838
Fax: 0151 648 9644
Website:
www.churchfarm.org.uk

Organic farm specializing in strawberries and asparagus. Deliveries throughout the Wirral, and farm-shop sales.

Clive Houlder: Mushroom Man
98 West Street
North Creake
Fakenham
Norfolk
NR21 9LH
Tel: 01328 738610

Wild mushrooms from East Anglia and Scotland. Mail order available; call for details.

Coleshill Organics
59 Coleshill
Swindon
Wiltshire
SN6 7PT
Tel/Fax: 01793 861070

Box scheme and farm sales of fruit, herbs and vegetables, including leeks.

Duchy Home Farm Organic Vegetables
Broadfield Farm
Tetbury
Gloucestershire
GL8 8SE
Tel/Fax: 01666 504287

Unusual variety of organic vegetables from the Prince of Wales' estate. Box scheme deliveries within a 10-mile radius; also available at Tetbury, Cirencester and Stroud farmers' markets and Bath Organic Farms (see Poultry suppliers, page 185).

Eddisbury Fruit Farm
Yeld Lane
Kelsall
Cheshire CW6 0TE
Tel: 01829 759157
Website: www.eddisbury.co.uk
E-mail:
m.dykes@btinternet.com

Fresh asparagus, raspberries and other soft fruit, available ready-picked from the farm shop, or pick your own.

Field 2 Kitchen
Wood Hall Farm
Codsall Wood
Wolverhampton WV8 1QR
Tel/Fax: 01902 766601
Website:
www.field2kitchen.co.uk
E-mail:
kjs@woodhallfarm.fsnet.co.uk

Farm shop and box scheme, delivering within a 30-mile radius. Much of the produce is home-grown, supplemented by produce from like-minded local farmers. A key aim is to send the produce out on the day it is harvested. Good range of fruit and vegetables, some organic.

Glendale Salads
19 Upper Fasach
Glendale
Isle of Skye IV55 8WP
Tel/Fax: 01470 511349

Unusual vegetables and salads, herbs and soft fruit, including kale buds, 3 varieties of courgette, mange tout and fine beans, all Soil Association certified. Sold through a box scheme, encompassing a wide area. Call for details.

Gourmet Mushrooms (UK) Ltd.
Morants Farm
Colchester Road
Great Bromley
Essex CO7 7TN
Tel: 01206 231660
Fax: 01206 231660
Website:
www.springfieldmushrooms.
co.uk

At least 20 different varieties of organic mushrooms. Available from many farmers' markets in the region; call for details.

Green Landscape Nurseries
Hurst Lane
Egham
Surrey TW20 8QJ
Tel: 01784 435545

Peppers, aubergines, Borlotti beans and many varieties of tomato, all from Italian seeds and grown without sprays or artificial fertilizers. Many famous restaurants in London buy their vegetables here. Available from the shop only.

Hollow Trees Farm Shop
Semer
Ipswich
IP7 6HX
Tel: 01449 741247
Fax: 01449 741799
Website:
www.hollowtrees.co.uk
E-mail: shop@hollowtrees.co.uk

Home-grown vegetables, home-reared meat, and produce from local small producers, including beer, honey and cream. Winner of the National Farmers' Union 'Best Farm Shop' Award, 2001. This was awarded not just for the quality of produce, but also for Hollow Trees' commitment to the community.

Isle of Wight Garlic
The Garlic Farm
Newchurch
Isle of Wight
PO36 0NR
Tel: 01983 865378
Fax: 01983 862294
Website:
www.garlic-gourmet.com

Farm shop and box scheme, delivering within a 30-mile radius. Much of the produce is home-grown, supplemented by produce from like-minded local farmers. A key aim is to send the produce out on the day it is harvested. Good range of fruit and vegetables, some organic.

Jekka's Herb Farm
Rose Cottage
Shellards Lane
Alveston
Bristol BS35 3SY
Tel: 01454 418878
Fax: 01454 411988
Website:
www.jekkasherbfarm.com
E-mail:
farm@jekkasherbfarm.com

Soil Association-certified organic herbs, sold as seeds or plants. Jekka has won dozens of awards from the Royal Horticultural Society and Chelsea Flower Show. Mail order available: minimum order value is £10 for plants; delivery charge from £7.00.

John Hurd's Organic Watercress
Stonewold
Hill Deverill
Nr Warminster
Wiltshire
BA12 7EF
Tel: 01985 840260
Fax: 01985 841346

Traditionally bunched and grown to maturity for a strong, peppery taste. Available direct from the farm, through the local organic box scheme (call for details), or from Waitrose.

Kingfisher Farm Shop
Guildford Road
Abinger Hammer
Dorking
Surrey
RH5 6QX
Tel: 01306 730703
Fax: 01306 731654

Watercress grown in natural springwater, with no fertilizers or insecticides. Farm-shop sales only.

Lang Meadow Farm Shop
Gardmenstone
Nr Dorchester
Dorset DT2 7AE
Tel: 01300 341779

Organic farm shop; also runs a local box scheme and sells vegetables and fruit from Orgarden Produce, winner of two Soil Association awards in 2000, and winner of best tomato in the Soil Association Awards 1999.

Lenshaw Organic Produce
Upper Lenshaw Farm
Rothienorman
Inverurie
Aberdeenshire AB51 8XU
Tel: 01464 871243
Fax: 01464 871416
E-mail:
jborganics@hotmail.com

Wide range of vegetables; also organic free-range Gloucester Old Spot pork and free-range chicken. Organic, 100 per cent home-produced seasonal vegetable box scheme, delivering within a 40-mile radius.

Lower Turley Farm
Cullompton
Devon EX15 1NA
Tel: 01884 32234

Box scheme and farm-gate sales of organic potatoes and vegetables. Winner of two Soil Association awards in 2001 and two in 2000.

Mrs Tees Wild Mushrooms
Gorse Meadow
Sway Road
Lymington
Hampshire SO41 8LR
Tel: 01590 673354
Fax: 01590 673336
Website:
www.wildmushrooms.co.uk
E-mail:
mrs.tees@wildmushrooms.co.uk

Fresh wild mushrooms from the New Forest and occasionally from the Continent. Mail order available, or from Mrs Tees' stall at Borough Market in London.

Old Spitalfields Organic Market
65 Brushfield Street
London E1 6AA
(near Liverpool Street Station)

Sundays only; full range of organic produce.

The Organic Farm Shop
Abbey Home Farm
Burford Road
Cirencester GL7 5HF
Tel: 01285 640441
Fax: 01285 644827
Website:
www.theorganicfarmshop.co.uk

Incredibly fresh, home-produced organic vegetables and herbs (over 100 varieties of vegetables). The farm has a dedication to strengthening the link between producer and consumer, and is creating an education centre on the farm. Everything is Soil Association certified. Free-range meat is also available. Farm-shop sales only.

Peppers by Post
Sea Spring Farm
Lyme View
West Bexington
Dorchester
Dorset DT2 9DD
Tel: 01308 897892
Fax: 01308 897735
Website:
www.peppersbypost.biz

Wide range of peppers and chillies. Mail order available.

Pumpkin Shed Walled Garden
Llanunwas
Solva
Pembrokeshire
SA62 6TU
Tel: 01437 721949

Vegetables, herbs and some soft fruit, grown biodynamically, though not registered. Good selection – only what is grown in the gardens is sold in the shop, and often vegetables are picked while the customer waits. Herbs will be available via mail order in October; call for details.

Riverford Farm Organic Vegetables
Wash Burn
Buckfastleigh
Devon
TQ11 0LD
Tel: 01803 762720
Fax: 01803 762718

Award-winning organic food producer, supplying fruit and vegetables by box scheme and farm shops (see below). Winner of six awards at the 2001 Soil

Association Awards. Farm shops are located at:

Riverford Farm Shop
Staverton
Devon
TQ9 6AF
Tel: 01803 762523
Fax: 01803 762571

Riverford at Kitley
Yealmpton
Nr Plymouth
Devon
Tel: 01752 880925

Rod and Ben's
Bickham Farm
Kenn
Exeter
Devon
EX6 7XL
Tel: 01392 833833
Fax: 01392 833832
Website: www.rodandbens.com
E-mail:
RodandBen@rodandbens.com

Organic staple vegetables, aubergines, peppers, fresh herbs and honey. The farm is run with a strong commitment to strengthening the connection between food producer and consumer. There are also open days, when customers are asked to come and find out how things are done. Produce is supplied by box scheme (Exeter and Exmouth) or by mail order.

Simply Wild
Scragoak Farm
Brightling Road
Robertsbridge
East Sussex
TN32 5EY
Tel/Fax: 01424 838420
E-mail:enquiries@
simplywildorganics.co.uk

Enormous range of vegetables: Simply Wild aim to offer a selection of varieties of each kind of vegetable, to encourage species diversity. Organic market garden, farm shop and box scheme, encompassing a wide area. Winners of two awards in the Soil Association Awards, 2000.

Test Valley Watercress
Stocks Cottage
Bishops Sutton
Nr. Alresford
Hants
SO24 0AG
Tel: 01962 734943

Tomatoes Direct.com
Main Road
Hale Common
Arreton
Isle of Wight
PO30 3AR

Tel: 01983 861000
Fax: 01983 862103
Website:
www.tomatoesdirect.com
E-mail:
sales@tomatoesdirect.com

Huge range of tomato varieties, including 10 different organically grown varieties, carefully chosen for the perfect balance of sweetness and acid, and grown in near perfect conditions. Ripened on the vine for as long as possible. Mail order available.

West Dean Gardens
West Dean College
West Dean
Chichester
Sussex PO18 0QZ
Tel: 01243 818210
Website: www.westdean.org.uk

Every August the gardens have a chilli fiesta, where you can buy unusual varieties of chillies in plant form to grow at home.

West Lea Farm Shop
Lady Croft
Alresford
Hampshire
SO24 0QP
Tel: 01962 732476

Freshly harvested watercress, available from the farm shop.

FISH

Alfred Enderby Ltd
Fish Dock Road
Grimsby
Lincolnshire
DN31 3NE
Tel/Fax: 01472 342984
Website:
www.alfredenderby.co.uk

Undyed smoked haddock, cod and salmon, smoked the old-fashioned way in a traditional smokehouse. Mail order available.

Andrew Keracher
73, South Street
St Andrews
Fife KY16 9PB
Tel: 01334 472541

Excellent selection of fish from Scottish waters.

Andy Race
The Harbour
Port-of-Mallaig
Inverness-shire
Scotland PH41 4PX
Tel: 01687 462626
Fax: 01687 462060
Website: www.andyrace.co.uk

Wide range of fish from Scottish waters, including wolf fish (rock turbot), mainly from day boats. Also farmed organic salmon; Andy is reluctant to sell wild salmon due to the pressure on stocks. Also undyed smoked fish (whiting, salmon (peat smoked), haddock, prawns and mussels), smoked in traditional kilns. Mail order available.

Argyle Fishmongers
273a Banbury Road
Oxford
OX2 7JF
Tel: 01865 515586

Daily deliveries from Lowestoft, of predominantly British fish from day boats. No mail order.

Bleikers Smoke House Ltd
Unit 88, Glasshouses Mill
Glasshouses
Harrogate
North Yorkshire HG3 5QH
Tel/Fax: 01423 711411
Website: www.bleikers.co.uk
E-mail: info@bleikers.co.uk

Kippers, smoked trout, smoked salmon. The company description of their processing is that 'nothing happens quickly'. Hand-fed salmon from low-density Western Isles sea farms is chosen for a taste and texture close to that of wild salmon. The fish is slow smoked the old-fashioned way, which results in a more moist end product. Bleikers have been awarded a gold and silver medal from the Guild of Fine Foods, and supply to numerous Michelin-starred restaurants. Mail order available.

Browse Seafoods
The Old Market House
The Quay
Brixham
TQ5 8AW
Tel: 01803 852942

Live local crabs and lobsters, or pick your lobster and have it boiled to order. Full range of local wet fish, too. No mail order.

Butley Orford Oysterage
Market Hill
Orford
Woodbridge
Suffolk IP12 2LH
Tel: 01394 450277
Fax: 01394 450949

Pacific oysters and fresh fish (including cod, skate, dover sole, brill and sea bass) caught by boats belonging to the shop; also smoked fish. No mail order.

Coakley-Green
Stall 41c
The Market
Oxford Street
Swansea
SA1 3PF
Tel: 01792 653416

Huge range of local fish from day boats, with an emphasis on freshness. The staff are very knowledgeable. No mail order.

The Company Shed
129 Coast Road
West Mersea
Colchester
Essex CO5 8PA
Tel: 01206 382700 (shop)
Fax: 01206 382284 (and mail order phone number)
E-mail:
caz@companyshed.fsnet.co.uk

Pacific and Native oysters available, harvested locally by a family who have been farming and selling oysters for six generations. No mail order.

Creelers of Arran
Home Farm
Arran
Argyll
KA27 8DD
Tel/Fax: 01770 302797

Lobsters from Argyll, available from the fish shop next to the seafood restaurant. All lobsters are from local waters and caught from the shop's own boat. No mail order.

Cross of York
3 & 4 Newgate Market
York
Yorkshire
YO1 2LA
Tel: 01904 627590

Fish from day boats landing at Scarborough and Whitby; also sea-farmed salmon from Scotland. The shop receives fresh fish two or three times a day. Winners of the Seafish Industry 'Best Fishmonger in Northern England' award. No mail order.

Crowe Fishmongers
No. 3 Provisional Market
Gentleman's Walk
Norwich
NR2 1ND
Tel: 01603 767411

A wide variety (40–50 kinds) of local fresh fish from Lowestoft, bought from day boats.

Direct Fish
High Street Market
Arndale Centre
High Street
Manchester
M4 2EB
Tel: 0161 832 8908

Wide range of fish to supply the diverse cultural mix that makes up Manchester. Lots of fish from north-west waters, from day boats; also warm water, Mediterranean whole fish. Wild salmon and wild sea bass are available, although Direct Fish say that the quality of farmed fish has improved lately and is worth a try. No mail order.

Donnington Fish Farm
Upper Swell
Nr Stow-on-the-Wold
Gloucestershire
GL54 1EP
Tel: 01451 830873

Brown trout and Rainbow trout from pure spring-water ponds. Brown trout takes twice as long to mature as Rainbow, which is why not many people sell it commercially, but it is available (with 1 day's notice – they have to find and catch it!) from Donnington Fish Farm. No mail order.

The Duchy of Cornwall Oyster Farm
Port Navas
Falmouth
Cornwall
TR11 5RJ
Tel: 01326 340210

Native and Pacific oysters. No mail order, but available from Martin's Seafresh (see below).

Eddie's Seafood Market
7, Roseneath Street
Edinburgh
EH9 1JH
Tel: 0131 229 4207
Fax: 0131 229 9339

Amazing range of unusual fish, including shark and octopus.

Fish at the Square
2 St Georges Road
Brighton
BN2 1EB
Tel: 01273 680808

Run by an ex-fisherman, and selling locally caught fresh fish, all from day boats. Nigel Sayers, the owner, is keen to encourage people to try fish with less pressurized stocks. His wife, Freia, makes a range of home-cooked fish products which are sold in the shop. No mail order.

Fishworks
6 Green Street
Bath
BA1 2JY
Tel/Fax: 01225 447794

Fish sourced from Cornwall and Scotland. The company have built up a relationship with many fishermen, and know which boats bring in the best fish. They stock 40-50 varieties of fish, and the staff in the shop are also chefs, who can advise on preparation and cooking. Also branches in Bristol (tel: 0117 974 4433) and Christchurch, Dorset (tel: 01202 487000).

Fortunes
22, Henrietta Street
Whitby
YO22 4DW
Tel: 01947 601659

Traditionally smoked kippers. No mail order

Fowey Fish
37 Fore Street
Fowey
Cornwall
PL23 1AH
Tel: 01726 832422
Fax: 01726 832887
Website: www.foweyfish.com
E-mail: buyfish@foweyfish.com

Good range of local Cornish fresh fish from Looe Fish Market or the boats that land at Fowey – fish from day boats is always chosen. Smoked fish is also available. Mail order available.

Frank Greenslade Ltd
Fish Market
New Quay Road
Poole
BH15 4AF
Tel: 01202 672199
Fax: 01202 667313

Most fish sold at Frank Greenslade Ltd is from the local waters around Bournemouth, from day boats. The range of fish available includes lobster, scallops and oysters, as well as wet fish. No mail order.

H. Forman & Son
6/14 Queensyard
Whitepost Lane
London
E9 5EN
Tel: 020 8985 0378
Fax: 020 8985 0180
Website: www.formans.co.uk
E-mail: info@formans.co.uk

One of the oldest smoking houses in the country, smoking wild salmon to a 1905 recipe. Described as 'sensational' by The Times. Mail order available.

Inverawe Smokehouses
Taynuilt
Argyll
PA35 1HU
Website: www.smokedsalmon.co.uk
Tel: 01866 822446

Trout and salmon, smoked slowly (for around 48 hours) over oak logs in a traditional brick smokehouse, without artificial colours or additives.

Isle of Skye Seafood Ltd.
Broadford Industrial Estate
Broadford
Isle of Skye
IV49 9AP
Tel: 01471 822135
Fax: 01471 822138
Website: www.skye-seafood.co.uk
E-mail: sales@skye-seafood.co.uk

Shellfish (including lobster and langoustines) from the clean waters around Skye; also smoked salmon. Mail order available.

John's Fish Shop
5 East Street
Southwold
Suffolk
IP18 6EH
Tel/Fax: 01502 724253
Website: www.johns-fish-shop.co.uk
E-mail: john@johns-fish-shop.co.uk

Owned and run by an ex-fisherman. Aiming to offer the largest range of fish possible, John buys from Southwold Harbour and Lowestoft Market, mainly from day boats. John hand picks the fish himself every morning. Winner of 13 Seafish Industry Authority awards. No mail order.

Ken Watmough
29 Thistle Street
Aberdeen
AB10 1UY
Tel: 01224 640321
Fax: 01224 315983

Ken buys his fish every morning from Aberdeen Market. He knows the schedule of landings, and knows whose boats he wants fish from – who follows good practices on the boat and looks after the fish. Can supply wolf fish, wild salmon, wild sea bass and turbot, scallops and lobster. Mail order available.

The Lobster Store
34 Shoregate
Crail
KY10 3SU
Tel: 01333 450476

Fresh lobsters and crabs from local waters.

Loch Fyne Oysters Ltd
Clachan
Clairndow
Argyll
PA26 8BL
Tel: 01499 600264
Fax: 01499 600234
Website: www.lochfyne.com
E-mail: info@lochfyne.com

Smoked salmon, haddock and trout; pickled herring, kippers and smoked eel; oysters from their own oyster beds, langoustines, mussels and scallops. The fish is chosen carefully from suppliers who operate sustainably, and organically if possible. Mail order available.

Loaves and Fishes
52 The Thoroughfare
Woodbridge
Suffolk
IP12 1AL
Tel: 01394 385650

Fantastic fish shop/grocer/deli. Wet, loose walnuts in season, some local, some from France; also a great selection of fish and local produce. No mail order.

McCallum's of Troon
944 Argyle Street
Glasgow
G3 8YJ
Tel: 0141 204 4456
Fax: 0141 204 4466

Huge range of exotic fish, but also lots of fish from local waters, including live lobsters, oysters, mussels and scallops.

Martin's Seafresh
St Columb Business Centre
Barn Lane
St Columb Major
Cornwall
TR9 6BU
Tel: 0800 027 2066
Website: www.martins-seafresh.co.uk
E-mail: sales@martins-seafresh.co.uk

Run by an ex-fisherman of 30 years standing, and supplying fresh Cornish fish, lobster, mussels and oysters (from the Duchy of Cornwall Oyster Farm). Fish from day boats is predominantly used, with a dedication to quality. Mail order available.

Matthew Stevens & Son
Back Road East
St Ives
Cornwall
TR26 1NW
Tel: 01736 799392
Fax: 01736 799441

Website: www.mstevensandson.com

Good range of Cornish wet fish and shellfish from Newlyn and St Ives. Mail order available.

Minola Smoked Products
Triley Mill
Abergavenny
Monmouthshire
NP7 8DE
Tel: 01873 736900
Fax: 01873 736909
Website: www.minola-smokery.com
E-mail: sales@minola-smokery.com

Enormous range of smoked produce, including unusual items like smoked vegetables, butter and salt. Mail order available.

Phil Bowditch
7 Bath Place
Taunton
Somerset
TA1 4ER
Tel: 01823 253500
Fax: 01823 421875
Website: www.philbowditch.co.uk

Fish from Brixham market, usually from day boats. Imports almost nothing – Phil is a firm believer that British fish is best. No mail order.

Quayside Fish Centre
The Harbourside
Porthleven
Cornwall TR13 9JU
Tel: 01326 562008
Fax: 01326 574386
Website: www.quaysidefish.co.uk (under construction)
E-mail: enquiries@quaysidefish.co.uk

Holders of 'Britains Best Fishmonger' award from Seafish Industries. They buy their fish only from day boats or inshore boats – no netted fish, only line caught, and all Cornish fish landed at Newlyn. A large range of fish, including wolf fish (known as catfish). Mail order available.

Richard & Julie Davies' Fish Shop
7 Garden Street
Cromer
Norfolk NR27 9HN
Tel: 01263 512727
Fax: 01263 514789

Local crab, said to be the sweetest tasting crab in the UK. Also available is a range of other wet fish and lobster, caught by Richard and his son in local waters. No mail order.

River Exe Shellfish Farms Ltd.
Lyson
Kenton, Exeter
Devon
EX6 8EZ
Tel: 01626 890133
Fax: 01626 891789
E-mail: David@resf.fsnet.co.uk
Fresh Pacific oysters, delivered overnight (prices include delivery cost).

Robertson's Prime
Unit 1D,
Willowtree Industrial Estate
Alnwick
Northumberland
NE66 2HA
Tel: 01665 604386
Fax: 01665 604386

A good selection of local fish from the nearby port of Amble, all from day boats, some line caught. Ian Robertson hand picks the fish for his shop every day, including local lobsters and oysters from Lindisfarne. Mail order for smoked fish only.

Salar Ltd
Lochcarnon
South Uist
Outer Hebrides
Scotland HS8 5PD
Tel: 01870 610324
Fax: 01870 610369
Website: www.salar.co.uk

Award-winning hot smoked salmon, given to Tony Blair on the opening of the Scottish parliament. The salmon is farmed on-site. Mail order available.

Severn & Wye Smokery
Chaxhill
Westbury on Severn
Gloucestershire
GL14 1QW
Tel: 01452 760190
Fax: 01452 760193
E-mail:
Shirley@severnandwye.co.uk

Traditionally smoked, hand-processed wild salmon; also smoked Glenarm salmon from a salmon farm in Northern Ireland. This farm has larger enclosures and lower stocking densities, so the salmon are healthier and more muscular, with a gamier flavour. Mail order available.

Shellwest Scotland Ltd
The Oyster Farm
Loch Nell Estate
Benderloch
By Oban
Argyll
PA37 1QU
Tel: 01631 720392

Mussels, live langoustines, wild salmon, crabs, lobsters and oysters, all from the clean west-coast waters around Oban.

Steve Hatt
88-90 Essex Road
Islington
London
N1 8LU
Tel/Fax: 020 7226 3963

Campaigner for UK fishing rights and quality fish within the UK. Can get hold of almost any fish you want. Stock comes from Billingsgate Market, from day boats. The company buying policy is to always buy on quality, never on price. No mail order.

Summer Isles Foods
Achiltibuie
Ross-shire
Scotland
IV26 2YR
Tel: 01854 622353
Fax: 01854 622335
Website:
www.summerislesfoods.com
E-mail:
sifsalmo@globalnet.co.uk

Smoked haddock, kippers, smoked sea bass, smoked eels, almost all from local Scottish waters. Oak shavings are used for a slow burn, which results in a sweeter flavour. The smoked salmon is slowly marinated in rum, molasses, juniper and garlic for an unusual flavour. Mail order available.

Swallow Fish Ltd
2 South Street
Seahouses
Northumberland
NE68 7RB
Tel: 01665 721052
Fax: 01665 721177
Website:
www.swallowfish.co.uk
E-mail:
wilkin@swallowfish.co.uk

Smoked haddock, cod and wild salmon, traditionally smoked without additives or colourings in a 19th-century smokehouse. Haddock and cod are from local waters. Mail order available.

Trafalgar Fisheries
Barford Fish Farm
Dourton
Wiltshire SP5 3QF
Tel: 01725 510448
Fax: 01725 511165
Website: www.trafish.com
E-mail: info@trafish.com

Farmed brown trout that are treated as wild fish – very low-density stocking, organically reared, and no artificial colouring

(the flesh is white). Available from most branches of Waitrose; each fish is tagged as organic. No mail order.

The Whitstable Shellfish Company
Westmeads Road
Whitstable
Kent CT5 1LW
Tel: 01227 282375
Fax: 01227 282379
Website: www.whitstable-shellfish.co.uk
E-mail: Phillp.Guy@whitstable-shellfish.co.uk

Scottish Rock oysters from the west coast of Scotland, available all year and transported live, and Whitstable Native oysters, harvested from wild beds in Whitstable Bay from September to April. The owner says that the Scottish oysters taste fresh and salty with a hint of cucumber, while the Natives have a mineral taste not unlike rusty nails! He says that connoisseurs always go for the Natives. Mail order available.

William's Kitchen
3 Fountain Street
Nailsworth
Gloucestershire
GL6 0BL
Tel: 01453 835507
Website:
www.williamskitchen.co.uk
E-mail:
food@williamskitchen.co.uk

Incredibly fresh fish from British ports. The fish comes from Cornwall, from day boats only, and from a few trusted suppliers; the shellfish comes from west-coast Scotland. All produce must meet exacting criteria before it is stocked in William's Kitchen: it has to be of the highest quality, and preferably unusual or interesting; in short, it has to be special, which includes the fish, the fruit and veg, and the deli products. No mail order.

Wing of St Mawes
4 Warren Road
Indian Queens
St Columb
Cornwall TR9 6TL
Tel: 01726 861666
Fax: 01726 861668
Website: www.cornish-seafood.co.uk
E-mail: admin@cornish-seafood.co.uk

Fresh Cornish fish from day boats. Staffed by experienced fishmongers who can prepare fish in any way required. Mail order available; Wing of St Mawes endeavour to have your fish with

POULTRY

Anne & Michael Moorhouse
Cefn Goleu
Pont Robert
Meifod
SY22 6JN
Tel: 01938 500128

Soil Association-certified farm selling organic, free-range turkeys which are hung properly before dressing. Large range of breeds: Norfolk Black, Bronze, Bourbon Red, Buff, Slate/Blue, Pied/Royal Palm and Nebraskan, all bred for a particularly gamey flavour. Call for details of outlets.

Aubrey Allen Direct
108 Warwick Street
Leamington
Warwickshire
CV32 4QP
Tel: 01926 315464
Fax: 01926 425119
Website www.aubreyallen.co.uk

Long-established family business. Whole guinea fowl and guinea-fowl supremes, whole Gressingham duck and breasts, free-range, slow-matured, corn-fed chickens; also a full range of meats, including free-range pork and Cornish lamb. Mail order available.

Barrow Boar
Fosters Farm
South Barrow
Yeovil
Somerset
BA22 7LN
Tel: 01963 440315
Fax: 01963 440901
Website:
www.barrowboar.co.uk

Guinea fowl available via mail order. Barrow Boar also supply Aberdeen Angus, Hebridean lamb, bison, venison, wild boar, kid, pigeon, wild rabbit, pheasant and partridge. Meat is sourced locally as much as possible.

Bath Organic Farms
6 Brookside House
High Street
Weston
Bath
BA1 4BY
Tel: 01225 421507

Fax: 01225 444436
Website:
www.bathorganicfarms.co.uk
E-mail:
robinsonp@btconnect.com

Soil Association-certified, organic, free-range chickens; also beef from the farm's own herd, and lamb and mutton from their own flock (hung properly). All other produce comes from organic farms within a 25-mile radius of Bath. Mail order available.

The Cornish Smoked Fish Company
Charlestown
St Austell
Cornwall
PL25 3NY
Tel: 01726 72356
Fax: 01726 72360
Website:
www.cornishsmokedfish.co.uk
E-mail:
cornishsmokedfish@cornwall-county.com

Great range of traditionally smoked duck, chicken and fish. Mail order available.

The Cotswold Gourmet
The Butts Farm
South Cerney
Gloucestershire
Tel/Fax: 01285 862224
Website:
www.cotswoldgourmet.com
E-mail:
goodfood@cotswoldgourmet.com

Free-range, traditionally slow-reared, dry-plucked chickens; also poussins, Gressingham ducks and black pudding. The Cotswold Gourmet offer rare-breed meats: 6 different breeds of cattle, 4 breeds of pig and 10 breeds of lamb – the website explains the taste variations of each. The company has a real feel for the heritage of British farming, and makes no apology when meats are out of season. Mail order available.

The Ellel Free Range Poultry Co.
The Stables
Ellel Grange
Galgate, Nr Lancaster
Lancashire
LA2 0HN
Tel: 01524 751200
Fax: 01524 752648
Website:
www.ellelfreerangepoultry.co.uk
E-mail:
info:ellelfreerangepoultry.co.uk

Free-range, slow-matured poultry, fed a rich, natural diet. All are reared with attention to animal welfare, with an end result of excellent texture and flavour.

Chickens are raised to 13 weeks (supermarket birds are raised to 6 weeks) and hung after slaughter. Mail order available.

English Natural Foods
Wormbridge Court
Wormbridge
Hereford
HR2 9EN
Tel: 01981 570767
Fax: 01981 570577
Website:
www.englishnaturalfoods.co.uk
E-mail:
sales@englishnaturalfoods.
co.uk

Award-winning free-range Trelough ducks, chickens and guinea fowl, from breeds that the owner, Barry Clark, has developed himself. The ducks are bred for flavour and a high meat-to-carcase ratio, and are less fatty than most mass-produced breeds. All the birds are reared without hormones, growth promoters or antibiotics. Also available are duck livers, duck fat and game birds in season. Mail order available.

G. G. Sparkes
24 Old Dover Road
Blackheath
London
SE3 7BT
Tel/Fax: 0208 355 8597
E-mail:
orders@ggsparkesorganic
butchers.com

A high-class butcher offering a full range of quality poultry and meat, including organic (Soil Association-certified), free-range Devon Red chickens. G. G. Sparkes has a policy of paying farmers a fair price to promote a sustainable rural economy. Free delivery is available within London and the home counties, subject to a minimum order.

Goodman's Geese
Goodman's Brothers
Walsgrove Farm
Great Witley
Worcester
WR6 6JJ
Tel: 01299 896272/896362
Fax: 01229 896889
Website:
www.goodmansgeese.co.uk
E-mail:
info@goodmansgeese. co.uk

Free-range geese and Bronze turkeys fed on grasses, corn and straw, without additives or growth promoters. Mail order available.

Great Grove Poultry
Whews Farm
Caston

Attleborough
Norfolk
NR17 1BS
Tel: 01953 483216
Fax: 01953 483808
E-mail:
great.grove.poultry@virginnet.
co.uk

Free-range chickens available all year; free-range Bronze turkeys and geese available at Christmas. Call for details of outlets.

Higher Hacknell Farm
Burrington
Umberleigh
Devon
EX37 9LX
Tel: 01769 560909
Website:
www.higherhacknell.co.uk
E-mail:
enquiries@higherhacknell.co.uk

Soil Association winners of 'Producer of the Year' Award, 1998. Free-range, organic chickens are sold by the box; also available are organic beef and lamb boxes. Mail order available.

Highland Geese
Corranmor Farm
Ardfern
By Loch Gilphead
Argyll
PA31 8QN
Tel: 01852 500609
Website:
www.highlandgeese.co.uk
E-mail:
corranmorhouse@aol.com

Free range geese from the farm's own laying stock, grass and grain fed. Available oven ready and fresh for Christmas, frozen for Easter. Mail order available.

Holly Tree Farm Shop
Chester Road
Tabley
Knutsford
Cheshire
WA16 0EU
Tel: 01565 651835

Free-range, grass- and corn-fed geese and ducks. Fresh geese available from Michaelmas to Christmas, frozen at all other times of the year. The farm is run in a traditional manner, with a strong ethos of respect for the environment and the animals. Ducks are not always available, as the farmer, Karol Bailey, insists on resting the land properly after a flock has grazed on it. Poultry are slaughtered on-site to reduce stress. The farm shop also sells free-range rare-breed pork (Saddleback and Gloucester Old Spot) and traditional lamb, sourced from local farms. The

criteria for the meat in the shop is that it must have been born, reared and finished on the same farm, and slaughtered at a local abattoir to minimise stress and travelling distance. All meat is fully traceable. Mail order available.

K. J. Eve
9 Corner House Parade
Epsom Road
Ewell
Epsom
Surrey
KT17 1NX
Tel/Fax: 0208 393 3043
Website: www.kjeve.co.uk

Organically fed, traditionally reared (no routine antibiotics; no growth promoters), free-range British Kelly chickens, all sourced from one local farm. Chickens are hung before sale. This Q Guild butcher also offers free-range pork and beef from Orkney. Free delivery is provided within the local area (within 15 to 20 miles); mail order available for the rest of the UK.

Kelly Turkey Farms
Springate Farm
Bicknacre Road
Danbury
Essex
CM3 4EP
Tel: 01245 223581
Fax: 01245 226124
Website:
www.kelly-turkeys.com
E-mail: info@kelly-turkeys.com

Organic, free-range chickens and turkeys, traditionally reared and slow growing. Dry-plucked by hand and hung for around 10 days – no mechanical processing. Turkeys are Bronze and organic Bronze (Christmas only), and won 'Best of British Speciality Produce' in the 1997 BBC Good Food Awards. Mail order available.

Lancashire Geese
Norman A. Lea Ltd
Tower View
Blindmans Lane
Ormskirk
Lancashire
L39 3AD
Tel: 01695 572023
Fax: 01695 581112

Free-range, grass-fed geese, traditionally reared with no growth hormones or antibiotics. Mail order available (seasonal).

Larkworthy Farm
Petrockstowe
Okehampton
Devon
EX20 3HQ
Tel: 01837 810691

Soil Association-certified farm selling organic, free-range poultry. Larkworthy sell at Taunton, Bovey Tracey, Crediton and Bridgewater farmers' markets and local outlets; call for details. Also available from Marshford Organic Produce (see below).

M. Feller, Son and Daughter Organic Butchers
54-55, The Oxford Covered Market
Oxford
OX1 3DY
Tel: 01865 251164
Website: www.mfeller.co.uk
E-mail: mfeller@mfeller.co.uk

A Soil Association-certified butcher, selling organic, free-range chicken, and organic beef, lamb, pork, bacon and sausages. Free local delivery if order value is over £15.

Marshford Organic Produce
Churchill Way
Northam
Nr Bideford
Devon
EX39 1NS

also:
Butchers Row
Barnstaple
Devon
EX31 3BB
Tel: 01237 477160
Website: www.marshford.co.uk
E-mail:
enquiries@marshford.co.uk

Organic shops selling Soil Association-certified produce, including free-range chickens and (sometimes) ducks from Larkworthy Farm (see above). Suppliers of their own organic fruit and vegetables, and an outlet for small, local organic farms. Delivery service offered throughout North Devon; call for details.

Owls Barn
Derritt Lane
Sopley
Christchurch
Dorset
BH23 7AZ
Tel/Fax: 01425 672239
Website: www.owlsbarn.com
E-mail: shop@owlsbarn.com

Farm shop selling free-range chickens, Poll Dorset sheep, which lamb in autumn, and Llanwenog sheep, which lamb in spring. Most produce is Soil Association-certified. No mail order. Produce is sold direct from the farm, or through Sunnyfields (see opposite page).

Peele's
Peele & Partners
Rookery Farm
Thuxton
Norwich
Norfolk NR9 4QJ
Tel: 01362 850237

Free-range Norfolk Black turkeys, slow-matured and reared in a traditional way. The turkeys are fed on home-grown wheat, barley and field beans. The farm also has a small flock of geese. Mail order available.

Providence Farm
Crosspark Cross
Holsworthy
Devon EX22 6JW
Tel/Fax: 01409 254421
Website:
www.providencefarm.co.uk
E-mail:
info@providencefarm.co.uk

Free-range, organic guinea fowl, ducks and chickens. Providence Farm was the Soil Association award winner for pork, duck and guinea fowl, 2001. Mail order available.

Richard Waller
Longrove Wood Farm
234 Chartridge Lane
Chesham
Buckinghamshire
HP5 2SG
Tel: 01494 772744
E-mail: aylesburydux@aol.com

Supplier of free-range Aylesbury ducks. Mail order available.

Seldom Seen Farm
Billesdon
Leicestershire
LE7 9FA
Tel: 0116 259 6742
Fax: 0116 259 6626

Free-range, slow-matured geese, not killed until 24–26 weeks. Fed on home-grown corn. Mail order available.

Sheepdrove Organic Farm
Warren Farm
Office Sheepdrove
Lambourne
Berkshire
RG17 7UU
Tel: 01488 71659
Fax: 01488 72677
Website: www.sheepdrove.com
E-mail:
andy_nash@sheepdrove.com

Free-range, organic chickens, matured to 12 weeks to give more flavour. The birds are strong and healthy due to the acreage available for them to range on. Free-range ducks, sourced from a local organic farm, are often *available, and Sheepdrove also produce organic, free-range pork, organic beef and lamb. Sheepdrove practise a high level of animal welfare and environmental conservation, with rough grass field margins and 11 miles of newly planted traditional hedgerows supporting a range of wildlife. They are also hosts of the Barn Owl Conservation Network. Mail order available (no farm gate sales). Local orders (within 40 miles) are delivered by Sheepdrove's own van free of charge.*

Somerset Farm Shop
Bittescombe Manor
Upton
Wiveliscombe
Taunton
Somerset TA4 2DA
Tel: 01398 371387
Fax: 01398 371413
Website:
www.somersetfarmdirect.co.uk
E-mail:
deawood@btinternet.com

Free-range chickens and Aylesbury X ducks, reared on natural feed without hormones or growth promoters. Also available is local Exmoor lamb. Mail order available.

Sunnyfields
Jacobs Gutter Lane
Totton
Southampton
SO40 9FX
Tel: 02380 871408
Fax: 02380 871146
Website:
www.sunnyfields.co.uk
E-mail:
orders@sunnyfields.co.uk

Sells Owls Barn produce (see above, left) direct from the shop, and also offer a wide ranging delivery service, which includes Bournemouth and London. Delivery charges from £2.

The Weald Smokery
Mount Farm
Flimwell
East Sussex
TN5 7QL
Tel: 01580 879601
Fax: 01580 879564
Website:
www.wealdsmokery.co.uk
E-mail:
info@wealdsmokery.co.uk

Hand-prepared, traditionally smoked fish and meat, with no artificial preservatives or colours. Weald Smokery won both the 2000 and 2001 'Great Taste' Award (from the Guild of Fine Food Retailers) for its smoked duck breasts. Mail order available.

W. E. Botterill & Son
Lings View Farm
10 Middle Street
Croxton Kerrial
Grantham
NG32 1QP
Tel/Fax: 01476 870394

Free-range geese and Bronze turkeys; also pheasants and partridges available seasonally. Available through farm-gate sales and local butchers; call for details.

Welsh Haven Products
Whitegates
Little Haven
Haverfordwest
Pembrokeshire
SA62 3LA
Tel: 01437 781552
Fax: 01437 781386
Website:
www.welshhaven.co.uk
E-mail: welshhaven@aol.com

Organic, free-range chicken and turkey over the Christmas period only. Farm-gate sales and some local outlets; call for details.

Woodlands Farm
Kirton House
Kirton
Boston
Lincolnshire
PE20 1JD
Tel: 01205 722491
Fax: 01205 722905
Website:
www.woodlandsfarm.co.uk
E-mail:
info@woodlandsfarm.co.uk

Free-range Original Bronze turkeys, with access to large paddocks at all times, and slaughtered on-site to limit stress. Mail order available, and suppliers from Woodlands Farm also attend seven Lincolnshire farmers' markets.

MEAT AND OFFAL

Ardalanish Farm
Bunessan
Isle of Mull
PA67 6DR
Tel: 01681 700265

Highland beef, Hebridean lamb and mutton, available from the farm gate, or delivered locally.

A. S. Portwine & Sons
24 Earlham St
London
WC2H 9LN
Tel: 0207 836 2353
Fax: 0207 813 0313

Highly respected old-fashioned, traditional butcher, selling a good selection of free-range, rare-breed and organic meats. No mail order.

Bumpy Lane Organics
Shortlands
Druidston
Haverfordwest
Pembrokeshire
SA62 3NE
Tel: 01437 781234
Website: www.bumpylane.co.uk
E-mail:
sales@bumpylane.co.uk

Organic, rare-breed lamb and beef, including White Faced Woodland, Grey Face Dartmoor and Kerry Hill sheep and White Park cattle. Animals graze on coastal pasture, giving a very specific flavour. Mail order available. Delivery is free within Pembrokeshire. Suppliers from Bumpy Lane also attend Haverfordwest and Fishguard farmers' markets.

C. Lidgate
110 Holland Park Avenue
London
W11 4AU
Tel: 0207 727 8243

Meat is either free range and/or organic. Some is sourced from the Highgrove and Gatcombe Royal estates. Game is also available in season. Mail order available.

C. H. Wakeling Ltd
41 Farncombe St
Godalming
Surrey
GU7 3LH
Tel/Fax: 01483 417557
Website: www.wakelings.co.uk
E-mail: info@wakelings.co.uk

Aberdeen Angus beef from a local farm – a herd that has never been affected by BSE. The animals are fed on unfertilized, unsprayed pasture, given no hormones, no GM food, no growth promoters and no routine antibiotics. Organic veal is also available. All local produce, with full traceability. The farm has countryside stewardship. Mail order available.

Chesterton Farm Shop
Off Chesterton Lane
Cirencester
Gloucestershire
GL7 6JP
Tel: 01285 642160

Large range of traditional British and rare-breed meats. Accredited by the Rare Breeds Survival Trust, Chesterton Farm Shop has a policy of full traceability. The shop also supplied the ham that was cooked in Kevin Minchew's perry (see page 92). Mail order available.

Cowmans Famous Sausage Shop
13 Castle Street
Clitheroe
Lancashire
BB7 2BT
Tel: 01200 423842
Fax: 01254 822611
Website: www.cowmans.co.uk

Huge range of sausages (60 varieties) from fifth-generation butcher, made using British meat. Mail order available.

The Cured Pig
Corachie Farm
Taynuilt
Oban
Argyll
PA35 1HY
Tel: 01866 822564

Tamworth free-range pork, sausages and bacon, slow-matured for 7 months for a dark, firm meat. Mail order available.

Curtis of Lincoln
Long Leys Road
Lincoln
LN1 1DX
Tel: 01522 527212
Fax: 01522 534669

Long-established Lincolnshire butcher, famous for Lincolnshire Chine. Mail order available.

Dairy Barn Farm Shop
North Houghton
Stockbridge
Hampshire
SO20 6LF
Tel/Fax: 01264 811405
Website: www.dairybarn.co.uk
E-mail: dairybarnshop@aol.com

Meat from a wide range of traditional British and rare breeds – Dexter, White Park, Belted Galloway and Highland cattle, Saddleback and Gloucester Old Spot pigs, and Portland and South Downs lambs. The farming is non-intensive, on unfertilized, herb-rich pasture. No growth hormones or antibiotics are used. Most meat comes from the farm's

own animals; some comes from other local farms who use the same farming ethics and techniques. All meat is fully traceable. Mail order available.

Denhay Farms Ltd
Broadoak
Bridport
Dorset
DT6 5NP
Tel: 01308 458963/422770
Fax: 01308 424846
Website: www.denhay.co.uk
E-mail: sales@denhay.co.uk

Award-winning air-dried hams, dry-cured bacon and gammon, including 3 awards from the Great Taste Awards 2001, and 5 awards from West Country Food Awards 2001. Denhay also make award-winning cheeses. Mail order available.

Donald Russell Direct
Harlaw Road
Inverurie
Aberdeenshire
AB51 4FR
Tel: 01467 629666
Fax: 01467 629434
Website:
www.donaldrusselldirect.com
E-mail:
info@donaldrusselldirect.com

Royal Warrant holder and supplier of award-winning meat from Scottish farms, including Aberdeen Angus, Black Face lamb, and free-range pork, all tradtionally reared and slowly matured on the bone. Game available in season, as well as smoked salmon, langoustine and scallops from Scottish waters. Mail order available.

Dove's
71, Northcote Road
London
SW11 6PJ
Tel: 0207 223 5191
Fax: 0207 801 0627
Email: doveandson@aol.com

Slow matured meat, including Aberdeen Angus beef, from trusted, named farms. Some free range and organic. Dove's operate a policy of fairly trading with farmers on price.

Eastbrook Farms Organic Meat
Bishopstone
Swindon
Wiltshire SN6 8PW
Tel: 01793 790340
Website:
www.helenbrowningorganics.co.uk
E-mail:
info@helenbrowningorganics.co.uk

Large company that upholds stringent levels of animal welfare. Most of the meat, which includes beef, veal, pork, lamb and free-range chicken, comes from Eastbrook's own stocks, although when necessary extra stock is sourced from local Soil Association-certified farms. Mail order available.

Eastwoods of Berkhamsted
15 Gravel Path
Berkhamsted
Hertfordshire HP4 2EF
Tel: 01442 865012
Fax: 01442 877212
Website:
www.eastwoodsofberkhamsted.
co.uk

Winner of the Q Guild of Butchers 'Top Shop' Award for 2001, this butcher operates with an emphasis on high animal welfare. Much of the range of meat is organic, and includes geese, duck and poussins. Mail order available.

Edward Hamer Ltd
Plynlimon House
Llanidloes
Powys
SY18 6EF
Tel: 01686 412209
Fax: 01686 411225
Website:
www.edwardhamer.com
E-mail:
Edward@edwardhamer.com

A traditional Welsh butcher, who always has Welsh Black Beef in stock. Mail order available.

Edwards of Conwy
18 High Street
Conwy
North Wales
LL32 8DE
Tel: 01492 592443
Website:
www.edwardsofconwy.co.uk
E-mail:
sales@edwardsofconwy.co.uk

The Edwards family buy their Welsh salt marsh lamb from a trusted local farm. They have a commitment to traceability and diversity – land is left to look after itself, and lambs feed on local grasses rather than grass from commercial seed, so the lamb is a truly local product. Staff are passionate about their products, and very friendly. Mail order available.

Eynon's of St Clears
Deganwy
Pentre Road
St Clears
Carmarthenshire
SA33 4LR

Tel: 0800 731 5816
Fax: 01994 231205
Website: www.eynons.co.uk

Holder of the Meat Trades Journal 'Wales No. 1 Butcher' Award for 2001. Eynon's specialize in Welsh Black Beef and salt marsh lamb, but also sell Aberdeen Angus, free-range Duroc x Hampshire pork, and tripe. All meat comes from farms with a high degree of animal welfare. Mail order available.

F. C. Phipps
Osbourne House
Mareham-Le-Fen
Boston
Lincolnshire
PE22 7RW
Tel: 01507 568235
Website: www.fcphipps.co.uk
E-mail:
enquiries@fcphipps.co.uk

This Q Guild butcher was voted Best British Butcher by Country Life in 2000, and is famous for Lincolnshire Stuffed Chine. Phipps offer a full range of meat, including rare-breed, free-range chicken – Cornish Red and White Rock – and local game. Mail order available

Farmer Sharp
Tel: 01229 832860
Website:
www.farmersharp.co.uk

Andrew Sharp is head of a group of Cumbrian farmers who get together to sell their Herdwick lamb by mail order. The sheep roam freely in the hills, feeding on heather and wild thyme, and this lifestyle leads to closely grained, uniquely flavoured lamb.

G. G. Sparkes
24 Old Dover Road
Blackheath
London
SE3 7BT
Tel/Fax: 0208 355 8597
E-mail:
orders@ggsparkesorganic
butchers.com

Stocks veal from Little Warren Farm (see below) and a wide range of organic meats. Free delivery within London and the home counties, subject to a minimum order.

George Payne
27 Princess Road
Brunton Park
Gosforth
Newcastle-Upon-Tyne
NE3 5TT
Tel/Fax: 0191 236 2992
Website:
www.georgepaynebutchers.co.uk

George Payne is a Q Guild member, and is also accredited by the Rare Breeds Survival Trust. Meat comes from trusted local Northumberland breeders who practise traditional, non-intensive farming, with no growth promoters, no hormones and no antibiotics. Breeds available include Belted Galloway, White Park (dark, gamey meat), Dexter and Pedigree Highland beef, Wensleydale and Longhair lamb, and Saddleback, Tamworth, Middle White and Gloucester Old Spot pork. No mail order.

George Stafford Ltd
130 Belper Road
Stanley Common
Derbyshire
DE7 6FQ
Tel: 0115 932 5751

Black puddings by mail order. If visiting the shop, call first to make an appointment.

Graig Farm Organics
Dolau
Llandrindod Wells
Powys
LD1 5TL
Tel: 01597 851655
Fax: 01597 851999
Website:
www.graigfarm.co.uk
E-mail:
whoweb@graigfarm.co.uk

Winner of 'Organic Retailer Of The Year' Award in the Soil Association Awards, 2001, and a winner of Soil Association awards every year since 1997. A large range of organic meats from the farm, or sourced from the 'Farmers Group' they have set up, comprising of mainly local producers. Meat is from slow-matured, properly hung animals. Mail order available.

Grayson & Start 'Sausages by Post'
9 George Street
Saffron Walden
Essex
CB10 1EW
Tel: 01799 513704
Website:
www.sausagesbypost.co.uk
E-mail:
enquiries@sausagesbypost.
co.uk

Range of traditional pork and Continental sausages. Mail order available – sausages are made on the day of ordering and sent by overnight courier.

Griffith David Williams
Cefn Trefor Fawr
Talsarnau
Gwynedd

LL47 6UF
Tel: 01766 770486

Farm-gate sales of Harlech salt-marsh lamb.

Happy Meats
Bank House Farm
Stanford Bridge
Worcestershire WR6 6RU
Tel: 01886 812485
Fax: 01886 812206
Website:
www.happymeats.co.uk
E-mail: info@happymeats.co.uk

Pork from free-range, traditional British breed pigs, with an emphasis on animal welfare. No additives, hormones or routine antibiotics are used, and cruelty-free husbandry is practised: no castration, and no teeth or tail clipping. Every pig is registered with the Rare Breeds Survival Trust. Mail order available.

Hindon Farm
Nr Minehead
Exmoor
Somerset TA24 8SH
Tel/Fax: 01643 705244
Website:
www.hindonorganicfarm.co.uk
E-mail:
info@hindonorganicfarm.co.uk

Organic, free-range pork – Gloucester Old Spot and Duroc boar. Also Aberdeen Angus cattle and Exmoor lamb, dry-cured bacon, sausages and gammon. Mail order available.

The Isle of Wight Bacon Company
Moor Farm
Godshill
Isle of Wight PO38 3JG
Tel: 01983 840210
Fax: 01983 840052
Website:
www.isleofwightbacon.co.uk
E-mail:
web@isleofwightbacon.co.uk

Free-range pork, dry-cured bacon and ham and sausages. Pigs are reared using humane husbandry, with a natural, additive-free diet. Mail order available.

J. Wicken's Family Butchers
Castle Street
Winchelsea
East Sussex
TN36 4HU
Tel: 01797 226287

Rare Sussex beef, sourced from only one local farm and hung for 3 weeks. Fine-grained, well-marbled, soft and sweet meat. Old-fashioned butcher – no website, no mail order, no credit cards!

Jack Scaife
Mill Lane
Oakworth
Keighley
West Yorkshire
BD22 7QH
Tel: 01535 647772
Fax: 01535 646305
Website: www.jackscaife.co.uk
E-mail: sales@jackscaife.co.uk

Traditional dry-cured bacon, available mail order. Jack Scaife also offer ham, sausages and black pudding, all from free-range, traditional British breed pigs.

Jamesfield Organic Farm
Abernethy
Perthshire
KY14 6EW
Tel: 01738 850498
Fax: 01738 850741
Website:
www.jamesfieldfarm.co.uk
E-mail:
jamesfieldfarm@btconnect.com

Aberdeen Angus, Black Face lamb and free-range pork from the farm's own land, and organic, free-range chickens from another local farm. Mail order available.

Lishman's of Ilkley
25 Leeds Road
Ilkley
West Yorkshire
Tel: 01943 609436

Winner of the 'Champion of Champions', 2001, for their sausages for the second time. The pork used is reared by the butcher himself, using Saddleback pigs, fed on a natural grain diet and matured slowly. Other rare-breed meats available. No mail order.

Little Warren Farm
Fletching Common
Newick
East Sussex
BN8 4JH
Tel: 01825 722545

Organic, humanely raised veal. Totally free range – calves have a natural upbringing, 'veaux de lait élève sous la mère', rather than being teat-fed. One of only two suppliers who rear their calves in this traditional, natural way (see Temple Farming, right). Cows are Jersey, so calves have a rich Jersey-milk diet, which the owners believe adds to the flavour of the meat. The veal calves are sent to a local abattoir to reduce stress. Available direct from the farm or from G.G. Sparkes (see opposite page).

Llwynheryg Farm Shop

Sarnau
Llandysul
Ceredigion
Wales
SA44 6QU
Tel: 01239 811079

Black beef and lamb from small, local farms; also free-range local pork and a range of 25 Welsh cheeses, home-grown vegetables, salad and herbs, and local honey.

Lower Hurst Farm

Hartington
Nr Buxton
Derbyshire
SK17 0HJ
Tel: 01298 84900
Fax: 01298 84732
Website:
www.lowerhurstfarm.co.uk
E-mail:
sales@lowerhurstfarm.co.uk

Organic beef from the farm's own herd of Herefordshire cattle. Slow-matured and hung for at least 3 weeks, a local abattoir is used to minimise stress. Traceability is a key policy – all meat is supplied to the customer with full ID, date of birth and slaughter. Mail order available.

Macbeths

11 Tolbooth Street
Forres
Moray
Scotland
IV36 1PH
Tel/Fax: 01309 672254
Website: www.macbeths.com
E-mail:
enquiries@macbeths.com

Aberdeen Angus Beef, Highland and Shorthorn cattle, all reared on Macbeths' own farms and slaughtered at a local abattoir ensuring full traceability. The beef is then hung for 2–3 weeks. Mail order available.

Malvern Country Meals

37 Church Street
Malvern
Worcestershire
WR14 2AA
Tel: 01684 568498
Fax: 01684 567858

Members of Guild of Q Butchers, and winner of 'National Champion of Champions' (Meat Trade Journal Awards) for their Classic Pork sausage. Also winner of the Q Guild's 'Diamond' Award for their Citrus Pork and Red Wine sausage. Meat comes from mainly local suppliers and is free range. Malvern Country Meals has a policy of total traceability. Mail order available.

Northfield Farm

Whissendine Lane
Cold Overton
Oakham
Rutland
LE15 7QF
Tel: 01664 474271
Website:
www.northfieldfarm.com
E-mail: nthfield1@aol.com

Northfield Farm sells meat from its own herd of Dexter cattle (which some people say is superior in flavour to Aberdeen Angus); the breed has never been affected by BSE. Mail order available, and Northfield also has a stall at Borough Market in London.

Northumbrian Quality Meats

Monkridge Hill Farm
West Woodburn
Hexham
Northumberland
Tel/Fax: 01434 270184
Website: www.northumbrian-organic-meat.co.uk
E-mail: enqs@northumbrian-organic-meat.co.uk

Mail-order organic Northumbrian lamb, which is naturally lean and sweet flavoured. Heather- and clover-fed lamb is also sometimes available, as is hill-bred beef and rare-breed free-range pork. Meat from Northumbrian Quality Meats is always from local farms, and always fully traceable.

Ormsary Farm

By Lochgilphead
Argyll
PA31 8PE
Tel: 01880 770700
E-mail: meat@ormsary.co.uk

Scottish beef, including sirloin steak. Mail order available.

Pipers Farm

Magdalene Road
St Leonards
Nr Cullompton
Exeter
EX15 1SD
Tel: 01392 881380
Fax: 01392 881600
Website: www.pipersfarm.com

A company dedicated to supplying excellent-quality produce, while preserving the infrastructure of small, family-run farms from which they buy produce. The Greigs control every aspect of the produce they sell, and even have specially formulated feed made for their farms. Animal welfare is a key concern, down to the choice of one small, local abattoir. Traditional breeds are used, including Devon Red Ruby cattle and Exmoor sheep. All animals are slow-matured without growth

hormones or routine antibiotics, and then hung for longer than usual. Mail order available.

Providence Farm

Crosspark Cross
Holsworthy
Devon EX22 6JW
Tel/Fax: 01409 254421
Website:
www.providencefarm.co.uk
E-mail:
info@providencefarm.co.uk

Free-range and organic pigs, slow-reared without growth hormones or antibiotics. Winner of the 'Best Pork' Award at the Soil Association Awards 2001 (also won Best Duck and Best Guinea fowl). Mail order available.

R. S. Ireland Black Pudding

Back Duke Street
Baronfold
Waterfoot
Rossendale
Lancashire
BB4 7HA
Tel: 01706 224990
Fax: 01706 210580

Traditional Lancashire Black Pudding

The Real Meat Company Ltd

Warminster
Wiltshire
BA12 0HR
Tel: 01985 840562
Fax: 01985 841005
Website: www.realmeat.co.uk
E-mail:
Richard@realmeat.co.uk

Very high attention to welfare – genuinely free range, no growth promoters, no hormones, no pre-emptive medication. Full transparency – will allow public to visit their farms and abattoirs. Animals have a varied and natural diet, a stress-free life, are killed humanely and live longer. The owner of the company believes that eating meat is a privilege, not a right, and that responsible farming and husbandry must come before price. Mail order available,

Richard Woodall

Lane End
Waberthwaite
Nr. Millom
Cumbria
LA19 5YJ
Tel: 01229 717237/717386
Fax: 01229 717007
Website:
www.richardwoodall.co.uk
Email:
admin@richardwoodall.co.uk

Traditional Cumbrian air dried ham.

Saulmore Farm Shop

Connel
By Oban
Argyll
PA37 1PU
Tel: 01631 710247

Highland beef and Black Faced lamb. The animals are raised on the farm, grazing on pasture next to the sea, which gives a specific flavour similar to Welsh salt marsh lamb. The meat is butchered and hung on the premises. Mail order available.

Swaddles Green Farm

Hare Lane
Buckland St Mary
TA20 3JR
Tel: 01460 234387
Fax: 01460 234591
Website: www.swaddles.co.uk
E-mail:
information@swaddles.co.uk

Organic meat from the winner of 'Best Pork' in the 2001 Soil Association Awards; also highly commended for their beef. Swaddles Green have won awards from the Soil Association every year since 1994. All meat is from old British breeds, reared slowly for unforced growth, and from local organic, registered farms. Beef is hung for 3 weeks, lamb for 1 week. Pork is free range, from Saddleback, Berkshire and Large Black. Lamb is reared on organic meadows, grazing on a wide range of grasses and herbs. Mail order available.

Sweet Ithon Lamb

Llanbadarn Fynydd Community Shop
Llandrindod Wells
Powys
LD1 6YA
Tel: 01597 840448
Website: www.lambdirect.co.uk
E-mail:
enquiry@lambdirect.co.uk

Welsh hillside lamb, grazing on natural unfertilized grasses and sorrel, giving the meat a sweet, herby flavour. The shop is owned collectively by the villagers as an outlet for their lamb (the community is dominated by sheep farming). There is a strong sense of pride and healthy competition among the farmers, ensuring that the lamb that arrives in the shop is always of the highest quality. Each joint is traceable back to the individual farmer. Mail order available.

T. Harper & Son Ltd

Bell Farm
Studham
Bedfordshire
LU6 2QG

Tel: 01582 872001
Fax: 01582 872902
Website: www.tasteandtry.co.uk

Member of Guild of Q Butchers, offering a wide range of deli products, including salt beef. Mail order available.

Temple Farming

Rockley
Marlborough
Wiltshire
SN8 1RU
Tel: 01672 514428
Fax: 01672 514116

Organic veal, reared 'veaux de lait élève sous la mère' (see Little Warren Farm above). Available from September to December. Mail order available.

The Tripe Dressers of Dewsbury

Kirkgate Market
George Street
Leeds
Yorkshire
Tel: 07808 016843

Owned by Mrs Hey. Suppliers of tripe to many butchers in West Yorkshire; call for details.

Wallaces of Hemyock

Hill Farm
Hemyock
Devon
EX15 3UZ
Tel: 01823 680307
Fax: 01823 680017
Website:
www.naturalmeats.co.uk
E-mail:
info@naturalmeats.co.uk

Bison and Aberdeen Angus, accredited by the Rare Breeds Survival Trust. Fully traceable meat. Mail order available.

Warren Farm Shop

Dymchurch Road
New Romney
Kent
TN28 8UE
Tel: 01797 363837
Website:
www.warrenfarmshop.co.uk

Free-range poultry, including geese; also beef, lamb and pork. Animals are not fed on growth hormones or animal by-products. Warren Farm's cattle herd have never had BSE. Mail order available.

Warren's of Tideford

1 Bridge Road
Tideford
Saltash
Cornwall
PL12 5HH
Tel: 01752 851224

Excellent local butcher, selling a good range of meats from local farms.

West Country Well Hung Lamb
Carswell
Holbeton
Plymouth
South Devon
PL8 1HH
Tel: 01752 830494
Fax: 01752 830565
Website:
http://lambs.future.easyspace.com
E-mail:
geoffreysayers@carswellfarm.co.uk

Well Hung are the winners of the 'Best Lamb' Award at the 2001 Soil Association awards. Lambs are organically reared and processed locally to minimize stress. They are hung for 9 days to improve texture and flavour. No hormone treatment, growth promoters or routine antibiotics are used. Mail order available.

Weylands Farm
Stoke by Nayland
Colchester
Essex
CO6 4SR
Tel/Fax: 01206 337283

Producers of pork from Large Black Suffolk pigs. Available at farm gate and from local butcher. Call for details of other outlets.

GAME

Aberdeen Scotch Meat
Duthie Road
Tarves
Aberdeenshire
AB41 7JX
Tel: 01651 852004
Fax: 01651 851794
(head office)

Full range of local game offered by this Q Guild butcher. Mail order is available for larger orders.

Ashbee & Son
100 High Street
Rye

East Sussex
TN31 7JN
Tel: 01797 223303
Website:
www.ashbeeandson.sageweb.co.uk
E-mail:
jayne55@btinternet.com

Local pheasant, grouse, duck, pigeon and rabbit. No mail order.

Brown's Speciality Meats
3 Cumbergate
Peterborough
Cambridgeshire
PE1 1YR
Tel: 01733 562104
Fax: 01733 552229
E-mail: browns-peterborough@breathE-mail.net

Pheasant, venison, wild boar and rabbit, most locally sourced. No mail order. Member of Guild of Q Butchers.

C & G Starkey
8 Wolsey Parade
Sherburn-in-Elmet
Leeds
LS25 6BQ
Tel: 01977 682696
Website: www.c-gstarkey.co.uk
E-mail: graham@c-gstarkey.co.uk

Full range of local game in season. Free delivery within a 15-mile radius of the shop. Mail order service available for the rest of mainland UK.

Chalcroft Farm Shop
Chalcroft Farm
Burnetts Lane
West End
Southampton
SO30 2HU
Tel: 02380 600558
Fax: 02380 602110

New Forest venison, pigeon and pheasant from the farm's own land. Large premises – 36 full-time butchers on the staff of this Q Guild butcher. No mail order.

D. J. MacDougall
Canal Side
Fort Augustus
Inverness-shire
PH32 4AU
Tel/Fax: 01320 366214

Full range of local game, including Scottish venison. The only butcher in the UK to hold a Q Guild Diamond award for haggis! Mail order available.

Dennis of Bexley
1-2 Bourne Parade
Bourne Road
Bexley

Kent
DA5 1LQ
Tel: 01322 522126
Fax: 01322 661164
Website:
www.dennisofbexley.co.uk

Traditional Q Guild butcher, selling local pheasant, rabbit and wild venison. No mail order.

Fletchers
Reediehill Deer Farm
Auchtermuchty
Fife
KY14 7HS
Tel: 01337 828369
Fax: 01337 827001
Website:
www.fletcherscotland.co.uk
E-mail:
info@fletcherscotland.co.uk

Farmed venison, slaughtered, hung and butchered on-site for complete traceability. All deer are slaughtered under 27 months for tenderness of meat. Naturally reared without growth promoters or hormones.

George Arthur Ltd
70 Guildford Road
Lightwater
Surrey
GU18 5SD
Tel: 01276 472191
Website:
www.georgearthur.com

Full range of British game, locally sourced. No mail order.

Hamblings
2 Moneyhill Parade
Rickmansworth
Hertfordshire
WD3 7BQ
Tel: 01923 772557/773289
Website:
www.hamblingsbutchers.co.uk
E-mail:
enquiries@hamblingsbutchers.co.uk

Local pheasant, partridge and venison available. No mail order.

Hutchinsons Butcher's
Main Street
Ripley
Nr Harrogate
North Yorkshire
HG3 3AX
Tel: 01423 770110
Fax: 01423 770025

Local wild rabbit and venison, traditionally butchered and hung, sourced from local gamekeepers. Also pigeon, duck and pheasant, available all year round. No mail order.

J & D Papworth Farms
16 Millers Walk
Fakenham
Norfolk
NR21 9AP
Tel: 01328 855039

Locally sourced pheasant and partridge. No mail order. Member of Guild of Q Butchers.

John Thorner's Ltd
Bridge Farm Shop
Pylie
Shepton Mallet
Somerset
BA4 6TA
Tel: 01749 830138
Fax: 01749 830301
E-mail:
johnthorner@freeuk.com

Full range of local game, including venison, fresh in season, frozen at other times. Local delivery service available within a 30-mile radius. Mail order available throughout mainland UK.

Kernow Wild Boar
Higher Hill
Cardinham
Bodmin
Cornwall PL30 4EG
Tel: 01208 821300
Fax: 01208 821705
Website:
www.kernowwildboar.co.uk
E-mail:
a.p.worden@farming.co.uk

Slow-growing wild boar, ranging free on Bodmin Moor and fed on natural feed with no additives. Mail order available, but one week's notice is required.

Lakings of Louth
33 Eastgate
Louth
Lincolnshire
LN11 9NB
Tel: 01507 603186
Fax: 01507 608778

Full range of locally sourced game from a Q Guild butcher. No mail order.

Lords of Middleton
18 Old Hall Street
Middleton
Manchester
M24 1AN
Tel: 0161 643 4160
Website:
www.lordsofmiddleton.co.uk
E-mail:
sales@lordsofmiddleton.co.uk

Wild Scottish venison from Red deer available for on-line ordering. Wider range of game in season; call for details. Mail order available.

McCabe's
5 Fore Street
Totnes TQ9 5DA
Tel: 01803 865846

Good quality butcher selling game from local shoots.

McGarrity's
21 The Foregate
Kilmarnock
Ayrshire
KA1 1LU
Tel: 01563 522086
Fax: 01292 611394
(head office)

Local game in season. Mail order available. Member of Guild of Q Butchers.

Manor Farm Game
96 Berkeley Avenue
Chesham
Buckinghamshire
HP5 2RS
Tel: 07778 706179
Fax: 01494 776723
E-mail:
info@manorfarmgame.co.uk

Game birds (pigeon, mallard, pheasant, partridge), rabbit and hare, and venison (fallow, roe and muntjack). Manor Farm run their own shoot, so all produce is traceable. Mail order available.

Manydown Farmshop
Scrapps Hill Farm
Worting Road
Basingstoke
Hampshire
RG23 8PU
Tel: 01256 460068
Fax: 01256 329288

Pheasant, partridge and hare from the farm's own land. No mail order. Member of Guild of Q Butchers.

O. Roberts a'i Fab
Corwas Amlwch
Ynys Mon LL68 9ET
Tel: 01407 830277
Website:
www.owenrobertsandson.com
E-mail:
mail@owenrobertsandson.com

Full range of game, including wild boar, some locally sourced, all British. Mail order available.

Palmers of Tavistock
50 Brook Street
Tavistock
Devon PL19 0BJ
Tel/Fax: 01822 612000
Website: www.palmers-tavistock.com
E-mail: sales@palmers-tavistock.com
Full range of local game. Mail order available.

Philip Warren & Son
1 Westgate Street
Launceston
Cornwall PL15 7AB
Tel: 01566 772089
Fax: 01566 779384
Website:
www.philipwarrenbutchers.co.uk

*Game from local sources,
including wild venison from
Dartmoor, partridge and pheasant
from local estates. Game is not
always available, as Warren's
insist on the finest quality, and
will not sell inferior meat.*

R. F. Burrows & Sons
Old Post Office
Bunbury
Nr Tarporely
Cheshire
CW6 9QR
Tel: 01829 260342
Fax: 01829 261162
Website:
www.burrowsandsons.co.uk

*Q Guild butcher, offering local
pheasant and wild duck, and wild
Scottish venison. Mail order
available.*

Ramsay of Carluke Ltd
Wellriggs
22 Mount Stewart Street
Carluke
Scotland
ML8 5ED
Tel: 01555 772277
Fax: 01555 750686
Website:
www.wellriggs.demon.co.uk
E-mail:
ramsay@wellriggs.demon.
co.uk

*Award-winning, traditional
Ayrshire bacon, dry cured to
Ramsay's 1857 recipe. Called
'the best bacon in Scotland' by
the BBC's Good Food Magazine.
Member of Guild of Q Butchers.
Mail order available.*

Randalls Butchers
113 Wandsworth Bridge Road
Fulham
London
SW6 2TE
Tel: 0207 736 3426

*Wide selection of game birds
from a local shoot. No mail order.
Member of Guild of Q Butchers.*

Saxmundham Foods
8 High Street
Saxmundham
Suffolk
Tel: 01728 602081

*Old-fashioned butcher, who sells
a good range of game birds in
season, with hard-to-come-by wild
goose and snipe. No mail order.*

Sillfield Farm
Endmoor
Kendal
Cumbria
LA8 0HZ
Tel: 01539 567609
Website: www.sillfield.co.uk
E-mail:
enquiries@sillfield.co.uk

*A variety of meats from pure wild
boar (four different breeds:
French, German, Russian and
Polish). The boar are free-range
and allowed to mature naturally.
Mail order available. Suppliers
from Sillfield also attend
Liverpool, Carlisle and
Manchester farmers' markets,
and Borough Market in London.*

Somerset Organics
Manor Farm
Rodney Stoke
Cheddar
Somerset
BS27 3UN
Tel: 0800 085 7669
Fax: 01749 870919
Website:
www.somersetorganics.co.uk
E-mail:
info@somersetorganics.co.uk

*Very wide selection of locally
sourced game, including game
birds, rabbit and hare, venison
and wild boar, all hand-picked by
Somerset Organics. Mail order
available.*

Steadman's
2 Finkle Street
Sedbergh
Cumbria LA10 5BZ
Tel: 01539 620431
Fax: 01539 621719
Website: www.steadmans-
butchers.co.uk
E-mail:
garth.steadman@talk21.com

*Traditional, award-winning Q
Guild butcher, with a huge range
of local produce. Almost
everything they sell originates in
Cumbria. Full range of local game
available; also award-winning
sausages and black pudding.
No mail order.*

Steve Brooks Butchers
25 High Street
Sandbach
Cheshire
CW11 1AH
Tel: 01270 766657

also:
13 Lawton
Stoke-on-Trent
ST7 2AA
Tel: 01270 882248
Website: www.qualitycuts.co.uk
E-mail:
enquiry@qualitycuts.co.uk

*Pigeon, hare, wild rabbit,
pheasant, partridge, fresh in
season, frozen at other times.
Mail order available.*

T. H. Checketts Ltd
Ombersley
Droitwich
Worcestershire
WR9 0EW
Tel: 01905 620284
Fax: 01905 620152
Website: www.checketts.co.uk
E-mail:
enquiries@checketts.co.uk

*Long-established local Q Guild
butcher, sells local pheasant,
hare and rabbit in season.
No mail order.*

T. Harper & Son Ltd
Bell Farm
Studham
Bedfordshire
LU6 2QG
Tel: 01582 872001
Fax: 01582 872902
Website:
www.harpersfood.co.uk

*Venison, wild boar, pheasant
and partridge cuts available;
also a wide range of deli
products available for on-line
ordering. Member of Guild of
Q Butchers.*

The Welsh Venison Centre
Middlewood Farm
Bwlch
Nr Brecon
Powys
LD3 7HQ
Tel: 01874 730929
Fax: 01874 730566

*Farmed Red deer venison,
slaughtered at local abattoir
and butchered on the premises.
Mail order available.*

Yorkshire Game Ltd
18 Leaside
Aycliffe Industrial Park
Newton Aycliffe
Co. Durham
DL5 6DE
Tel: 01325 316320
Fax: 01325 320634
Website:
www.yorkshiregame.co.uk
E-mail:
sales@yorkshiregame.co.uk

*Sources a huge range of game
birds, rabbit, hare and venison
from local, traditional suppliers.
A member of the National Game-
dealers Association, their ethos is
sympathetic game management.
Mail order available, but for larger
orders only (eg 10 birds).*

FRUIT DESSERTS, CAKES AND BREAD

Adamson's Bakery
29 High Street
Pittenweem
KY10 2LA
Tel: 01333 311336

*Traditional Scottish oatcakes, also
available at Neal's Yard Dairy in
London, and Iain Mellis in
Edinburgh and Glasgow (see their
entries in the cheese section).*

Artisan Bread
Units 16-17, John Wilson
Business Park
Whitstable
Kent CT5 3QZ
Tel: 01227 771881
Fax: 01227 278661
Website:
www.artisanbread.ltd.uk

*Artisan Bread mill their own
grain to make flour, often using
unusual varieties of grain. No
yeast or tap water is used (only
spring water) and less salt.
This is the UK's first biodynamic
bakery, where a holistic
approach is taken to bread –
from health to the impact on
the environment to maintaining
the biodiversity of the
ingredients used. Call or see
website for stockists.*

The Authentic Bread Company
Strawberry Hill
Newent
Gloucestershire
GL18 1LH
Tel: 01531 828181
Fax: 01531 828151
Website:
www.authenticbread.co.uk
E-mail:
info@authenticbread.co.uk

*Organic, traditionally baked
bread, including rye bread,
walnut bread, spelt and
Continental varieties. Authentic
Bread say that 'taste rather than
cost is paramount'. No flour
improvers are used; the dough
is allowed to ferment naturally
twice, a time-consuming process
that most commercial bakers
won't use. Winner of six national
awards.*

Baker & Spice
46 Walton Street
London
SW3 1RB
Tel: 020 7328 2300

also:
75 Salusbury Road
Queens Park
London
NW6 6NH
Tel: 020 7604 3636

*Traditional breads, baked the old-
fashioned way with no additives.
No mail order.*

The Bakery
Station Road
Kelly Bray
Nr Callington
Cornwall
PL17 8ER
Tel: 01579 383362

*For Michael Pearce's famous
Saffron cake. No mail order.*

Bankhead of Kinloch
Meigle
Tayside
PH12 8QY
Tel: 01828 640265
Fax: 01828 640687

*Tayside raspberries – the finest
raspberries in Britain are said to
come from Tayside. Pick your
own, or buy them ready-picked
from the farm shop.*

Barbara Lake
Priors
Coads Green
Launceston
Cornwall
PL15 7LT
Tel: 01566 782547

*Traditionally made cream,
available from Barbara herself or
from local outlet; call for details.*

Billingtons Sugar
The Billington Food Group
The Cunard Building
Liverpool
L3 1EL
Tel: 0151 243 9001
Fax: 0151 243 9011
Website: www.billingtons.co.uk
E-mail: bfg@billingtons.co.uk

*Billingtons sugar is available from
Sainsbury's, Waitrose, Safeway,
Tesco, Asda, Morrisons and Co-op.*

Boddington's Berries
The Ashes
Tregoney Hill
Mevagissey
Cornwall
PL26 6RQ
Tel/Fax: 01726 842346 /
842549
Website:
www.boddingtonsberries.co.uk
E-mail:
info@boddingtonsberries.co.uk

*Strawberry specialists, growing
different varieties to create a*

very long growing season. The strawberries are sweeter than most, due to a full, slow ripening process (the sea breezes allow the berries to ripen slowly, allowing the sugar to develop properly). Available from the farm shop May to September, with pick-your-own available in July and August.

Brogdale Horticultural Trust
Brogdale Road
Faversham
Kent
M13 8XZ
Tel: 01795 535286
Fax: 01795 531710
Website: www.brogdale.org.uk
E-mail: info@brogdale.org.uk

Home to the National Fruit Collections, with literally hundreds of varieties of apple; also mulberries, blueberries, raspberries and nuts. Maintaining the diversity of species is the guiding objective.

The Chocolate Society
Clay Pit Lane
Roecliffe
Nr Boroughbridge
North Yorkshire
YO51 9LS
Tel: 01423 322230
Website: www.chocolate.co.uk
E-mail: info@chocolate.co.uk

also:
36 Elizabeth Street
London
SW1W 9NZ

All varieties of Valrhona chocolate, plus much more.

& Clarkes
122-124 Kensington Church Street
London
W8 4BH
Tel: 020 7229 2190
Fax: 020 7229 4564
Website: www.sallyclarke.com
E-mail: shop@sallyclarke.com

Great range of traditional British and Continental breads, from the chef Sally Clarke's shop. All baked without artificial colours, preservatives or improvers. Also available from Carluccios, Selfridges and Harvey Nichols.

Clay Barn Orchard
Fingringhoe
Colchester
Essex
CO5 7AR
Tel/Fax: 01206 735405

Quinces available via mail order (when in season – from beginning of October).

Constantine Stores Ltd.
30 Fore Street
Constantine
Falmouth
Cornwall
TR11 5AB
Tel: 01326 340226
Fax: 01326 340182
Website: www.drinkfinder.co.uk
E-mail: sales@drinkfinder.co.uk

More whiskies than you knew there were, and rare, aged sherries. Mail order available; delivery from £6.95.

Court Farm
Tillington
Burghill
Hereford
HR4 8LG
Tel: 01432 760271

Great range of pick-your-own and ready-picked soft fruit, including blueberries, cherries, raspberries and redcurrants. Asparagus is also available.

Cyrnel Bakery Ltd
Lower Road
Forest Row
East Sussex
RH18 5HE
Tel: 01342 822283

Huge variety of breads, some organic, made with local flour. Cakes are made with local free-range eggs. Available from several Sussex farmers' markets; call for details.

De Gustibus
53 Blandford Street
London
W1H 3AF
Tel: 020 7486 6608

also:
4 Southwark Street
London
SE1 1TQ
Tel: 020 7407 3625

and:
53–55 Carter Lane
London
EC4V 5AE
Tel: 020 7236 0056

Traditional Mediterranean breads, all hand-made with traditional ingredients. The dough is allowed to mature slowly; they even make a 6-day sour dough – the dough is fermented for a full 6 days before baking. De Gustibus hold several national awards for their bread.

Dorset Blueberry Company
Church Cottage
352 Hampreston Lane
Wimborne
Dorset

BH21 7LX
Tel: 01202 579342
Fax: 01202 579014
Website: www.dorset-blueberry.com

Many varieties of blueberry. Available via mail order, from the farm shop, from farmers' markets in Dorset, Hampshire and London, or from Marks and Spencer.

Durleigh Marsh Farm Shop
Durleigh Marsh Farm
Rogate Road
Petersfield
Hampshire
GU31 6AX
Tel: 01730 821626
Fax: 01730 821581
E-mail: grange@ukgateway.net

Farm shop and pick-your-own strawberries, raspberries, blueberries and asparagus.

El Rey Chocolate
123 Buspace Studios
Conlan Street
London
W10 5AP
Tel: 020 7854 7770
Fax: 020 7854 7772
Website: www.elrey.co.uk
E-mail: info@elrey.co.uk

Venezuelan chocolate from single bean cocoa, a rival to Valrhona in terms of quality. Six different kinds available, varying from 41 per cent cocoa content to 73.5 per cent. Available from Waitrose, Safeway and many delicatessens.

Essington Fruit Farm
Bognop Road
Essington
Wolverhampton
Staffordshire
WV11 2BA
Tel: 01902 735724

Farm-shop sales and pick-your-own soft fruit, including blueberries; also potatoes, leeks and other vegetables. Essington Fruit Farm carefully selects fruit and vegetable varieties for maximum flavour, often using old-fashioned varieties. The blueberries are only available in July and August, but freeze well.

The Food Company
London Road
Marks Tey
Colchester
Essex
CO6 1ED
Tel: 01206 214000
Fax: 01206 214019
Website: www.thefoodcompany.co.uk
E-mail: info@thefoodcompany.co.uk

A large food shop with twelve departments, including a bakery, a fishmonger, a butcher and green grocery. The company mission is to get as far away from manufactured and processed packaged foods as possible. Traceability and freshness are key concepts for the Food Company. The bakery section produces traditional and unusual breads – some you may never have heard of – all baked traditionally on the premises.

The Fruit Garden
Groesfaen Road
Peterston-Super-Ely
Cardiff
South Glamorgan
Tel: 01446 760358

Specialist soft fruit growers, including 18 varieties of strawberry. The Fruit Garden continually experiment with varieties to achieve the best flavour. Pick-your-own and ready-picked available, and suppliers from The Fruit Garden attend many local farmers' markets; call for details or look at www.sewafm.org.uk. Also available is home-made, high-quality ice cream.

Gourmet's Lair
8 Union Street
Inverness
IV1 1PL
Tel: 01463 225151
Website: www.gourmetslair.co.uk

Heather and blossom honey from Struan Apiaries in Scotland, alongside a range of high-quality deli items from around the world. Mail order available.

Hobbs House Bakery
Unit 6, Chipping Edge Estate
Hatters Lane
Chipping Sodbury
Bristol
BS37 6AA
Tel: 01454 321629

also:
4 George Street
Nailsworth
Gloucestershire
Website: www.hobbshousebakery.co.uk
E-mail: clive@hobbshousebakery.co.uk

Award-winning baker's, with a huge variety of breads, including excellent sour dough. Clive Wells runs the Chipping Sodbury branch, while his son, recently named Baker of the Year, runs the Nailsworth branch. Many outlets in the South West, and also available via mail order.

Janet Oldroyd-Hulme and Neil Hulme
Ashfield House
Main Street
Carlton
Wakefield
WF3 3RW
Tel: 0113 2822245

Farm-gates sales of rhubarb

North Elmham Bakery
Eastgate Street
North Elmham
Dereham
Norfolk
NR20 5HD
Tel: 01362 668548
Fax: 01362 668577
Website: www.breadbaker.co.uk

Run by a baker obsessed by freshness and the baking of bread in the old-fashioned way, without additives. The owner, Norman Ollie, is a tireless campaigner for 'real bread'. Many outlets in Norfolk; call for details.

Park Fruit Farm
Pork Lane
Great Holland
Nr Frinton-on-Sea
Essex
Tel: 01255 674621
Website: www.parkfruitfarm.co.uk
E-mail: s.elsworth@farmline.com

Pick-your-own farm (also has ready-picked fruit), with 40 varieties of apple, 10 varieties of plum, pears and raspberries (also frozen raspberries out of season). Wet walnuts, local untreated honey, cider vinegar and vegetables, all grown on the farm or sourced locally. No mail order.

Plaisir du Chocolat
251-253 Canongate
Edinburgh
EH8 8BQ
Tel: 0131 556 9524
Fax: 0131 556 6553
E-mail: sales@plaisirduchocolat.co.uk

High-quality chocolate, including Valrhona and Michel Cluizel. Mail order available.

Poilane
46 Elizabeth Street
London
SW1W 9PA
Tel: 020 7808 4910
Website: www.poilane.fr

French bakery famous for their sour dough, baked on-site in a wood and brick oven, an exact copy of a Roman bread oven. Available from numerous London delis; call for details.

Rococo Chocolates

321 Kings Road
London
SW3 5EP
Tel: 020 7352 5857
Fax: 020 7352 7360
Website:
www.rococochocolates.com
E-mail:
web@rococochocolates.com

Valrhona and organic 'couverture' chocolate. Mail order available.

Ryton Organic Gardens

Ryton on Dunsmore
Coventry
CV8 3LG
Tel: 02476 303517
Website: www.hdra.org.uk

National Centre of Organic Gardening, and headquarters of the Henry Doubleday Research Association and Heritage Seed Library. Hundreds of different varieties of apple; also locally produced fruit and vegetables.

Shipton Mill

Long Newnton
Tetbury
GL8 8RP
Tel: 01666 505050
Fax: 01666 504666
Website: www.shipton-mill.com
E-mail: jlister@shipton-mill.com

Old-fashioned stone-ground flour from a water-powered mill. Shipton Mill produce 60 varieties of mainly organic flour, which complement traditional breads – the grist is matured for longer for a more rounded flavour. Available via mail order; call and ask for Flour Direct. Shipton Mill will also provide advice for home bakers.

Tony's Bakery

1 Peel Street
Kidderminster
Worcestershire
DY11 6UG
Tel: 01562 636463

Tony's use recipes going back 130 years, and hand-make their bread without help from machines. Customers can see their bread being made in the open kitchens. The resulting quality is such that customers will travel from larger neighbouring towns just for the bread.

Trewithen Farm Foods

Greymare Farm
Lostwithiel
Cornwall
PL22 0LW
Tel: 01208 872214
Fax: 01208 873693
E-mail: greymarefarm@aol.com

Clotted cream made from milk from the farm's own cows, which are fed on feed made from the farm's own crops, using traditional methods. Mail order available.

The Village Bakery

Melmerby
Penrith
Cumbria CA10 1HE
Tel: 01768 881515
Website: www.village-bakery.com
E-mail: info@village-bakery.com

Totally organic bakery, with a wide range of bread varieties, including some suitable for people with yeast and wheat intolerances. Available mail order, and also from Waitrose and Sainsbury's.

Wilkin & Sons

Tiptree
Essex
CO5 0RF
Tel: 01621 815407
Fax: 01621 814555
Website: www.tiptree.com
E-mail: info@tiptree.com

Mulberry jam, available from most supermarkets. Wilkin & Sons have less than 20 mulberry trees, which are all very old; mulberry trees often don't bear fruit for the first 20 years.

W. & H. Marriage & Sons Ltd

Chelmer Mills
Chelmsford
Essex
CM1 1PN
Tel: 01245 354455

Flour traditionally milled from Canadian wheat – said to be the best for bread-making. 14 varieties are available, some certified organic. Available from health food shops across the UK.

SPECIAL INGREDIENTS

Aberfeldy Water Mill

Mill Street
Aberfeldy
PH15 2BG
Tel: 01887 820803

Traditional stoneground oatmeal. Mail order available.

Adnam's Plc

Sole Bay Brewery
Southwold
Suffolk
IP18 6JW
Tel: 01502 727200
Fax: 01502 727201
Website: www.adnams.co.uk

Adnam's ales are available from Tesco, Waitrose and Sainsbury's.

Aspall's

The Cyder House
Aspall Hall
Debenham
Suffolk
IP14 6PD
Tel: 01728 860510
Fax: 01728 861031
Website: www.aspall.co.uk
E-mail: info@aspall.co.uk

Cider and aged cider vinegars. Call for details of stockists.

Avonbank

Core Food and Drink
Pershore College of Horticulture
Avonbank
Pershore
Worcestershire
WR10 3JP
Tel: 01386 551200
Fax: 01386 556865

Award-winning single-variety and blended cider and perry, some using unusual and rare varieties of fruit; also some organic ciders. No mail order.

Berry Bros & Rudd

3 St James Street
London
SW1A 1EG
Tel: 0870 900 4300
Fax: 01256 340106
Website: www.bbr.com
E-mail: orders@bbr.com

Lots of interesting, unusual high-quality sherries. Mail order available.

Brindisa

9B Weir Road
Balham
London
SW12 0LT
Tel: 020 8772 1600
Fax: 020 8772 1666
Website: www.brindisa.com
E-mail: sales@brindisa.com

Wide range of hard-to-find Spanish ingredients, including Judion de la Granja butter beans. Mail order available, but large minimum order applies. Brindisa also have a shop at 32 Exmouth Market, London EC1 4QE, Tel: 0207 713 1666, and a stall at Borough Market in London.

Carluccio's

28a Neal Street
Covent Garden
London
WC2H 9PS
Tel: 0207 240 1487
Fax: 0207 497 1361

Italian deli-style produce with a good selection of wild mushrooms. Carluccio's also stock saba, the Trebianno grape sauce referred to in the recipe for Ragoût of hare with red wine from the Loire (see page 130).

Clarke's

124 Kensington Church Street
London
W8 4BH
Tel: 020 7221 9225
Website: www.sallyclarke.com

Sally Clarke's restaurant.

Club Chef Direct

Lakeside
Bridgwater Road
Barrow Gurney
Bristol
BS48 3SJ
Tel: 01275 475 252
Fax: 01275 475167
Website:
www.clubchefdirect.co.uk
E-mail:
info@clubchefdirect.co.uk

A company which aims to provide the home cook with the quality of food top chefs expect. The meat, game and fish are endorsed by a panel of legendary chefs. Mail order available.

The Cool Chile Company

PO Box 5702
London
W11 2GS
Tel: 0870 902 1145
Website: www.coolchile.co.uk
E-mail: dodie@coolchile.co.uk

Many different kinds of dried chillies and Mexican ingredients, such as masa harina. Mail order available. They also stock tortilla presses.

Eatalia Direct Ltd

PO Box 84
Tonbridge
Kent TN11 8ZD
Tel: 0800 027 7959
Fax: 020 8675 8567
Website: www.eataliadirect.com
E-mail: info@eataliadirect.com

Italian deli with a good variety of artisan pastas, oils, charcuterie and polenta. Mail order available.

Esperya

Via Trieste 7
60025 Loreto
Italy
Tel: +39 071 759 2274
Fax: +39 071 759 7249
Website: www.esperya.com
E-mail: Alison.b@esperya.com

Italian regional oils, vinegars, pasta, cheese, charcuterie, honey, etc. Mail order available.

Fratelli Camisa

Unit 4, I. O. Centre
Lea Road
Waltham Cross
Hertfordshire
EN8 7PG
Tel: 01992 763076
Fax: 01992 652775
Website: www.camisa.co.uk
E-mail:
sales@fratellicamisa.co.uk

Good range of Italian deli products, including authentic Italian sausages, such as Luganega. Mail order available.

George Bateman & Son Ltd

Salem Bridge Brewery
Wainfleet
Lincolnshire
PE24 4JE
Tel: 01754 880317
Website: www.bateman.co.uk
E-mail:
batemansbrewery@bateman.co.uk

Mail order real ale, from CAMRA award-winning brewery. Their XXXB ale has won CAMRA 'Premium Beer of the Year' Award 5 times. Also organic and fruit beers.

Gourmet World

101 Lonsdale Road
London SW13 9DA
Tel: 020 8748 0125
Fax: 020 8741 4980
Website: www.gourmet-world.co.uk
E-mail: info@gourmet-world.co.uk

Continental deli items from small, artisan producers, often exclusive to Gourmet World in the UK. Winner of 'Guild of Fine Food Retailers' award.

The Grapevine Delicatessen
77 High Street
Odiham
Hampshire
RG29 1LB
Tel/Fax: 01256 701900
Website: www.grapevine-gourmet.com
E-mail: info@grapevine-gourmet.com

Selection of Spanish, Italian and Eastern foods; also traditional British and local Hampshire products. Mail order available.

Hoo Hing
Hoo Hing Commercial Centre
Freshwater Road
Chadwell Heath
Romford
Essex
RM8 1RX
Tel: 0208 548 3636
Fax: 0208 548 3688
Website: www.hoohing.com
E-mail: enquiries@hoohing.com

Enormous range of Chinese spices, soy sauces, and any other Chinese ingredients you might need. Mail order available.

The Ingredient Company Ltd
Freepost ANG 3751
Market Deeping
Peterborough
Cambridgeshire
PE6 8BR
Tel: 01778 380088
Fax: 01778 380052
Website: www.theingredientcompany.co.uk
E-mail: mail@theingredientcompany.co.uk

Good range of beans, lentils, herbs and flours that supermarkets may not carry. Mail order available.

Lefktro U.K. Ltd
Somerville House
High Street
Hinton St George
Somerset
TA17 8SE
Tel: 01460 72931
Website: www.getoily.com
E-mail: feedback@getoily.com

Vast choice of unusual oils from Greece, Italy, Spain, France, Australia and New Zealand, plus related products. Mail order available.

The Lizard Pasty Shop
Beacon Terrace
The Lizard
Helston
Cornwall
TR12 7PB
Tel: 01326 290889
Fax: 01326 290153
E-mail: LIZARDPASTY@connexions.co.uk

Ann Muller's famous Cornish pasties, available mail order November to February.

Lupe Pinto's Deli
24 Leven Street
Edinburgh
EH3 9LJ
Tel/Fax: 0131 228 6241

also:
313 Great Western Road
Glasgow
G4 9HR
0141 334 5444
Website: www.lupepintos.com
E-mail: lupep@globalnet.co.uk

Specialist importer of Mexican and Spanish foods, with some southern US, Spanish, Caribbean, Thai and Japanese foods. The emphasis is on spice!

Minchews Real Cyder and Perry
Rose Cottage
Aston Cross
Tewkesbury
Gloucestershire
GL20 8HX
Tel: 01684 773427
E-mail: ask.us@minchews.co.uk

The perry used to cook the gammon on page 92. Sold through Orchard Hive and Vine (see below).

Mrs King's Pork Pies
Unit 30, Manvers Business Park
Hollygate Lane
Cotgrave
Nottingham
NG12 3JW
Tel/Fax: 0115 989 4101

Pork pies made to a very old traditional recipe. Mail order service available.

The Oil Merchant Ltd
47 Ashchurch Grove
London
W12 9BU
Tel: 020 8740 1335
Fax: 020 8740 1319
E-mail: the_oil_merchant@compuserve.com

Specialist importer of single estate olive oils from small

producers throughout Europe, Australia, New Zealand and South Africa. Mail order available.

Orchard Hive and Vine
6 The Buttercross
Leominster
Herefordshire
HR6 8BN
Tel/Fax: 01568 611232
Website: www.orchard-hive-and-vine.co.uk
E-mail: sales@ohv.wyenet.co.uk

Mail order sales of cider and perry from a range of small producers, who often use hand-picked, unsprayed, single-variety fruit.

Pata Negra
12 Haynes Lane
London
SE19 3AN
Tel: 020 8653 9628
Fax: 020 8653 8504
Website: www.patanegra.net
E-mail: info@patanegra.net

Shop and mail order company that carry Brindisa products (see page 193), available in smaller quantities.

Provender
3 Market Square
South Petherton
Somerset
TA13 5BT
Tel: 01460 240681
Fax: 0870 169 4835
Website: www.provender.net

Artisan cheeses, cider, air-dried ham, smoked meat and fish, all sourced locally.

Reid Wines
The Mill, Marsh Lane
Hallatrow
Nr. Bristol
BS39 6EB
Tel: 01761 452645
Fax: 01761 453642
E-mail: redwines@aol.ocm

Mail order available.

Roots Deli
33 Crendon Street
High Wycombe
Buckinghamshire
Tel/Fax: 01494 524243
Website: www.rootsdeli.demon.co.uk
E-mail: sales@rootsdeli.demon.co.uk

British cheese, wine, beer, charcuterie and smoked salmon.

Sagebury Cheese Delicatessen
21 Cheap Street
Frome
Somerset

BA11 1BN
Tel: 01373 462543

Fantastic deli selling unusual cheeses, oils, pasta, high-quality chocolate and hard-to-find ingredients. Mail order available.

Seasoned Pioneers
12a Beswicks Road
Northwich
Cheshire
CW8 1AP
Tel: 0800 068 2348
Website: www.seasonedpioneers.co.uk
E-mail: info@seasonedpioneers.co.uk

Over 100 varieties of spices from all over the world, some organic. Spice blends are created in house, using original, traditional recipes.

The Spice Shop
1 Blenheim Crescent
London
W11 2EE
Tel: 020 7221 4448
Website: www.thespiceshop.co.uk

Every spice you can imagine. Mail order available.

Springbank Distillers
85 Longrow
Campbeltown
Argyll
PA28 6EX
Tel: 01586 552009

Springbank whisky, available mail order from:
Loch Fyne Whiskies
Inverary
Argyll
PA32
Tel: 01499 302219
Fax: 01499 302238
Website: www.lfw.co.uk

Stein's Seafood Delicatessen
South Quay
Padstow
Cornwall
PL28 8BL
Tel: 01841 533466
Fax: 01841 533868

Canned seafood like tuna, anchovies and sardines, fresh seafood and shellfish, take-away food, 'Rick Stein' products and a selection of high-quality specialist ingredients.

Valvona & Crolla
19 Elm Row
Edinburgh
EH7 4AA
Tel: 0131 556 6066
Fax: 0131 556 1668
Website: www.valvonacrolla.co.uk

E-mail: sales@valvonacrolla.co.uk

Huge range of Italian products, available mail order.

Websites

www.farmshopping.com
www.bigbarn.co.uk

Both these websites can tell you where your nearest farm shop is.

www.soilassociation.org

Find your nearest organic food producers or retailers.

www.farmersmarkets.net

Find your nearest farmers' market.

ireland

A Taste of Italy
37 Dunnlie Avenue
Dublin 6
Tel: (01) 497 3411

Italian breads, charcuterie, cheeses, pastas, oils.

Ballycotton Seafood
46, Main Street
Midleton
County Cork
Ireland
Tel: (00353) 2164 13122

Legendary Cork fishmongers, selling exceptionally fresh fish from local waters.

Burren Smokehouse
Lisdoonvarna
Co. Clare
Tel: (065) 707 4432
Fax: (065) 707 4303
Website:
www.burrensmokehouse.ie

Irish Atlantic smoked salmon; also smoked trout and mackerel. All slowly smoked over oak in a traditional smoke box. Mail order available.

Caherbeg Free-Range Pork
Caherbeg
Rosscarbery
West Cork
Tel: (023) 48474
Fax: (023) 48966
Website:
www.caherbegfreerangepork.ie
E-mail:
caher@caherbegfreerangepork.ie

Slowly matured, traditionally reared Saddleback X Great White pigs, slaughtered locally to minimize stress. The pigs are fed on a diet of grain and boiled barley, and are allowed to root freely. All pork cuts are available, as well as dry-cured bacon, from the farm gate, or delivered locally.

Caviston's Seafood
59 Glasthule Road
Sandycove
Dun Laoghaire
Tel: (01) 280 9245

Fantastic fresh local fish and artisan Irish foods.

Cheese etc
Beside the Bridge
Carrick-on-Shannon
Leitrim
Tel: (078) 22121

Irish cheeses from small-scale producers that you may not find anywhere else, alongside a choice of British and Continental cheeses. Available from the shop or from Belfast Farmers' Market.

Continental Sausages
Fossa
Killarney
Co. Kerry
Tel: (064) 33069

Sausages and charcuterie, hand-made with Irish meats.

Cork English Market

O'Connells for really fresh south coast fish; Eddie Sheehan's for salt ling. Also of note in Cork English Market are Stephen O'Reilly's tripe stall and Arbutus Breads for sour dough.

Country Choice
25 Kenyon Street
Nenagh
Tipperary
Tel: (067) 32596

Renowned small shop selling an enormous array of artisan Irish produce, including cheeses from small producers (ripened on site), duck, Maran and hens' eggs, and fresh produce from farm gardens. Also stocks a selection of unusual Continental produce.

Cuan Sea Fisheries
Sketrick Island
Killinchy
Co. Down BT23 6QH
Tel: (028) 9754 1461

Pacific and Native oysters from Strangford Lough, also scallops and Queenies, available via main order.

Danny O'Toole
138 Terenure Road North
Dublin 6W
Tel: (01) 490 5457

Properly butchered and hung (for 3 weeks) local beef, organic free-range local chicken and pork.

David Burns
112 Abby Street
Bangor
Ulster
Tel: (028) 9127 0073

Locally sourced meat, free-range chicken, organic eggs, and beef from their own herd.

Ditty's Bakery
33 Rainey Street
Magherafelt
Derry
Tel: (028) 7963 3944

also:
44 Main Street
Castledawson
Derry
Tel: (028) 7946 8243

Northern Irish ethnic breads, including soda, wheaten and potato. Artisan Italian breads, all traditionally made.

Doyle's Family Butchers
Village Gate Arcade
Bray
Co. Wicklow
Tel: (01) 282 8530

also:
Tesco Shopping Centre
Greystones
Co. Wicklow
Tel: (01) 287 2181

Member of the Association of Craft Butchers of Ireland, selling traditionally butchered meats, including local grass-fed beef, properly hung. Also stocks a good range of sausages, including Italian varieties.

Dunne and Crescenzi
14 South Frederick Street
Dublin 2
Tel: (01) 677 3815

Italian deli selling unusual ingredients.

Finnebrogue Venison Company
35 Finnebrogue Road
Downpatrick
BT30 9BL
Tel: (028) 4461 7525

Farm-gate sales of young, tender, farmed red-deer venison. Finnebrogue call their venison Oisin, which means 'little fawn', to differentiate it from the tougher, gamier venison most people are used to – the venison is all under 15 months old and is mildly flavoured. Also available from Marks and Spencer.

Goya's
Kirwan's Lane
Galway
Tel: (091) 567010

Bakery that insists on high-quality ingredients and making everything by hand, including traditional Irish soda bread and fantastic pastries.

John David Powers Butchers
57 Main Street
Dungarvan
Co. Waterford
Tel: (058) 42339

Traditional butchers renowned for their dry-cured bacon.

Knockanore Farmhouse Cheese
Ballyneety
Knockanore
Co. Waterford
Tel: (024) 97275

Gold medal award winner at the British Cheese Awards, Knockanore make a semi-hard cheese from unpasteurized milk. Can be bought from Sheridan's Cheesemongers (see opposite page) or direct from the dairy.

Limerick Saturday Market
Every Saturday. Local cheeses, vegetables, free-range eggs and local meats.

Marc Michel
Tinna Park
Kilpedder
Co. Wicklow
Tel: (01) 281 0545

Farm shop selling an amazing range of very fresh, organic fruit, vegetables, oils and grains. The fresh produce is all home-grown.

McCartney's
56–68 Main Street
Moira
Co. Down
BT67 0LQ
Tel: (028) 9261 1422

Traditional butchers and champion sausage makers.

McDonagh's Seafood House
22 Quay Street
Galway
Tel: (091) 565001
Fax: (091) 526246

Fish bought direct from trusted local fishermen. Also, legendary oysters from Clarinbridge.

McGeough's
Lake Road
Oughterard
Galway
Tel: (091) 552351

Traditional butchers, specializing in air-dried ham.

McGrath's Butchers
Main Street
Lismore
Co. Waterford
Tel: (058) 54350

Local pork, and lamb and beef from the herds on their own farm. McGrath's have their own abattoir, so meat is fully traceable.

Michael Hickey
Gortrua
New Inn
Tipperary
Tel: (062) 72223

Organic, slow-matured, grass-fed Irish Angus beef, slaughtered locally for full traceability. Local deliveries.

Molloys of Donnybrook
Donnybrook Road
Dublin 4
Tel: (01) 269 1678

Fresh fish from local waters, mostly from day boats. Molloys buy on quality, not price. Also, game in season.

Mortons
9 Bayview Road
Ballycastle
BT54 6BP
Tel: (028) 2076 2348
Fax: (028) 2076 3043

Fish from their own and other local day boats, including wild salmon.

Moyallon Foods
The Farm
Crowhill Road
Craigavon
Co. Armagh
BT66 7AT
Tel: (028) 3834 9100
Website:
www.moyallonfoods.com

Rare breed meats, wild and farmed venison, free-range, corn-fed chicken, poussins, matured Belted Galloway beef, heather-fed lamb, and dry cured bacon from free-range pigs. Moyallon have a high regard for traceability, animal welfare and non-intensive farming.

Nicky's Plaice
Store F
Howth West Pier
Dublin
Tel: (01) 832 3557

Mostly local white fish, with salmon smoked traditionally on-site. With 42 years' trading behind him, Nicky and his son Martin know which boats bring in the best fish, and that's who they buy from.

O'Doherty's Butchers
Belmore Street
Enniskillen
Co. Fermanagh
Tel: (028) 6632 2152
Website: www.blackbacon.com

Famous for their black bacon made with free-range Tamworth, Saddleback and Gloucester Old Spot pork. Also, Irish Angus beef, venison, game in season and wild boar. Mail order is available.

O'Flynn's Butchers
36 Marlborough Street
Cork
Tel: (021) 427 5685

Free-range chicken, Irish Hereford beef, dry-cured bacon, local pork, game in season, guinea fowl and quail. Also, a good range of sausages.

Olive Tree Company
353 Ormeau Road
Belfast
Tel: (028) 9064 8898

Deli selling all kinds of Mediterranean ingredients.

Sheridan's Cheesemongers
11 South Anne Street
Dublin 2
Tel: (01) 679 3143

also:
Kirwan's Lane
Galway
Tel: (091) 564829
Website: www.irishcheese.com

Huge selection of Irish and British cheeses (including Colston Bassett), local artisan produce and charcuterie. Mail order available.

Temple Bar Market
Meetinghouse Square
Dublin

Great selection of local cheeses, breads, Italian, Spanish and Mexican delis, local sausages and organic meat.

Tir na nOg
Grattan Street
Sligo
Tel: (071) 62752

Natural food shop selling seasonal Irish fruit and vegetables, Irish artisan cheeses, local honey, organic eggs. The emphasis is on local produce.

Tormey's Butchers
Harbour Place
Mullingar
West Meath
Tel: (044) 45433

Properly butchered and hung local beef, lamb and pork.

Walter Ewing
124 Shankill Road
Belfast BT13 2BD
Tel: (028) 9032 5534

Wet fish and shellfish from local day boats; also smoked salmon, oysters and mussels.

Woodcock Smokery
Castletownshend
Co. Cork
Tel: (028) 36232

Undyed, traditionally smoked salmon, haddock, mackerel and kippers. Mail order available.

Wysner Meats
18 Anne Street
Ballycastle
Co. Antrim
Tel: (028) 2076 2372

Traditionally made sausages and black pudding.

Find your nearest market:
Irish Country Markets
Association
Swanbrook House
Morehampton Road
Dublin 4
Tel: (01) 668 0560

australia

A. C. Butchery
174 Marion Street
Leichhardt
Sydney
NSW 2040
Tel: (02) 9569 8687

Free-range pork, chicken and duck; own-reared organic beef, organic lamb, guinea fowl and pheasant.

Adelaide Central Market
Between Gouger and Grote Streets
Adelaide
Tel: (08) 8203 7494

Barossa Fine Foods
Stall 60, Central Market
Adelaide
South Australia
Tel: (08) 8231 2575

Continental butcher's, with free-range and organic meats available.

Bayside Meats
638 Sandy Bay Road
Sandy Bay
Tasmania 7005
Tel: (03) 6225 1482

Excellent quality beef, lamb, pork and chicken; also tripe.

Belconnen Fresh Food Markets
Lathlain Street
Canberra
Tel: (02) 6251 1680

Black Pearl Epicure
36 Baxter Street
Fortitude Valley
Queensland
Tel: (07) 3257 2144

Local and imported speciality foods, unusual ingredients and deli items. Mail order available

Bottega Rotola
7 Osmond Terrace
Adelaide
Tel: (08) 8362 3376

Bouchiers of Malvern Road
551 Malvern Road
Toorak
Victoria
Tel: (03) 9827 3629

Butchers selling excellent-quality veal, beef, lamb and free-range chicken.

Byron Bay Butcher's
Shop 6
The Plaza
Johnston Street
Byron Bay 2481
Tel: 2 6685 6216
Fax: 2 6680 9275

Free-range and organic meat, with some interesting breeds being used.

Canals, The Seafood Appreciation Centre
703 Nicholson Street
North Carlton
Melbourne, Victoria
Tel: (03) 9380 4537

Great range of locally caught fish.

Carl Torre & Sons
41–43 Lake Street
Northbridge
Western Australia 6003
Tel: (08) 9328 8317

Free-range chicken and pork, aged beef and local lamb.

Casa Iberica
25 Johnston Street
Fitzroy
Melbourne
Victoria 3065
Tel: (03) 9419 4420

Spanish ingredients and charcuterie.

The Chicken Pantry
Stall 85-86, Dairy Produce Hall
Queen Victoria Market
Corner of Elizabeth and Victoria Streets
Melbourne, Victoria
Tel: (03) 9329 6417

Free-range and corn-fed chickens, duck, quail, turkey, pheasant and squab, plus native meats.

Christopher Hiller
151a Rokeby Road
Subiaco
Western Australia 6008
Tel: (08) 6380 2000

Lots of Australian cheeses alongside imported cheeses,

ripened in the maturing rooms on-site. Mail order available.

Cleaver's
Shop 6, The Grove
174 Military Road
Neutral Bay
NSW
Tel: (02) 9953 2129

Organic butcher's with a good selection of free-range meats.

Cliff Penny's Quality Butcher
18 Bungan Street
Mona Vale
NSW
Tel: (02) 9997 1581

also:
880 Military Road
Mosman
NSW
(02) 9969 3372

Free-range chicken from Barossa, properly aged beef, pheasants and goose; organic meat also available.

Enoleca Sileno
21 Amess Street
North Carlton
Victoria
Tel: (03) 9347 5044

Great range of Italian ingredients.

The Essential Ingredient
Shop 8, 531 Hay Street
Perth
Tel: (08) 9380 4799

Exquisite Flavours
GPO Box 2201
Tasmania 7001
Tel: (03) 6234 3489
Fax: (03) 6234 3020
Website:
www.exquisiteflavours.com

Australian cheeses, including award-winning Heidi Farmhouse and cheese from the Woodside Cheesewrights. Also pancetta, Tasmanian honey, spices, aged vinegars and good-quality chocolate from France. Mail order available.

The Farmers Market
Brisbane Powerhouse
117, Lamington Street
New Farm, Brisbane

Five Star Gourmet Foods
13 Willoughby Road
Crows Nest
Sydney
NSW
Tel: (02) 9438 5666

Good-quality dry goods and a selection of local cheeses and meats.

Footscray Market
Corner Leeds and Hopkins Streets
Melbourne
Tel: (03) 9687 1205

Fountaindale
Fountaindale Road
Robertson
NSW 2577
Tel. (02) 48852115

Fox Studios Farmer's Market
Fox Studios
Lang Road
Moore Park
Sydney
NSW
Tel: (02) 9383 4000

Fyshwick Fresh Food Markets
Corner of Canberra Avenue and Mildura Street
Canberra
Tel: (02) 6295 0606

Game Birds
Shop 32, Cosmopolitan Centre
Knox Street
Double Bay
NSW
Tel: (02) 9327 6126

Full range of game birds and chickens; also duck and goose fat.

Glenloth Game
RMB 1024
Wycheproof
Victoria 3527
Tel: (03) 5493 7383

Corn-fed, free-range chicken, and game birds including pigeon and pheasant. All birds are reared, killed and butchered on-site. Call for details of stockists.

Good Living Grower's Market
Pyrmont Bay Park
Pirrama Road
Pyrmont
Sydney
NSW
Tel: (02) 9699 4100

The Grocer
145 Stirling Highway
Nedlands
Western Australia 6009
Tel: (08) 9389 8144

Free-range, corn-fed chickens from Barossa Valley; also deli goods and other meats.

Hagen's Organic Meats
Stall 16, Queen Victoria Market
Corner of Elizabeth and Victoria Streets
Melbourne
Victoria
Tel: (03) 9329 5534

also :
Stall 509, Prahran Market
Commercial Road
South Yarra
Victoria
Tel: (03) 9827 1899

Organic and free-range beef, lamb, pork and chicken, and a wide range of sausages.

Herbie's Spices
745 Darling Street
Sydney
NSW
Phone: (02) 9555 6035

Illabo Lamb
Hillside Farm
Illabo
NSW 2590
Tel: (02) 6924 5404

Award-winning tender, young lamb, with a unique buttery flavour. Available from several Sydney butchers. Call for details of stockists.

John Cester Poultry and Game
Stall 506, Prahran Market
Commercial Road
South Yarra
Victoria
Tel: (03) 9827 6111

Local free-range and organic poultry, and game birds.

Jones the Grocer
68 Moncur Street
Woollahra, NSW
Tel: (02) 9362 1222

Great deli stocking all kinds of dry goods, with cheese rooms stocking local and imported cheeses.

Joseph Olive Oil
PO Box 77
Virginia
South Australia 5120
Tel: (08) 8380 9442
Website:
www.primoestate.com.au
E-mail:
info@primoestate.com.au

Voted Australia's best olive oil for four years in a row. Available from gourmet food shops. Call for details of stockists.

Kailis Bros Fish Markets
101 Oxford Street
Leederville 6007
Western Australia
Tel: (08) 9443 6300
Fax: (08) 9443 6299
Website:
www.kailisbros.com.au

Lobsters, oysters and fresh wet fish, often line caught. Good website explaining where and how the fish is caught.

Mondo di Carne
824 Beaufort Street
Inglewood
Perth, Western Australia
Tel: (08) 9371 6350
Website: www.mondo.net.au

White Rocks veal and other meats, including free-range and organic.

New Norcia Bakery
163 Scarborough Beach Road
Mount Hawthorne
Western Australia
Tel: (08) 9443 4114

Award-winning artisan bakery, hand-making traditional sour dough without additives, baked in a 100-year-old wood-fired oven. New Norcia's bread is available in other outlets – call for details.

Ordway's Kangaroo Island Poultry
PO Box 468
Kingscote
Kangaroo Island
South Australia 5223
Tel: (08) 8553 5219
Fax: (08) 8553 5325

Award-winning, slow-reared, corn-fed, free-range poultry. Call for details of stockists.

Pino's Quality Meats
45 President Avenue
Kogarah, NSW 2217
Tel: (02) 9587 4818

Huge range of sausages and black pudding.

Providor Central Market
Stall 66–67,
Central Market
Adelaide
South Australia
Tel: (08) 8231 5977

Local corn-fed, free-range chickens; also free-range turkey, goose, duck and pheasant.

Queen Victoria Market
Corner Elizabeth and Victoria
Streets
Melbourne
Tel: (03) 9320 5822

Richmond Hill Café and Larder
48–50 Bridge Road
Richmond, Victoria
Tel: (03) 9421 2808

Co-owned by Stephanie Alexander, this shop offers a good range of local and imported cheeses, ripened in their own maturing rooms. Mail order available.

Rosalie Gourmet Market
164 Baroona Road
Brisbane
Tel: (07) 3876 6222

Samtass Bros Seafoods
Stall 46–48, Central Market
Adelaide, South Australia
Tel: (08) 8211 8600

An enormous range of whole, filleted and smoked fish, and shellfish.

Schulz Butcher's
42 Murray Street
Angaston
South Australia 5353
Tel: (08) 8564 2145

Award-winning traditionally cured and smoked bacon.

Simon Johnson, Purveyor of Quality Foods
181 Harris Street
Pyrmont
NSW 2009
Tel: 1800 655522
Website:
www.simonjohnson.com.au
E-mail:
orders@simonjohnson.com.au

Smoked salmon and trout, pasta, olive oils, Valrhona chocolate, aged vinegars. Mail order available.

South Melbourne Market
Corner Cecil and Coventry
Streets
Melbourne
Tel: (03) 9209 6295

Steve Costi Seafoods
Shop 74–75, Greenwood Plaza
Blue Street
North Sydney
NSW
Tel: (02) 9955 6727

also:
Northbridge Plaza
Sailors Bay Road
Northbridge
NSW
Tel: (02) 9958 0974

Top-quality fishmongers, with a wide range of wet fish and shellfish.

The Sweet Pork Company
12 Station Road
PO Box 90
Bangalow
NSW 2479
Tel: (02) 6687 1744
Freecall: 1800 736 606
Fax: (02) 6687 1746
Website:
www.sweetpork.com.au

Very high-quality, traditionally reared and butchered pork, without additives, hormones or growth promoters. Outlets in Sydney, Brisbane, Gold Coast and Northern Rivers; call for details.

Sydney Fish Market
Bank Street (Corner of Pyrmont
Bridge Road)
Sydney
NSW
Tel: (02) 9660 1611
Fax: (02) 9552 1661
Website:
www.sydneyfishmarket.com.au

Fresh fish every morning, from as far afield as New Zealand.

Victoire French Bakery
285 Darling Street
Balmain
NSW 2041
Tel: (02) 9818 5529

Award-winning, traditional French bakery, making Continental

breads, including sour dough. Call for details of stockists.

The Vital Ingredient
206 Clarendon Street
South Melbourne
Victoria
Tel: (03) 9696 3511

Spices, oils, pasta and a range of deli goods, both local and imported. Mail order available.

Wrights The Butcher's
32 Clovellie Road
Randwick
NSW
Tel: (02) 9398 1038

Milk-fed lamb, White Rock veal, aged beef, game birds including pheasant and poussins; also salmon, local cheeses and fresh pasta.

Wursthaus Kitchen
1 Montpelier Retreat
Hobart
Tasmania 7000
Tel: (03) 6224 0644

A cross between a deli and butcher's, with good-quality, corn-fed, free-range chicken, grass-fed beef, duck and game birds. Most of the meat is from local farms, and is always fresh, never frozen. Also available is a wide range of local and imported cheeses.

Clark's Organic Butchery
356 West Coast Road
Glen Eden
Auckland
Tel: (09) 818 6526
Fax: (09) 818 6592

Organic beef, lamb and free-range chicken. Delivery available within North Island.

Clean GreeNZ Organics
39 Queen Street
Blenheim 7301
Tel: (03) 577 6323

Organic capsicums, tomatoes, aubergines, chillies, herbs, salad leaves and unusual vegetables.

Commonsense Organics
260 Wakefield Street
PO Box 9206
Wellington
Tel: (04) 384 3314
Fax: (04) 385 3383

Local meat and fish, free-range chickens, organic fruit and vegetables.

Eco Egg Co Ltd
PO Box 678
Levin
Tel: (06) 368 6889
Fax: (06) 368 5060
Website: www.ecoegg.co.nz

Totally free-range eggs, available from Countdown, Foodtown and New World stores.

ExtraOrdinary Eggs
446 Gorge Road
Otaki
Tel: (06) 364 3405
Fax: (06) 364 3905

Free-range hens' eggs, duck eggs, organic free-range chicken, and free-range Saddleback and Large White pork. Farm-gate sales only.

Good Things
163 High Street
Christchurch
Tel: (03) 366 3894
Fax: (03) 366 3895
Website: www.goodthings.co.nz

Walnuts, oils, pasta, spices, puy lentils, cheeses.

Gourmet Direct
Richmond Stortford
Plunket Street
Hastings
Tel: 0800 737 800
Website:
www.gourmetdirect.com
E-mail:
sales@gourmetdirect.com

Aged beef, veal and venison, air-dried bacon; poussins, duck, pheasant and quail; smoked salmon. Mail order available.

Kapiti Cheeses Ltd
136–142 Fanshawe Street
Auckland
Tel: (09) 377 2473

also:
12–18 Moorhouse Avenue
Christchurch
Tel: (03) 377 7077

and:
57 Teroto Drive
Paraparaumu
Tel: (04) 297 0329

Winner of 22 awards in the New Zealand Cheese Awards this year, including Supreme Champion. The cheeses can be found at the retail outlets above, or from supermarkets.

Mountain Valley Organic Meats
Mangapiri Downs Organic
Stud Farm
2RD
Otautau
Southland 9653
Tel: (03) 225 5283
Website:
www.organicmeats.com
E-mail: tim@organicmeats.com

Opawa Meats
124 Opawa Road
Opawa, Christchurch
Tel: (03) 332 4311
Fax: (03) 338 1091

Locally reared beef, lamb, free-range chicken and organic pork.

Pandoro Panetteria
290 Dominion Road
Mount Eden, Auckland
Tel: (09) 631 7416
Fax: (09) 631 7432

Specialist Continental bakery, making French and Italian breads and sour doughs.

Sabato Ltd
57 Normanby Road
Mount Eden
Auckland
Tel: (09) 630 8751
Website: www.sabato.co.nz
E-mail: info@sabato.co.nz

Ortiz tuna, artisan pastas, oils, vinegars, spices, Valrhona chocolate and cheeses.

South Island Gourmet Distributors
366 Cashel Street
Linwood
Christchurch
Tel: (03) 377 1030
Website: www.sig.co.nz

Organic free-range chickens.

Swiss Delicatessen and Fine Meats
68-70 Greenmount Drive
East Tamaki
Auckland
Tel: (09) 274 4455

Pork specialists, selling a range of high-quality cuts.

Traiteur
Corner of Aikmans and Papanui
Roads
Christchurch
Tel: (03) 355 7750
Fax: (03) 355 6696

also:
300 Columbo Street
Christchurch
Tel: (03) 332 5325
Fax: (03) 332 5026
Website: www.traiteur.co.nz

Continental butchers selling a wide range of meats, including free-range chicken, and venison.

Vinotica
Unit D, 3 Henry Rose Place
Albany
Auckland
Tel: (09) 9415 5942

New Zealand and Italian cheeses, oils and all kinds of deli items. Mail order available.

Weka Hill Orchard
Weka Road
Mariri
RD2
Upper Montere
Nelson
Tel: (03) 526 6738

Huge range of apple and pear varieties, many old varieties that are seldom grown these days. Mail order available.

Wick's Fish
389a Worcester Street
Linwood
Christchurch
Tel: (03) 389 7675

Good range of fresh local fish.

bibliography & acknowledgements

Bibliography

I have been greatly aided in looking for producers
and suppliers for the book by reference to the
following:

Brown, Lynda, New Shoppers Guide to Organic Food
(Fourth Estate, 2002)
Davidson, Alan, The Oxford Companion to Food
(Oxford University Press, 1999)
Fearnley-Whittingstall, Hugh, Cuisine Bon Marché
(Macmillan, 1994)
Green, Henrietta, Food Lovers' Guide to Britain
(BBC Worldwide Ltd, 1995)
Green, Henrietta, The Farmers Market Cookbook
(Kyle Cathie, 2001)
Grigson, Sophie and Black, William, Organic
(Headline, 2001)
Harbutt Juliet, Cheese, (Mitchell Beazley, 1999)
Hartley, Dorothy, Food in England (Little, Brown,
1999)
Mason, Laura and Brown, Catherine, Traditional
Foods of Britain (Prospect Books, 1999)
McKenna, John and Sally, The Bridgestone Food
Lover's Guide to Ireland (Estragon Press, 2001)
Richardson, Paul, Cornucopia (Abacus Books, 2001)
Slow, The Magazine of the Slow Food Movement,
UK (Tel. 01844 339 362)

For Australian Suppliers:
Alexander, Stephanie, Cooking and Travelling
in South West France (Viking, 2002)

Acknowledgements

I am indebted to Debbie Major who helped test and
write up the recipes for this book. As well as
producing the food for the photography, she
prepared the food for the TV series, which it
accompanies. As I said of her in my last book,
Seafood, without her this book would have been
years in the making.

Though my name appears on the front cover, this
sort of book is very much a team effort. Much of the
enjoyment of creating something like this lies in
working with a group of talented people who are
also friends. So, once again, I must applaud the
food photography of James Murphy and the
landscape photography of Craig Easton, the
beautiful design work of Paul Welti and Art
Directors, Pene Parker and Sarah Ponder, the very
watchful eye of Commissioning Editor Viv Bowler
and the enlightened hard work of the Project Editor
Rachel Copus. Finally, I would like to add a big
thank you to Christina Burnham who did the lion's
share of the research for the produce directory.

Credits

Thanks are due, too, to the following individuals and
organisations:

The Guild of Q Butchers
Fionnuala Jay-O'Boyle (A Taste of Ulster)
The Soil Association
The Marine Stewardship Council
Paul Rankin, Chef/Patron, Cayenne, Belfast,
Northern Ireland
Michele Curtis and Allan Campion (Australian Food
Writers,www.campionandcurtis.com)
Babak Hadi, Black Pearl Epicure, Queensland,
Australia
Jaguar/Australian Gourmet Traveller Awards for
Excellence
The Soil and Health Association of New Zealand, Inc.